PINK, PURPLE, GREEN

Women's, Religious, Environmental and Gay/Lesbian Movements in Central Europe Today

Edited By
HELENA FLAM

HQ
1587
.P565
2001
West

EAST EUROPEAN MONOGRAPHS, BOULDER
DISTRIBUTED BY COLUMBIA UNIVERSITY PRESS, NEW YORK

2001

EAST EUROPEAN MONOGRAPHS, NO. DLXXVII

CONTENTS

PART IV: GAY MOVEMENTS

ACKNOWLEDGMENTS

Putting together a volume like this is a hazardous game. Every section is a matter of contingencies. In this part of Europe it is easier to identify experts on gender, environment, religion or gay-lesbian cultures than on social movements as such. I am glad that in spite of several dramatic moments of uncertainty everything worked out in the end.

My work as an editor of this book started in fall of 1998 when I finally decided to devote my time to identifying and contacting native experts in what used to be *Eastern Europe* before 1989. It took somebody two decades younger than I am to point out to me that I did not have to visit each of these countries to accomplish this task. I could rely on e-mail. Indeed. Most of the back and forth of various drafts, comments, missing references, latest news, sporadic pieces of gossip and friendly greetings went over e-mail. This means, however, that I have never seen and perhaps will never meet most contributors to this volume. Here then, on the first page of this book, I would like to thank all of them for participating. My special thanks go to those who cared for the contents of their own chapters as much as I did.

E-mail worked wonders, except in the Czech and Slovak Republics which I bombarded with all types of mail and to which I sent all sorts of messengers. Of all the people who tried to help Eva Stehlíková's persistence deserves special mention. For a long time it looked like that there would be no native Czechs or Slovaks ombord. In this case, however, my in person appearance in Prague helped. A brand new issue of the *Czech Sociological Review* fell into my hands. It included an article on the Czech environmental policy and the e-mail address of the author. Within two weeks Petr Jehlička joined us as a contributor.

Two more moments of doubt should be noted. Remembering Janusz Mucha from the European conferences devoted to social movements, I tried my e-mail luck with him. He mentioned one of his doctoral students to me, but, as it turned out much later, forgot the other. Anyhow, Paweł Załęcki's joining made thinking of a section on religious movements more realistic, so I contacted Klaus Hartmann. No Hungarian, Czech or Slovak authors responded to my search for experts on this topic. But I sat there with only one essay on the eastern German gay movement. A befriended literary journal from Poznań, *Czas Kultury*, supplied me with fax numbers of two gay magazines which, however, did not react. It appeared likely that I would have to drop the idea of having a section on gay(-lesbian) movements in Central Europe - the first of a kind. Jochen Kleres came to my rescue. He provided me with a list of gay organizations in Central Europe which I wrote or faxed asking them to assist me in locating suitable authors. To my relief Krzysztof Kliszczyński contacted me after a while. A few months later, much too late, the editor of an important Polish gay magazine, *Inaczej*, also expressed his interest. I then asked my friend to buy this magazine during his next trip to Poland. In it I found an ad for the first sociological study of gays in Poland. Its female author thanked Janusz Mucha for his sponsorship! Luckily she did not want to displace Kliszczyński and he agreed to have his article expanded in light of her work.

I am very grateful to the Head of the British Council in Leipzig, Mr. Stephen Ashworth, for his generosity. He eliminated the worst of our English language errors. I also want to express my gratitude to many other native speakers of English - colleagues and friends - who labored over our first drafts. Their help made this volume possible.

I am also very much obliged to the consecutive directors of my Institute of Sociology, Professors Kurt Mühler and Steffen Wilsdorf, for providing me with student assistants when I most needed them. Speaking of which: Tanja Täubner helped with references. My special thanks, however, go to Jochen Kleres, who while assisting me in making these pages presentable, offered sound advice and good laughs in spring of 1999 and Fall of 2000. I am sure glad I did not have to do this alone!

I would also like to thank Mario Diani, Hank Johnston and Professor Stephen Fischer-Galati for their support.

NOTES ON CONTRIBUTORS

HELENA FLAM, Fil.Kand. at the University of Lund, Sweden and Ph.D. at Columbia University, New York. Researcher at the Swedish Collegium for Advanced Study in the Social Sciences, fellow at the Max Planck Institute (Köln) and assistant professor at the University of Konstanz, since 1993 professor of Sociology at the University of Leipzig. She is co-author of *The Shaping of Social Organization*, London, Sage 1987 and editor of *States and Anti-Nuclear Movements*, Edinburgh, Edinburgh University Press, 1994. She also wrote *Mosaic of Fear: Poland and East Germany before 1989*, East European Monographs distributed by Columbia University Press, 1998 and *The Emotional 'Man' and the Problem of Collective Action*, Frankfurt a.M., Peter Lang, 2000.

PIOTR GLIŃSKI, Ph.D. and *Habilitation* at the Institute of Philosophy and Sociology of the Polish Academy of Sciences. Head of the Civil Society Division at the Institute of Philosophy and Sociology of the Polish Academy of Sciences in Warsaw, professor of Sociology at the University in Białystok. Affiliated with the Polish Sociological Association (vice-president), the Service Office for the Environmental Movement, the Social Ecological Institute (co-founder and currently president), the Ecological Forum of the Union of Freedom (vice-president) and the Academy for the Development of Philanthropy in Poland (co-founder). He is author of *Polish Greens: Social Movement in the Time of Transformation* (1996) and of numerous articles on culture, social movements and non-governmental organizations.

KLAUS HARTMANN, has a Ph.D. in Social Sciences and Theology and is a researcher and a lecturer in Sociology at the Faculty of Cultural Studies, Central European University "Viadrina" in Frankfurt/Oder. He is author of numerous articles and co-author of *Gegen den Strom. Kircheneintritte in Ostdeutschland nach der Wende*, Opladen, Leske+Budrich, 1998.

PETR JEHLIČKA, is Research Fellow at the Institute of International Relations in Prague and Lecturer in Social Geography at the Faculty of Science at Charles University in Prague. He is a specialist on environmental policy, politics and political geography. He is currently engaged in research on the effects of eastern enlargement on environmental policies of the European Union and on the environmental NGOs in Slovakia and the Czech Republic. He is the co-editor of *Dilemmas of Transition: The Environment, Democracy and Economic Reform in East and Central Europe* which appeared with Frank Cass in London.

JOCHEN KLERES, born in 1975, studies for a *Diplom* Degree in Sociology and Law at the University of Leipzig. Fellow of the Heinrich Böll Stiftung 1999-2001, enrolled in the Gay-Lesbian Study Program at the University of Amsterdam. Contributor to the special issue of the *Journal Neue Soziale Bewegungen*, named "Queering Democracy", to appear in 2000.

KRZYSZTOF KLISZCZYŃSKI, born in 1968, specializes in Polish minorities. He has *Magister* Degree in the Applied Social Sciences and is a graduate of the Institute for the Applied Social Sciences at the Warsaw University and of the School of Human Rights at the Helsinki Foundation for Human Rights. He holds a research position at the Collegium for the Social Sciences and Administration at the Warsaw Polytechnique.

INGRID MIETHE, born in 1962, was a long-standing member of the East German dissident movement. She has a Ph.D. in Social Sciences and is a specialist in Gender Studies and qualitative methods. She is a lecturer at Free University Berlin and a senior researcher at Greifswald University. Author of *Frauen in der DDR-Opposition*, Opladen, Leske + Budrich, 1999 and co-editor of *Biographies and the Division of Europe*, Opladen, Leske + Budrich, 2000. Her most recent article on female dissidents appeared in *Social Politics*, 1999.

ANDREA PETŐ, born in 1964, Ph.D. in Contemporary History, assistant professor at the Central European University of Budapest between 1991 and 1998, since 1998 in its Gender and Culture Program. Publications: *Women's Stories. From History of Hungarian Women in Politics (1945-1951)*, Budapest 1998. She is author of numerous articles published in prestigeous English language journals and an editor of several collected volumes. She is also a member of the board of several journals on women's history, such as, *Gender and History, and Clio*. Currently: President of the Feminist Section of the Hungarian Sociological Association.

KATY PICKVANCE is a Research Fellow at the University of Kent at Canterbury. Her research has focused on environmental and housing movements in Hungary, Estonia and Russia, on local environmental policy implementation in Hungary and on young people's housing opportunities in the U.K. A well-known specialist on the environmental movements, she is author of *Democracy and Environmental Movements in Eastern Europe. A Comparative Study of Hungary and Russia*. Boulder. Westview Press, 1998 and co-editor of *Environmental and Housing Movements: Grassroots Experience in Hungary, Russia and Estonia*. Aldershot. Avebury, 1997. Her articles have appeared in *Sociology, Sociological Review* and *European Sociological Review*.

DIETER RINK, born in 1959, gained his Ph.D. in Philosophy at the University of Leipzig. He held a research position at the *Wissenschaftszentrum Berlin* before 1994 when he switched to the Environment Research Center Leipzig-Halle. Co-author of *Soziale Bewegungen auf dem Weg zur Institutionalisierung?* New York, Campus, 1997 and co-editor of *Zwischen Verweigerung und Protest*. New York, Campus, 1997. His assistant, SASKIA GERBER, studies Social Sciences at the Technical University of Dresden.

MIHALY RISZOVANNIJ, born in 1973, M.A. in German Philology and Gender Studies at ELTE/ Budapest. Currently Fellow at the Free University Berlin. Author of several articles in such international journals as the *Zeitschrift für Semiotik* and *The European Journal for Semiotics*.

STEVEN SAXONBERG, received his Ph.D in Political Sciences at the University of Uppsala. Awarded STINT post-doctoral stipend in 1999. He was a recipient of several other Swedish, German and American scholarships and a guest researcher at the Charles University of Prague 1997-1998 and at the Central European University in Prague 1995. Author of *The Fall. Czechoslovakia, East Germany, Hungary and Poland in a Comparative Perspective*, Gordon & Breach, 2000 and of numerous articles in international journals, including Czech.

EDWARD SNAJDR, received his Ph.D. in Anthropology from the University of Pittsburgh in 1998 where he was also engaged in research and teaching. He now teaches Cultural Anthropology at The Florida State University. He is also a visiting researcher in the School of Criminology and Criminal Justice at the same university where he is currently working on a U.S. State Department grant concerned with women's NGOs in Central Asia. His field research in the Slovak Republic was funded by the U.S. National Science Foundation, Fulbright-IIE and the International Research and Exchanges Board. His articles on the Slovak greens appeared recently in the journal *Problems of Post-Communism* and in *Intellectuals and Politics in Central Europe*, Central European University Press, 1998.

ANNE ULRICH-HAMPELE, was born in 1961. She has a Ph.D. in German Philology and Social Sciences. She was assistant researcher at Central Institute for Social Scientific Research at the Free University Berlin 1989-1994. Currently she is assistant at the board of directors of the Heinrich Böll Stiftung. Contributor to *Gender Politics and Post Communism*, New York, Routledge, 1993 and *Frauen in Deutschland 1945-1992* Berlin, Bundeszentrale, 1993.

PAWEŁ ZALĘCKI, has a Ph.D. in Sociology. Currently research assistant in the Cultural Studies Department at the Institute of Sociology, Nicholas Copernicus University, Toruń. Awarded Florian Znaniecki's Award of the Polish Sociological Association in 1995 and a Scholarship of the Foundation for Polish Science in 1997. Author of *Wspólnota Religijna Jako Grupa Pierwotna* (Religious Community as a Primary Group), Cracow, NOMOS Publishing House, 1997 and co-author of *Słownik Socjologiczny* (Dictionary of Sociology), Toruń, Graffiti BC Publishing House, 1997, 1998, 1999.

Introduction*
In Pursuit of Fundable Causes?

Helena Flam

In this introduction I would like to deal with some issues which I hope will turn out to be as disquieting to the reader as they are to me. Is this volume really about social movements? Can bureaucratic organizations which do not mobilize the public and/or which are inspired and sustained chiefly by domestic and international funds be classified as social movements? Are they in a position to invigorate post-communist democracies? Although this introduction is intended merely as a sensitizing framework, by raising these issues I hope to rekindle the general debate about the nature of social movements. I also hope to assist the reader in coping with the variety of material this volume presents.

When I started this project, I drew up a list of questions which were to guide the work of each contributor to the extent that she or he found the questions pertinent. These questions were: Which movement is addressed (ethnic, religious, women's, environmental, gay, etc.)? How many organizations make up this movement (if several, list the names of the most important organizations)? When did this movement emerge? How many active members does it have (compare before and after 1989)? What issues/themes does this movement pursue? What is its organizational structure? What is its range of protest forms? Any innovations? Is it willing to resort to violence? What symbols does it use frequently? What lines of conflict are prominent within the movement? What is the mobilizing power of the movement? Does the movement wish for/have access to government, business or trade unions? What is its public resonance? What sources of finances does this movement have? Does it have any allies? Any other additional information?

Not all authors were able or willing to respond to all these queries, but each offers enough substantive information to make comparisons possible. In what follows I rely on these comparisons to address the disquieting issues and, by the same token, say a bit about each chapter. Finally, the information provided by the contributors to this book makes it possible to outline an agenda for the future studies on the Central European social movements.

But before I turn to the main task of this chapter, I would like to put the social movements presented in this volume in a historical perspective. I will do so by very sketchily describing the past thirty years of social movement research.

THE PRIMACY OF DISSIDENTS

While in the US researchers, such as Charles Tilly, Mayer Zald, John McCarthy, Douglas McAdam or Myra Marx Ferree concentrated on developing the "resource mobilization" approach, Europeans, such as Alain Touraine, Alberto Melucci or Jürgen Habermas, advanced the "identity" approach (Cohen 1985). Although at first hardly aware of each other, they shared two attributes. They wanted to understand the emergence of "new" social movements mobilized by young, well-educated people and they wanted to understand Western liberal democracies. Initially at least, and Americans more so than the Europeans, they had little interest in repressive regimes or in Central

Europe (see Jenkins 1988:6-7). Until this day for most American social movement experts Asia or Central Europe are too far to register. Such researchers as Craig Calhoun (1991, 1994) or Hank Johnston (1989; 1991) who themselves do research on repressive regimes and encourage others to do so are still exceptional.[1]

We have to be thankful to some prominent refugees, their colleagues and friends in the US and Europe, Jürgen Habermas and his disciples in Germany, one Canadian and several British social scientists that Central Europe remained on the social science map before 1989 (e.g. Arato 1981/2; Cohen 1985; Keane 1988; Skilling 1989). Their keen interest in the conditions accounting for the emergence and functioning of the *civil society* kept Central Europe from completely turning into regional - Soviet or East European - studies. But most of all we should be thankful to the Polish oppositional movement the Committee for the Defence of Workers (*KOR*), the Czechoslovak dissident movement *Charta 77,* and the Polish mass movement *Solidarność* for their spectacular and heroic emergence in 1976, 1977 and 1980. They generated a virtual writing flurry, even among such absolute strangers to such themes as protest or social movements as Anthony Giddens or Jeffrey Alexander. These movements not only contributed to a temporary merger of the European and American research interests, but, thanks to several enthusiasts and many patient translators, helped to introduce Central European writers and their writings to the Western public.[2]

Less than a decade after the worker and student revolts in Western Europe and before Western feminist, environmental or gay-lesbian movements captured Western imagination, West European neo-romantic idealism became transferred and firmly attached to the Central European dissidents and their movements. This transfer of idealism, oft accompanied by solid scholarship, pumped new life into the concept of *civil society* previously used mainly by the students of totalitarianism.

Students of totalitarianism argued that totalitarian states aim to eradicate any free initative, any independent, organized elements of the *civil society*, such as free associations, trade and business unions or foundations, in order to subjugate this society and its members to its undisputed rule (Feher and Heller 1987; Lefort 1986). For this purpose they engage ideological and policiary terror (Aron 1969). In contrast, in the 1970s at the heart of the revived concept of the *civil society* was the belief in its rebirth (Pelczynski 1988:361). Everybody was certain that a genuine revolution was taking place in Central Europe before their very eyes. Most Western and Central European contributors to the debate about the reborn *civil society* were also quite sure that new organizations and institutions, yet to be established or already established in the very womb of the totalitarian society, had to put pressure on the official society to affect change. At the same time they agreed that this *civil society* had to exercise self-discipline in order not to awaken the sleeping Russian bear. One had to acknowledge geo-political realities which one was powerless to change. Hence the term "self-limiting revolution." There was also an agreement in distaste expressed in relationship to political power which dissidents associated with the communist party-state and its machinations. Hence the second key term, here in Havel's rendition, "politics outside politics." Dissent was and had to be a moral and existential, not a political undertaking, it was a matter of speaking and living the truth (Skilling 1989:134-135).[3]

From this perspective on historical developments, years of solidary, both open and clandestine activities, paid off. The ever more mature and expansive *civil society* accelerated and avalanched to produce *Solidarność* - a massive social movement which, as Ken Jowitt (1993) argues, convinced Gorbachev it was time for the relaxation of the Soviet grip on its European satellites. Gorbachev's conviction that the popular demands for more national autonomy were legitimate moved him to support dissident and popular movements at crucial points. This produced unintended consequences. Together, Gorbachev and these movements, were instrumental in toppling the Soviet giant.

This heroic narrative needs some correction. Indeed, Polish *KOR* - the first alliance between workers and intellectuals - evolved in the late 1970s into a broadly mobilizing oppositional movement which managed to challenge the legitimacy of the communist party. In many ways it set the stage for the emergence of *Solidarność* which within months became a movement supported by 10 million members. However, dissident movement in Czechoslovakia, Hungary and East Germany was confined to a narrow group of intellectuals and did not enjoy much societal support (Skilling 1989; Bugajski and Pollack 1989; Flam 1998). They managed to create dissident subcultures, but not a *civil society*. In Hungary and East Germany they were virtually unknown. This accounts for the differences in the transition years 1989-1990. In Poland no mass demonstrations were necessary to overthrow the communist regime. The reform-wing of the communist party invited prominent dissidents to join in the Round Table talks and so they co-determined the transition process. The voters accomplished the rest. The intransigent Czechoslovak and East German party-states, even the Hungarian one which already was on a negotiating and reform course, had to be confronted with mass demonstrations, before they toppled. In contrast to Poland, in East Germany and Hungary dissidents had to fight for the recognition of the reform-wing of the communist party. They finally managed to press party reformers into the Round Table talks. In Czechoslovakia mass demonstrations brought dissidents a long overdue recognition and with it seats at the negotiating tables (Oberschall 1996:107-108; Flam 1998:270-279).

CIVIL SOCIETY AFTER 1989

The new question was whether and how a *civil society*, once repressed and restricted, then reborn, would avail itself of new opportunities? Would this society continue to self-organize and articulate itself?

After their initial massive venture into parliamentary politics, most leading dissidents are now found in politics, mass media and research. At their international meeting in Podkowa Leśna in 1996, a meeting which was sponsored by the Batory Foundation (Soros) and organized on the initiative of Zbigniew Gluza, the chief adminstrator and editor of the Polish *Ośrodek Karta*, the main issue on the agenda was the future role of dissidents. Most participants did not see any particular role for themselves. Others defined it as defense of human rights at home and abroad.

Some of the leading dissidents of the past are now also found in what is conventionally understood as the social movements. They join hands with old and new movement activists concerned chiefly with women's, environmental, gay-lesbian or other "movement" issues. They seem to be exhausted by their past in dissent and keen on enjoying its fruits - the comforts of institutionalization.

A short digression is necessary to dispel the notion that these movements are an entirely new phenomenon. In the Soviet bloc the environmental movements received much support from the public worried about the air, water and ground pollution, dam construction, mining sites, industrial and nuclear waste, and dying forests. In the region where Poland, East Germany and the Czechoslovak Republic met (the Black Triangle), environmental pollution was truly scary. In south-western Poland alarming proportions of children were born handicapped and equally alarming percentage of adults and children developed cancer. Similarly, concern with health mobilized large sectors of the Czechoslovak and even the East German population. In East Germany contaminated rivers as well as the mining sites, such as the lignite mining site near Leipzig or the uranium mining site near Wismut, destroyed entire regions. Clear air became a scarce good. Cancer spread. Villages singled out for destruction were neglected and abandoned. The environmental movements in these three countries and Hungary started developing in the early 1980s (Pickvance 1998:75; Gliński 1996:149). By their mobilization they all contributed to the peaceful revolutions of 1989. They also affected agendas of the Round Table talks and political parties in their respective countries. During the very process of regime transformation the Hungarian Danube Circle managed to stop the construction of a gigantic dam on the Danube on the Hungarian side.

Unofficial women's movements were rather modest but nevertheless active in Poland, Hungary and Czechoslovakia before 1989. Only East German female dissidents, however, took the step to organize separately from male dissidents already in the early 1980s. They were important initiators of the events of 1989 and participated in the Round Table talks. Also East German gays started their movement earlier than their Polish and Hungarian counterparts who established their first organizations in 1987. Finally, Poland but even much more restrictive East Germany allowed some religious movements and sects even before 1989.

All these movements, at the peak of their activity between 1989 and roughly 1993, appear to suffer from the mobilization fatigue now, some ten years after 1989-1990. As comparative studies indicate, this is no isolated phenomenon. In all four countries political parties find it very difficult to mobilize voters (Schmitter 1999). From a classical sociological perspective (Durkheim), we should actually expect that a period of frenzied activity is followed by a period of calm. Social movement theory (Tarrow 1989) also suggests that movements go through cycles of protest. They go from the first stirrings of protest through institutionalized conflict and enthusiastic peak to their ultimate collapse.

Not satisfied with these interpretations of the present-day political tranquility among social movements in Central Europe analyzed in this volume, I will turn now to the question: In what sense can we speak of social movements, if there is no mobilization? Is this volume really about social movements? If so, what are their specific characteristics.

SOCIAL MOVEMENTS WITHOUT COLLECTIVE MOBILIZATION?

When we envision social movements, we think of strong protest forms - demonstrations, marches, human chains, vigils or hunger strikes. We tend to associate collective mobilization with speeches, raised fists, joyous or angry voices, banners and flags flapping in the wind. We expect moving gestures.

As a matter of fact one renown theorist of collective action, Charles Tilly, went as far as to argue that for more than a century the basic repertoire of protest has not changed. Protesters demonstrate, rally, strike, block access or occupy sites. They form associations, organize public meetings, draw up and make public their declarations or petitions (Tilly 1983; 1988:14-16). These activities lead to so-called contentious gatherings between the protesters and their opponents, gatherings which scientists can study as protest events.

An alternative view suggests, however, that the basic repertoire of protest has become modified in the second part of this century (Flam 1994:16-17; Ferree and Roth 1999:136; Beisheim and Zürn 1999). In liberal democratic states the initially powerless contenders are no longer confined to private or public spaces. They are not sentenced to addressing "the state and sympathetic members of the general public, by means of actions that dramatize the conflict and attract the attention of mass media." (Tilly 1988:15) Mass media and public drama are not their only hope of gaining attention. On the contrary, they often make it as far as the "house of power" - to use Weber's metaphor for the state.

In liberal democratic states a partial transformation and relocation of collective protest takes place. Protest assumes forms of dry statistics, shocking and distressing photographs, eye-witness accounts, fliers, posters, graffitti, protest e-mail, lobbying or scientific expertise. Protest becomes expressed in publications, legal challenges, film festivals, art exhibits, training-programs, conferences, national and international networking efforts. It penetrates universities, mass organizations, courts, public hearings, inquiries, governmental offices and commissions. It confronts international business and political organizations. These are the newer forms and loci of contentious action.

Seen from the first perspective, there is little in a way of protest in Central Europe today. Contributors to this volume who write on the German women's, environmental, gay and even religious movements agree and Rink hits a ringing phrase - institutionalization without mobilization best depicts their state (see also Blattert et.al. 1995:404,409; Schmitt-Beck and Weins 1997:330). Although most explicitly argued by the German contributors, this thesis is also advanced for the women's movements. On the definition of protest as an open-air drama, only (some of) the environmental movements in Poland, Hungary, Slovakia and the Czech Republic would qualify as protest movements at all. They would be joined by the most important religious (Catholic) "Oases" movement in Poland.

The second perspective compeletely reverses our assessment. Collective mobilization is easily detectable if one does not look for it in the streets but at the universities and formal organizations as well as in research, assistance or counselling projects. As Gliński puts it, movements make an effort to consolidate and to professionalize themselves (but see also Blattert et.al. 1995; Schmitt-Beck and Weins 1997). They learn how to tap resources, how to use modern technology to communicate with each other and the public, and also how to play political games in new party democracies. Among their other main activities we find out-reach, mutual help and assistance programs, lobbying, critical scientific reporting, and, when feasible, conflictual negotations with governments and politicians.

In sum, if we define social movements as mobilizing agents who are capable of staging open-air collective protest, then several chapters included in this volume do not deal with social movements at all. If, however, we define social movements as social agents who tap and command resources in order to put issues across to the public and to influence the agenda in their polity, then this entire book deals with social movements and our task is to understand and recognize their specificity.

SOCIAL MOVEMENT OR THE NONPROFIT SECTOR?

Let me continue in the same vein. If there is so little mobilization, do the essays contained in this volume deal with social movements or with a mere nonprofit sector?[4] Can the issue-related nonprofit sector be always treated as part and parcel of a social movement?

As far as theory is concerned, it is more than compatible with McCarthy and Zald's (1977) by now classical "resource mobilization" approach that a movement industry would include not only movement organizations proper but also non-governmental organizations (NGOs). These are to be understood as yet another - professional, specialized, formalized - way of generating issues and appropriating resources for a movement.

In a recent German-language collected volume on social movement, several authors deal with this issue in a more or less explicit way (Rucht 1999:19-24; Roth 1999:59; Wahl 1999:281-83). Rucht, echoing his and Neidhardt's original formulation (Neidhardt and Rucht 1993), argues that German social movements have become more professional, specialized and formalized, but argues for the view that we still deal with movement organizations since these organizations considered together challenge their society and polity. They keep it on the move.

Wahl argues that, even if the movement activists and the representatives of the by-issue-related NGOs reject each other, one should consider the NGOs as the continuation of the movement by other means in times of de-mobilization (Wahl 1999:282). One should also be open to the empirical possibility that some social movements and NGOs are related by common concerns and by their creators, while it is not the case for others. He does not stop to consider what it means if the nonprofit sector is unrelated to the original movement in these two ways.

As we know, NGOs are dependent on governments, business, national and international organizations for their funding. Western or international organizations, interested in furthering specific issues and/or civic society in the former Soviet satellites account for much of the NGO-factor also in Central Europe. Organizations such as the Greens, the Soros Foundation or the European Union's PHARE-program animate the process of the NGO-formation by offering know-how and/or financial assistance as an incentive to formalization.

The question is **whether or not** this dependence undermines the position of the national NGOs as issue-generators. We should not rest comfortable with the assumption that the national and transnational NGOs pick each other based on issue-compatibility and that they enjoy reciprocal relations, although I do not deny that this is sometimes the case. If we allow for the possibility that an issue-mismatch is frequent, however, we are forced to consider its implications. We should realize that only when these NGOs retain their ties to the issue-related social movement (Wahl) or local social milieus (Roth) do they stand a chance of avoiding co-optation and irrelevance. In contrast to Wahl, moreover, we have to stop and ask how we should classify such organizations, if they lose/ do not have such ties and/or become co-opted.

Based on these remarks, we can use several criteria to decide whether seemingly movement-related organizations are to be considered as part of a given social movement:

(a) continuity with the past: are movement activists among the important founders of the nonprofit organizations claiming to represent their movement? is the nonprofit sector an outgrowth of the social movement: does a phase of mobilization parallel/ precede the establishment of the NGOs?

(b) autonomous issue-generation: are the organizations in question capable of issue-generation or do they serve as a mere issue-conveyor?

(c) autonomous mobilizing strategies: do these organizations invent their own mobilizing (and fund-raising) strategies or do they rely on imports?

(d) moral and political support by movement activists: do these organizations enjoy links to and support of an issue-related movement or do they live a lonely bureaucratic existence? are these organizations capable of mobilizing movement activists/the public around key issues on occasion or only other nonprofit organizations?

(e) source of funding: do these organizations rely on the contributions of movement members and interested public to a considerable extent or do most of their funds come from their government, business or foreign/international organizations?

Ultimately, even these criteria are not helpful in strongly mixed cases, but they should hasten the process of information-gathering and classification. They can help to make systematic our search for an answer to the question as to whether or not a given set of organizations is to be considered part of a social movement or instead should be classified as part of the nonprofit sector.

The need to rely on several criteria to decide how we want to characterize any given movement or apparently movement-related organizations becomes even more clear when we tie it to the empirical material presented in this volume. Using the first criterion, Miethe, who was a long-term dissident, and her co-author, Ulrich-Hempele, stress that the nonprofit sector which deals with women's issues in eastern Germany is not to be identified with the East(earn) German women's movement after 1989. One senses their dislike for paid-for political engagement, and for movement members who now dominate the NGOs although they had not achieved rank prior to 1989. Since these NGOs rely predominantly on government funds, pursue issues on its agenda, and are not anchored in local social milieus or movement networks (Roth 1999:59; see also Rink 1999:185-193), they should not be considered part of the women's movement even on these grounds. That the nonprofit sector does not enjoy much of a movement or any other social support is confirmed by Anheier and Seibel,[5] specialists on the nonprofit sector, who point out that the scarcity of public funds is not a serious problem in eastern Germany. Instead they find that "[w]hat is missing is the local embeddedness... a sufficient degree of volunteer input..." (1998:182). In the eastern part of Germany volunteers, local elites and managers of NGOs are hard to come by. Anheier and Seibel conclude: "The effect is, presumably, a much more centralized and 'artificial' third sector with a higher degree of state dependency than that in West Germany" (Anheier and Seibel 1998:182).

The eastern German gay or the Czech and Polish environmental movements all appear to contrast with the eastern German women's movement since in these cases we find predominantly former dissidents and movement activists as the founders of new movement organizations which emerged at the latest about 1989. Or they are the incumbents of positions provided by the movement NGOs or the government after 1989.

However, even such "genuine" movements are bound to have some newcomers. As Jehlička notes, this is the case with the Czech Greenpeace and the Czech Children of the Earth. These organizations are difficult to disassociate from the movement which they purport to represent because of the international reputation their mother organizations enjoy and since they pursue issues which identical movements elsewhere do. At home, however, they receive very little activist or public support and they (have to) rely on their mother organizations, Western foundations and governments for funds.[6] Jehlička predicts that if they will not learn to mobilize and to generate resources on their own, they are bound to disappear once the external resources of funds dry up. His reflections upon how the public within a specific nation may reject a movement because of its use of "inappropriate," "imported" strategies stress the importance of the third criterion.

Saxonberg's chapter helps to underscore that rules for the allocation of domestic and international funds often influence which issues are put on the organizational agenda. He draws our attention to the fact that some Czech women's groups do not even deal with specific women's issues! International and public funds earmarked for specific projects not only account for the growth of the newcomer NGOs, but are also a chief reason for goal-displacement even among some genuine movement NGOs. Movement members often end up running in pursuit of fundable causes rather than those which they had initially placed on their agenda.

In their pursuit of fundable causes, Central European NGOs do not differ much from some of their Western counterparts. Seen from the point of view of those who work for the NGOs, the nonprofit sector, whether movement-related or not, opens up new opportunites to those who earlier had jobs in the state sector or could count on financial family support. In particular in Poland,[7] but also in the other countries, this form of employment offers a way out of overcrowded labor markets and social assistance. When NGO-staff are recruited from the ranks of people who had little earlier movement experience, this contributes to their issue-shifting.

From the students of the nonprofit sector we can learn about yet another factor - the national cleavage structure - which sometimes fully determines and sometimes only co-shapes the structuring and the issue-spectrum of a given movement/nonprofit sector (Anheier and Seibel 1998). In our future research we should take seriously the notion that a pillarized polity produces a pillarized social movement sector. The influence of this pillarization on the eastern German, Hungarian and Polish women's movements is much in evidence. In Poland the abortion issue pitted Church-affiliated groups against secular groups. Eastern German, Hungarian and Polish women, moreover, find it hard to break away and organize themselves apart from the traditional set of political parties and trade unions. It is puzzling why the environmental movements do not seem to be affected in their structure in the same way.

On the other hand, both national governments and social movements suffer under the competitive pressures. The inability of the movements to gain more attention for "their" issues[8] has very much to do with the predominance of privatization, employment and social issues on the national agendas of their countries. In trying to position themselves in the capitalist world order, their governments initiate criss-crossing debates about the haunting communist past, the advantages and disadvantages of joining the European Union and the latest demands of the International Monetary Fund and World Bank. To this overcrowded national agenda social movements which have been granted some political and public recognition, such as women's, the eastern German gay and most environmental movements, react by turning into experts and bureaucrats. Those still fighting for recognition, such as the Slovak environmental or the Polish gay and Hungarian gay-lesbian movements, withdraw or take to protest, for which they, however, receive only very meager support.

Apart from the national cleavage structure, transnational NGOs (TNGOs), already mentioned above, influence the issue- and strategy-spectrum. It is the saving grace of these TNGOs that not all of them act the part of "friendly hegemons" who provide funds in exchange for the pursuit of issues and mobilizing strategies which they prefer. Two TNGO-experts single out Friends of the Earth International as one of the most democratic TNGOs. It has a very decentralized, federated structure which consists of loosely coupled networks and is open to participatory inputs (Beisheim and Zürn 1999: 312). Their differentiated assessment of the Greenpeace, World Wide Fund International, Friends of the Earth International and Climate Action Network implies that as social movement researchers we have to make fine, well-informed distinctions at the TNGO level in order to adequately assess local NGOs and their activities. We have to ask whether we deal with TNGOs which are hierarchical or federated (see also Rucht 1999a:208). We have to grant the possibility that issue- and/or strategy-shifts are not due to the influence of TNGOs or financial dependence on TNGOS after all, but to the internal movement dynamic or other factors at the national-level. This same argument applies to other sponsors.

WHOSE *CIVIL SOCIETY* ANYHOW?

Many researchers find it so important that social movements (or the nonprofit sector for that matter) speak with their own voices because their shared ideal is that of *civil society/* public in which a plurality of distinctive, yet autonomous and democratically organized actors, engage each other in a public debate about issues of social and political importance. Their second ideal is to have elites open to their influence.

This ideal becomes problematic when we convert it into an export product. The literature on TNGOs, in particular on those which are engaged in promoting human rights, environmental and development issues, is generally enthusiastic about their democratizing potential at the national and international level (Beisheim and Zürn 1999; Wahl 1999; Windfuhr 1999:527,529,531,534; della Porta and Kriesi 1999:14-21; Rucht 1999a:210-217). It also praises their expertise, resources and monitoring capacities which have the potential of enforcing the processes of democratization and policy implementation at the local and national level. Finding in TNGOs a new outlet for their neo-romantic idealism, Western researchers herald them as the modern bearers of the (international) *civil society*. TNGOs have become the conscience of the world - for this reason they can "shame" single states into observing international standards (Nölke 1997:88) and expand international bargaining and decision-making regimes by one crucial factor - "arguing" (Beisheim and Zürn 1999:311,314).[9]

This is only one side of the coin, however - the Western one. In developing countries TNGOs or their local representatives are understood as funding or sponsoring organizations whose excessive influence is to be avoided (Windfuhr 1999:530). This can be accomplished by relying on several sponsors or pooling resources with similar organizations. From this perspective only native social movements or community-based organizations qualify as genuine participants in the *civil society*. The reader may recall that Wahl and Roth argued in a similar manner: only if NGOs retain their ties to their social milieus or social movements, do they stand a chance of neutralizing the influence of their sponsors. If they let their dependence on their sponsors guide their politics and activities, they run the risk of co-optation. If they are co-opted, even if they contribute to the national debate or influence the stage of policy deliberation, their independent input is negligible.

The point is that we cannot have it both ways. We cannot export our organizations and standards for the *civil society* and claim that by virtue of some miraculous transformation they turn domestic at their place of destination. As true democrats we should support native products. This is quite problematic, however, when native products include a good measure of xenophobia, damage to environment or violations of human rights. Still we have to choose and make our criteria of choice explicit.

HOMEMADE AND IMPORTED MOVEMENT ORGANIZATIONS

In all populations mentioned here a deep cleavage runs between the "cosmopolitan," "European" and the "nationalist" parts of the public. In eastern Germany it joins the cleavage between the Ossis (eastern Germans) and the Wessis (western Germans). Hatred of foreigners, although it is expressed with more violence in eastern Germany than elsewhere, is found in all four countries addressed in this volume. The nationalists are against any form of foreign influence on domestic debates and affairs. They oppose foreign investments, foreign ownership of property, even international aid. In all countries analyzed in this book, TNGOs play a very important role in helping movement organizations to emerge, build their organizational structures, professionalize, use modern technology/know-how and engage in networking. How are they perceived? This is another issue to which social movement theorists pay too little attention. In *Social Movements in a Globalizing World*, for example, the editors, della Porta and Kriesi (1999:4-22), place their emphasis on the new opportunities created by globalization. Global mass media, recent advances in the computer technology and in the consolidation of the international negotiating regimes hasten movement diffusion and expand international movement co-operation. TNGOs, their activities and the negotiating arenas they create are understood as part and parcel of this globalization. The intellectual effort is invested in understanding the many ways in which they help to expand opportunities for diffusion and co-operation, and not in understanding the obstacles to them. The assumption prevails that "good guys" from the developed and developing countries will together confront the powerful, "bad guys" of this world. True, a constraint, such as national culture, is briefly mentioned, but this is not where the thrust of the argument is (della Porta and Kriesi 1999:9,13).

As Koopmans' (1999:57-70) article in the same volume reminds us, however, national culture and history constitute reservoirs of meaning upon which a public draws to frame events, issues and itself. In situations of conflict, the parties involved in a national debate can draw upon these reservoirs to frame the events, issues, their opponents and themselves in a way which they hope will pull the public their way. Koopmans implies that each national culture provides a certain historically conditioned attitude towards the past and an image of a given nation's role in it. It also has a rather stable view of other nations and nation states. These are ranked. Only a few belong to a group of favorites. All this conditions how a given country reacts to an event.

Unmentioned is nationalism - itself a great obstacle to unhindered diffusion of social movements and international co-operation. Nationalism makes for a rejection of nearly everything foreign in the phases of intense mobilization, which we can expect to last long past the actual moment of achieving national independence and which we can also expect to re-surface in times of economic crises. But even every-day nationalism exercises a powerful influence on the issues which are being debated at the national level. If a movement attacks what broad sectors of the public perceive as national achievements or virtues, if it violates the national sacrum, it is bound to lose public credibility and support, even if it is "right" or "just" by international standards. A transplanted movement enhances its chances of winning acceptance when it acknowledges and defers to key national symbols, traditions and values (Snow and Benford 1999:26,34-37). It can only risk playing the role of a trend-setter, if it ranks high in the hierarchy of favorites of the host nation and the countering nationalist movement is rather weak.

At stake in the truly heated debates between the conflicting domestic parties is what and who is moral, who is a good or a bad German, Swede, or Pole. A bad co-national is marginalized and then ostracized. There are no higher stakes. In the case of transplanted movements, Czechs, Slovaks or Poles who co-operate with foreigners risk being similarly condemned and disowned. They risk being deprived of the moral right to belong to the national community. Their arguments are rejected as illegitimate.

Without taking this issue head on, several contributors to this volume note a distinction between "ours" and "foreign" which is of key importance to many social movements and publics in Central Europe. In echoing these movements and publics, they introduce an analytical distinction between outsider and insider movement organizations, between imported and homemade "movement products," between domestic and Western sponsors (see, for example, Gliński's chapter).

We can expect some animosity on the part of eastern Germans towards their western German "benevolent colonizers" after the re-unification of the two Germanies in 1990, but it is not clear whether the NGO sector is rejected as part of the women's movement for this reason. Rink (1999: 185-193 and in this volume), in contrast, although without any hint of emotion, explicitly introduces a distinction between western German and eastern German movement organizations, funds and mobilization activities. Rink (1999:185,188) argues that there is no continuity between the dissident activities, citizen committees of 1989 and the present-day citizen initiatives. Based on empirical research, he gives credence to the thesis that new eastern German groups and initiatives should be treated as transplants from western Germany (Zimmer in Rink 1999:188). Between 1991 and 1993 the initiatives turned less radical and more professional. Institutionalization, spurred by government subsidies, made for the withdrawal of the activists, de-mobilization and loss of public appeal. In this case, the foreign explains de-mobilization. The next case is even clearer. Jehlička portrays the contrast between the homemade and the imported NGOs. The original national movement stands for the familiar and appealing, its new organizations stand for the foreign, their strategies for the appalling. They suffer public rejection. Similarly, Snajdr in his chapter on the Slovak environmental movement connects foreign funding to the expansion of the movement, but also to its rejection by the public. He convincingly argues that without massive international and Western assistance, this particular movement may actually not be able to sustain itself. With this assistance, however, it does not make much headway either. For some countries this is a characteristic dilemma. Hungarian contributors to this volume do not address this problem. However, another Hungarian researcher, Szabó (1996) takes care to distinguish between domestic and foreign movement activities. Between 1989 and 1994, the Hungarian environmental movement managed to mobilize many different sectors of the public and on its own stood for 5-8% of all protest events (Szabó 1996:509-510). Szabó points out that the Dutch financed almost all publications of this movement. They also supplied organizational, technological and financial help.

All these are homemade distinctions, yet their recurrence suggests that they have analytical relevance. Future research should pay more systematic attention to how, if at all, the basic cleavage between national and foreign plays a role or affects the (self-)perception and mobilization capacities of social movements in this part of the world. Only then will we be able to say more about the con- straints on movement diffusion and co-operation, and also about the extent to which the genuine as opposed to the imported social movement organizations affect public debates, national affairs and the implementation of various policy programs.

POLITICS OF INFLUENCE AND POLITICS OF RECOGNITION

When we turn to the question of the political influence exercised by various social movements we have to focus on these movements and the nation states within whose territory they operate. In the literature on social movements, it is argued, based on many empirical studies, that social move- ments have the greatest chances of gaining political influence if they are (a) active in liberal societies which bestow legality on organizing and mobilizing; (b) operate in states which offer multiple points of access and contestation and/or competitive party systems and/or systems with divided elites, so that at least some political parties, formal organizations or elite factions can be enlisted as allies; (c) deal with states which are capable of determined policy implementation; (d) mobilize in old, secure democracies; (e) face a conciliatory rather than a repressive conflict management style, that is, do not encounter policiary repression but rather the opening up of new arenas for policy contestation, etc. etc. (but see della Porta and Diani 1999:196-237; Flam 1994).

The question of access and political influence, however, pertains to social movements which have already gained at least a modicum of public and political recognition. Movements which still struggle for it face multiple tasks. They have to construct their own collective identity, convince the public that they should be allowed to enter the *civil society* (which amounts to expanding its boundaries to make room for one more social category) and, finally, wrest a set of rights from the state (Melucci 1980; Touraine 1981; Habermas 1984; Cohen 1985) These movements can be said to be engaged in the *politics of recognition* (Calhoun 1995:213-214).

Next I wish to show that in Central Europe we find both social movements aiming to stablize their political influence and those still struggling for recognition. I will first address the environmental movements, most of whom seem to be concerned with maintaining their political influence. I will then briefly turn to the gay(-lesbian) movements to show that these movements for recognition respond to the same nation-states in a different way. In this way I want to stress that the nature of the nation-state interacts with the type of the movement to produce a particular set of movement strategies. Older social movements which aim to retain their access and political influence come to resemble interest groups in their orientations and strategies. They turn themselves into experts and lobbyists. The movements which still struggle for recognition are more inclined to rely on mobilization and protest - they have to, if they are to attract attention to the plight of their members and to lay foundations for a new collective identity.

It turns out that the Czech, eastern German and Polish environmental movements have experienced a falling from grace in the last ten years. The Hungarian movement seems to be favored by its government, while the Slovak has to work hard against its.

The Polish case has very clear contours. As a result of widespread environmental concerns and social movement pressure, long before 1989 several agencies and a ministry were set up to deal with environmental reforms (Tews 1999). When the party-state started to skirt the issue, its major opponent, *Solidarność*, provided an umbrella for the women's, environmental and gay movements. A separate table set up for ecological issues during the Round Table talks showed the great importance attached at the time to the environmental issues and the environmental movement. When the scramble for state power began, however, *Solidarność* fell apart. Since then, it is the color of the national government which determines which persons, interests and social movements are in and which are out. Although the Polish ennvironmental movement is very large and played an important role during the Round Table talks, afterwards some of its most professional organizations had privileged but only informal access to the Ministry of Environment. This allowed politicians to completely ignore these organizations as well as some of the key environmental issues since 1997.[10]

So far, the trajectory of the Czech environmental movement has very much resembled that of its Polish counterpart. Numerous and in part tied to the dissident movement before 1989, the Czech environmentalists were well represented in the Civic Forum during the November revolution of 1989 and later in the Czechoslovak government. A few environmental movement organizations, moreover, became members of a policy network which had privileged access to the Ministry of Environment. The Klaus-government caused a complete u-turn on the environmental issue. By 1994-1995 the environmentalists became the new subversives, on the list of major public enemies. Like their Polish counterparts, they switched their emphasis from protest to expertise and regular politics, although as in the Polish case, grassroots mobilization continues to play a role.

The supporters of the eastern German environmental movement feel bitter about its demobilization, the betrayal suffered at the hands of "its" Green Party and the inactivity of the New Forum. At the same time, this movement, even more than the Polish and Czech movements, managed to institutionalize itself in associations, political parties, citizens' initiatives, environmental projects, ecological villages as well as in legislation. As in Poland and in the Czech Republic, scattered local and regional protest is rather frequent in eastern Germany. As in these two countries, there is no massive mobilization. It is the fall from grace, the inability of the environmental movement to keep up public and political interest or to realize its grand visions, I believe, rather than the actual extent of policy or institutional failure that is problematic for its proponents.

The chapter on the Hungarian environmental movement tells three success stories. Although it mentions demonstration fatigue among the Hungarian public and so implies de-mobilization (see also Szabó 1994), it creates an impression of an amicable communication between the environmental movement and the Hungarian government, no matter what color the latter has. Interestingly, each of the three depicted movements seems to influence the national government in a different way. The Danube Circle relies on its 10 years old reputation and on mass mobilization in emergency situations, Green Future on advocacy of the public interest and the Air Group on regular politics. The fact that the movement as such is fragmented is portrayed as its strength rather than its weakness.

The chapter on the Slovak enviromental movement creates the opposite impression. Although the Slovak movement seems to have grown, radicalized and linked up to important international organizations, it has neither access to the government nor much public support. Snajdr poignantly conveys its dilemma: to resign from international support, but risk obliteration, or to continue relying on this support, but risk continued public rejection. This movement, as the two gay movements to which I will turn next, is actually still at the stage where it is struggling hard for recognition.

Gay and gay-lesbian movements with their *politics of recognition* constitute a complete novelty in the Polish and Hungarian[11] cultural and political contexts (Melucci 1980; Touraine 1981; Habermas 1984; Cohen 1985; Calhoun 1995:213-214). Like the labor movement or the Western women's, environmental or gay-lesbian movements at their historical points of origin, these Central European movements face a triple task: to forge their own mobilizable, collective identity, to gain entry into and expand the *civil society*, and to secure/have enacted the legal recognition of the state. The two chapters depict several major parallel problems: to gain staff members, activists and supporters who would not be afraid to appear and act in public; to establish solidary gay communities and self-help groups - which in turn calls for mobilization to have gay and lesbian organizations legalized and registered; to initiate and gain control over the public debates about homosexuality so as to affect its public definitions; to secure and expand protective legal rights; and, last but not least, to help prevent and treat HIV/AIDS.

For my purposes only the political dimension is of interest: Since the general public is rather conservative and homophobic, even liberal political parties in Central Europe are still very far from daring to look for the gay vote. This applies also to eastern Germany where gay-lesbian rights enjoy legal protection. In Hungary it seems that only because parliamentary work often escapes the attention of the public that at times a piece of legislation favorable to gays and lesbians is passed. In Poland the gay community has several champions in parliament and government. In their view, shared by parts of the gay community,[12] they are unable to accomplish more in view of the uncertain and weak mobilization of the gay community. Polish gays have not been able to set up a stable and effective lobby. Nor are they able to stage protest events when necessary. Confronted with an intolerant general context, gays in Poland oscillate between defensive and offensive collective actions (Cohen 1985:704). At times they seek retreat in their own community institutions, at times they venture out to engage in the struggle for recognition. The Hungarian chapter, in contrast, conveys the impression that the unintimidated younger gays have taken over the initiative. They are resolved to push the Hungarian public and polity towards more tolerance. The eastern German case seems to suggest that where gay-lesbian rights are institutionalized and commercialized, the gay movement has to decline. In eastern Germany the new legal-political framework brought more freedom but also de-mobilization, even though there are enough issues around which mobilization could occur.

THE STRUCTURE OF THE BOOK

The aim of this book is to present introductory information about four types of social movements - women's, religious, environmental and gay(-lesbian) - in Central Europe. The first part of the book focuses on the women's movements in eastern Germany, the Czech Republic and Hungary. It shows that women's social and political engagement takes a variety of forms. They organize nonprofit organizations, mutual aid groups, lobbies, expert committees, political party or trade union clubs. But, as is also the case in Poland (see note 10), none of these countries can claim that it has a mobilized, integrated, independent women's movement. The next part of the book addresses religious movements in Poland and eastern Germany. While in Poland new religious sects experienced a brief period of expansion after 1989, in eastern Germany the expected sect-expansion did not occur at all. Moreover, a massive exodus from the Protestant Church took place between 1989-1992. It has not stopped since. In this sense we can speak of religious de-mobilization. The third part of the book deals with the environmental movements in the Czech Republic, Slovakia, Hungary and Poland. It shows that, apart from the Slovak case, these movements have become institutionalized and enjoy some, more or less continuous, more or less unquestioned and uninterrupted, access to the state. There is little national, but some local and regional mobilization. The final part of the book is unprecedented. It is devoted to the gay movements in eastern Germany and Poland, and to the gay-lesbian movement in Hungary. It shows that these movements still have to wrest public acceptance from their societies and polities, even though they are making headways as far as institutionalization and legalization of gay and lesbian rights is concerned. Their mobilization is capricious in Poland, carried out but the younger generation in Hungary and on decline in eastern Germany.

NOTES

* I am thankful to one embittered and hateful and one laid-back anonymous reviewer for convincing me that a short introduction to this volume would not do. I would also like to thank Petr Jehlička for his criticisms, and Dieter Rucht and Andreas Moerke for sending me books from Berlin. I am also indebted to Sim Lee who so carefully corrected and refined my English.

1. For Calhoun's students see, for example, Pfaff 1996; 1999 or Yang 2000a; 2000b. Johnston in his capacity as an editor of the international journal on social movements, *Mobilization*, encourages articles on repressive regimes and Eastern Europe. For his Ph.D. students see, for example, Deess 1997.
2. For numerous examples see Keane 1985. See also "notes and references" in Bugajski and Pollack 1989 and in Skilling 1989. I purposely use the term Central Europe rather than Eastern Europe in this text for two reasons. First I wish to join those past dissidents who defied the political division of Europe into Western and Eastern. They engaged historiography to remind us that this used to be Central Europe and so kept hope alive that it would be again. Secondly, for reasons which I explain at length elsewhere (Flam 1998) I want to employ a term which includes East/eastern Germany. Just as the mainstream Western scholars excluded "Eastern Europe" from their research, so did the

specialists on totalitarianism and civil society for a long time exclude East Germany from theirs. It was only when East German dissidents stirred in the late 1970s and the early 1980s and created a modicum of a *civil society* by mid-1985, that they made it onto the research agenda. It was only after that time that, when specialists spoke of Central Europe, they usually also included East Germany.

3. Among its useful conceptual offspring we find such terms as "second" or "independent" society and "parallel politics" or "second polity" and their extremely useful indicator *samizdat* (Skilling 1989:158-164; Ekiert 1991:298-303).

4. The Polish case, if typical, suggests that we have witnessed a remarkable increase in the number of nonprofit formal organizations in Central Europe. In Poland the number of formal women's organizations rose from 59 to 107 between 1993 and 1997, the number of environmental organizations from 700 to 1,000 between 1995 and 1999 alone and the number of religious organizations from 30 in 1989 to 300 in 1999 (see two chapters in this volume and note 10). Before 1989 several hundred large, centralized, "official" associations and organizations existed, while by early 1995 researchers gathered data on 4,328 associations and foundations, 6,050 local chapters of these organizations and some 6,500 other organizations ("Jawor" in Ekiert and Kubik 1999:338).

5. As most Western and western German commentators they fail to see that eastern Germans reject these organizations in part because they see them as imposed. Instead they single out such factors as the experience of totalitarianism and the flight of "the bulk of the East German intellectuals and entrepreneurs to West Germany [before 1961] which accounts for the relative absence of local middle classes in East Germany" (Anheier and Seibel 1998:182).

6. We do not have any figures for the Polish movement organizations, but 64% of the entire nonprofit sector came from private and foreign sources while 26% came from the state budget by early 1995 ("Jawor" in Ekiert and Kubik 1999:338).

7. By the early 1995 NGOs employed 53,000 full-time employees ("Jawor" in Ekiert and Kubik 1999:28).

8. To cite one good example: Not only eastern German movements, but also eastern German politicians find it difficult to make themselves heard in the capital, although they much more than their western German colleagues (85% vs. 68%) are interested in environmental protection (Machatzke 1997:336-Tabelle X-2).

9. See Nölke 1997, however, for interesting empirical findings and Rucht 1999a:217-219 for some reflections about the limitations of the NGOs.

10. Somewhat in contrast, the independent Polish women's movement, although it is not particularly large and at this point can be reduced to its numerous NGOs of which many were organized by the women who turned "feminist" at their universities prior to 1989, enjoyed formalized access to the government since mid-1996. With the ascent to power of a new party coalition in 1997, however, it lost this access. The range of concerns of the Government Plenipotentiary to whom it had enjoyed access was also narrowed: from family and women's issues to family issues only. Women's organizations reacted with renewed efforts to gain some political influence. They set up the Parliamentary Women's Group in 1997 (based on a ms. prepared for this volume by Anna Titkow and Danuta Duch, two gender specialists engaged in research at the Institute of Philosophy and Sociology at PAN in Warsaw. The authors withdrew their contribution a few days before the book manuscript was to be sent to the publisher).

11. I leave out the eastern German movement which, in part due to its own pre-1989 efforts, in part because of the legal-institutional effects of the German re-unification, has already won the battle for recognition on several fronts.

15

12. Sergiusz Wróblewski, a historian who is the editor of a well-known, high quality gay magazine, *Inaczej*, published in Poznań, argues for this point of view in his 3-page long comment on Kliszczyński's contribution to this volume (see note 4 in Kliszczyński's chapter).

REFERENCES

Anheier H. K. and W. Seibel. 1999. "The Nonprofit Sector and the Transformation of Societies: A Comparative Analysis of East Germany, Poland, and Hungary" in *Private Action and the Public Good*. Edited by W.W. Powell and E.S. Clemens. New Haven. Yale University Press, pp. 177-189

Arato A. 1981/1882. "Civil Society Against the State: Poland, 1981-1982" *Telos* 50:19-48

Aron R. 1969. *Democracy and Totalitarianism*. New York. Frederick A. Praeger, Publisher

Beisheim M. and Michael Z. 1999. "Transnationale Nicht-Regierungsorganisationen" in *Neue Soziale Bewegungen*. Edited by A. Klein, H.-J. Legrand and T. Leif. Opladen/Wiesbaden. West-deutscher Verlag, pp. 306-319

Blattert B., D. Rink and D. Rucht. 1995. "Von den Oppositionsgrouppen der DDR zu den neuen sozialen Bewegungen in Ostdeutschland" *Politische Vierteljahresschrift*, Jg. 36 Heft 3:397-422

Bugajski J. and M. Pollack. 1989. *East European Fault Lines. Dissent, Opposition, and Social Activism*. Boulder. Westview Press

Calhoun C. 1995. *Critical Social Theory. Culture, History, and the Challenge of Difference*. Oxford. Blackwell

Calhoun C. 1991. "The Problem of Identity in Collective Action" in *Macro-Micro Linkages in Sociology*. Edited by J. Huber. Newbury Park. Sage, pp. 51-75

Calhoun C. 1994. *Neither Gods nor Emperors: Students and the Struggle for Democracy in China*. Berkeley. University of California Press

Cohen J. L. 1985. "Strategy or Identity: New Theoretical Paradigms and Contemporary Social Movements" *Social Research* Vol. 52 Nr. 4:663-716

Deess E.P. 1997. "Collective Life and Social Change in the GDR" *Mobilization* Vol.2 Nr. 2:207-225

della Porta D. and H. Kriesi. 1999. "Social Movements in a Globalizing World: an Introduction" in *Social Movements in a Globalizing World*. London. MacMillan Press Ltd, pp. 3-22

della Porta D. and M. Diani. 1999. *Social Movements: An Introduction*. Oxford. Blackwell Publishers

Ekiert G. 1991. "Democratization Process in East Central Europe: A Theoretical Reconsideration" *British Journal of Political Science* 21:285-313

Ekiert G. and J. Kubik. 1999. "Protest Event Analysis in the Study of Democratic Consolidation: Poland, 1989-1993" in *Acts of Dissent. New Developments in the Study of Protest*. Edited by D. Rucht, R. Koopmans and F. Neidhardt. Lanham, Maryland. Rowman and Littlefield Publishers, pp. 317-48

Feher F. and A. Heller. 1987. *Eastern Left, Western Left. Totalitarianism, Freedom and Democracy*. Cambridge. Polity Press

Ferree M. M. and S. Roth. 1999. "Kollektive Identität und Organisationskulturen. Theorien neuer sozialer Bewegungen aus amerikanischer Perspektive" in *Neue Soziale Bewegungen*. Edited by A. Klein, H.-J. Legrand and T. Leif. Opladen. Westdeutscher Verlag, pp. 131-143

Flam H. 1994. *States and Anti-Nuclear Movements*. Edinburgh. Edinburgh University Press

Flam H. 1998. *Mosaic of Fear: Poland and East Germany before 1989*. Boulder, Colorado. East European Monogragraphs distributed by Columbia University Press

Gliński P. 1996. *Polscy Zieloni*. Warszawa. Wydawnictwo IFiS PAN

Habermas J. 1984. *The Theory of Communicative Action*. Boston. Beacon Press

Jenkins C. J. 1988. "States and Social Movements: Recent Theory and Research" *States and Social Structures Newsletter* No. 8:4-8

Johnston H. 1989. "Toward an Explanation of Church Opposition to Authoritarian Regimes: Religious-Oppositional Subcultures in Poland and Catalonia" *Journal for the Scientific Study of Religion* Vol . 28 Nr. 4: 498-508

Johnston H. 1991. *Tales of Nationalism: Catalonia, 1939-1979*. New Brunswick, N.J. Rutgers University Press

Jowitt K. 1993. "Nowy światowy nieład" *Gazeta*, 27-28 luty, p. 13 (Interview with K. Jowitt conducted by T. Grabowski)

Keane J., ed. 1985. *The Power of the Powerless: Citizens against the State in Central-Eastern Europe*, by Václav Havel et al. London. Hutchinson

Keane J., ed. 1988. *Civil Society and the State. New European Perspectives*. London. Verso

Koopmans R. 1999. "A Comparison of Protests against the Gulf War in Germany, France and the Netherlands" in *Social Movements in a Globalizing World*. London. MacMillan Press Ltd, pp. 57-70

Lefort C. 1986.*The Political Forms of Modern Society. Bureaucracy,Democracy,Totalitarianism*. Cambridge. Polity Press

McCarthy J. D. and M. N. Zald. 1977. "Resource Mobilization and Social Movements: A Partial Theory" *American Journal of Sociology* Vol. 82 Nr. 6:1212-1241

Machatzke J. 1997. "Einstellungen zum Umfang staatlicher Verantwortung - Zum Staatsverständnis der Eliten im vereinten Deutschland" in *Eliten in Deutschland*. Edited by W. Bürklin, H. Rebenstorf et.al. Opladen. Leske + Budrich, pp. 321-350

Melucci A. 1980. "The New Social Movements: A Theoretical Approach" *Social Science Information* Vol. 19 Nr. 2:199-226

Neidhardt F. und D. Rucht. 1993. "Auf dem Weg in die 'Bewegungsgesellschaft'" *Soziale Welt*, Heft 3, pp. 305-326

Nölke A. 1997. "Transnationale Nichtregierungsorganisationen als 'Internationale Zivilgesellschaft'? Vergleichende Perspektiven" *Comparativ* 4:87-95

Oberschall A. 1996. "Opportunities and framing in the Eastern European revolts of 1989" in *Comparative Perspectives on Social Movements*. Edited by D. McAdam, J. D. McCarthy and M. N. Zald. Cambridge. Cambridge University Press, pp. 93-121

Pelczynski Z. A. 1988. "Solidarity and 'The Rebirth of Civil Society' in Poland, 1976-81" in *Civil Society and the State. New European Perspectives*. Editedy by J. Keane. London. Verso, pp. 361-380

Pickvance K. 1998. *Democracy and Environmental Movements in Eastern Europe. A Comparative Study of Hungary and Russia*. Boulder. Westview Press

Pfaff S. 1996. "Collective Identity and Informal Groups in Revolutionary Mobilization: East Germany in 1989" *Social Forces* Vol.75 Nr. 1:91-118

Pfaff S. 1999. "From Revolution to Reunification: Popular Protest and Social Movements in the Transformation of East Germany" Doctoral Thesis. New York University

Rink D. 1999. "Mobilisierungsschwäche, Latenz, Transformation oder Auflösung?" in *Neue Soziale*

Bewegungen. Edited by A. Klein, H.-J. Legrand and T. Leif. Opladen/Wiesbaden. Westdeutscher Verlag, pp. 180-195

Roth R. 1999. "Neue soziale Bewegungen und liberale Demokratie. Herausforderungen,Innovationen und paradoxe Konsequenzen" in *Neue Soziale Bewegungen*. Edited by A. Klein, H.-J. Legrand and T. Leif. Opladen/Wiesbaden.Westdeutscher Verlag, pp. 47-63

Rucht D. 1999. "Gesellschaft als Projekt - Projekte in der Gesellschaft. Zur Rolle sozialer Bewegungen" in *Neue Soziale Bewegungen*. Edited by A. Klein, H.-J. Legrand and T. Leif. Opladen/Wiesbaden. Westdeutscher Verlag, pp. 15-27

Rucht D. "The Transnationalization of Social Movements: Trends, Causes and Problems" in *Social Movements in a Globalizing World*. Edited by D. della Porta, H. Kriesi and D. Rucht. London. MacMillan Press Ltd, pp. 206-222

Schmitt-Beck R. and C. Weins. 1997. "Gone with the wind (of change). Neue soziale Bewegungen und politischer Protest im Osten Deutschlands" in *Politische Orientierungen und Verhaltensweisen im vereinigten Deutschland*. Edited by O. W. Gabriel. Opladen. Leske + Budrich

Schmitter P. C. 1999. "Critical Reflections on the 'Functions' of Political Parties and their Performance in Neo-Democracies" in *Demokratie in Ost und West*. Frankfurt a.M. Suhrkamp, pp. 475-495

Seifert W. 1996. "Systemunterstützung und Systembewertung in Ostdeutschland und anderen osteuropäischen Transformationsstaaten" in *Wohlfahrtentwicklung in vereinten Deutschland*. Edited by W. Zapf and R. Habich. Berlin. Edition Sigma, pp. 309-328

Skilling G. H. 1989. *Samizdat and an Independent Society in Central and Eastern Europe*. Columbus. Ohio University Press

Snow David A. and Robert D. Benford. 1999. "Alternative Types of Cross-national Diffusion in the Social Movement Arena" in *Social Movements in a Globalizing World*. Edited by D. della Porta, H. Kriesi and D. Rucht. London. MacMillan Press Ltd, pp. 23-39

Szabó M. 1996. "Politischer Protest im postkommunistischen Ungarn 1989-1994" *Berliner Journal für Soziologie*, Vol. 6 Nr. 4:501-515

Szabó M. 1994. "Soziale Bewegungen und politischer Protest im post-kommunistischen Ungarn (1990-1994)" in *Konfliktregulierung durch Parteien und politische Stabilität in Ostmitteleuropa*. Edited by D. Segert. Berlin. Peter Lang

Tarrow S. 1989. *Struggle, Politics, and Reform: Collective Action, Social Movements, and Cycles of Protest*. Western Societies Program Occasional Paper no 21, Cornell University, Center for International Studies

Tews K. 1999. *EU-Erweiterung und Umweltschutz. Umweltpolitische Koordination zwischen EU und Polen*. Leipzig. Leipziger Universitätsverlag

Tilly Ch. 1988. "Social Movements, Old and New" in *Social Movements as a Factor of Change in the Contemporary World, Research in Social Movements, Conflicts and Change*, Vol. 10, JAI Press, pp. 1-18

Tilly Ch. 1983. "Speaking Your Mind Without Elections, Surveys, or Social Movements" *Public Opinion Quarterly* 47:461-78

Touraine A. 1981. *The Voice and the Eye*. Cambridge. Cambridge University Press

Wahl P. 1999. "Perspektiven der Solidaritätsbewegung" in *Neue Soziale Bewegungen*. Edited by A. Klein, H.-J. Legrand and T. Leif. Opladen/Wiesbaden. Westdeutscher Verlag, pp. 272-291

Windfuhr M. 1999. "Der Einfluß von NGOs auf die Demokratie" in *Demokratie in Ost und West*. Edited by W. Merkel and A. Busch. Frankfurt a.M. Suhrkamp, pp. 520-548

Yang G. 2000a. "The Liminal Effects of Social Movements: Red Guards and the Transformation of Identity" *Sociological Forum* Vol. 15 Nr. 3:379-406

Yang G. 2000b. "Achieving Emotions in Collective Action: Emotional Processes and Movement Mobilization in the 1989 Chinese Student Movement" *The Sociological Quarterly* Vol. 41 Nr 4:593-614

PART I

WOMEN'S MOVEMENTS

1. Preference for Informal Democracy - the East(ern) German Case

Ingrid Miethe and Anne Ulrich - Hampele

Ingrid Miethe and Anne Ulrich - Hampele

LOOKING BACK: THE WOMEN'S MOVEMENT UNDER SOCIALISM[1]

In contrast to other Eastern European countries, there were informal women's groups in the German Democratic Republic which considered themselves part of an independent women's movement which was separate from state-sanctioned organizations at least since the beginning of the 1980s (Kenawi 1995). The existence of such groups was a condition for the mobilization of women which occurred in the Fall of 1989 (Ferree 1994:601-602). The question whether the term "women's movement" is appropriate for the GDR in the period before 1989 remains subject to debate in view of the low number of women involved and the lack of a public in the Western-democratic sense of the word, but more important than these issues is the fact that the movement defined itself as such. Moreover, this definition is justified by a degree of networking and semi-public communication among women that was considerable by socialist standards.

Because in state socialism it was difficult to find spaces in which the government did not claim access, the term "independent women's movement" here signifies the attempt to create such a space in the first place. The state-organized women's association (*Demokratischer Frauenverband Deutschlands*, or *DFD*), which had some 1.4 million members, claimed exclusive status as the official women's organization in the GDR. The *DFD* remained almost completely isolated from new and critical discussions, and when the independent women's movement developed in the 1980s, the *DFD* was used and played off against the new informal women's groups by the *SED* government (Hampele 1993a).

By organizing largely under the roof of the Protestant Church, the independent women's groups took advantage of the only means of gaining access to public found outside the sphere of state institutions. They addressed issues that were ignored by the state, such as women and peace, anti-militaristic child-raising and non-ideologized child care, feminism, lesbianism, domestic violence, etc.

A small proportion of these groups consisted of women active in the Church, and dealt with Christian topics such as feminist theology. The vast majority of the groups - mainly women's pacifist groups and lesbian initiatives - included Christian women and women active in the Church, but considered the Church mainly as an umbrella. The "Women for Peace" groups, founded in 1982, were the first major mobilization of women that attained a certain public visibility. These groups formed in response to a government plan to include women in compulsory military service. The petition against the new draft law is said to have been signed by some 200 women (Kukutz 1995), an extremely high number by East German standards. The women's peace groups considered themselves primarily as pacifist groups with a critical stance toward the regime, and only inci-dentally as women's groups (Kukutz 1995; Miethe 1999a). The first networking meetings among women's groups took place beginning in 1984, initiated by the Women for Peace groups (Kukutz 1995), and were increasingly structured by feminist groups from 1986 on (Hampele 1993b).

It can thus be argued that work for peace had led to the development of the unofficial women's movement (Kukutz 1995:1333). Some of the "Women for Peace," especially in the southern GDR, increasingly turned toward the groups with a stronger feminist orientation when the peace movement lost momentum after 1985. Others focused more strongly on the issue of human rights, and some of them were among the founders of the Initiative for Peace and Human Rights (Miethe 1999b). The formation of the "Inititative for Peace and Human Rights" (*IFM*) in 1986, which came from the Church-backed peace movement, but deliberately positioned itself outside the Church, became a catalyst for new human right dissidence.

A typical "career" of a female dissident in the GDR began in a subgroup of "Women for Peace," progressed to more involvement in the *IFM* and peaked when she became a founding-mother of one of the many citizen initiatives in the Fall 1989 (Miethe 1999b). The most well-known case in point is Bärbel Bohley who initiated The New Forum - which was to become the largest of the citizen initiatives - in September 1989. She was no exception. As Miethe showed (1996:88) East German women constituted 40% of the signatories of the very first proclamation of the New Forum which called on East German citizens to become its members by signing it. However, they withdrew their engagement from the New Forum and similar institutions, once they became confronted with their "male" emphasis on formal procedures and structures (Miethe 1996, 1999b). Among the actual members of the New Forum, only 20% were women.

In general the potential numbers of the women's groups in the 1980s, many of which existed only ad hoc, can only be roughly estimated. Although only seven women's groups are documented in the files of the State Security service (*Ministerium für Staatssicherheit, Stasi*),[2] Samira Kenawi (1994) has identified some 100 women's groups. The national networking meetings were attended by 60 to 300 women (Hampele 1995:423; Hampele-Ulrich 2000).

These women's groups differed in their view of the state and patriarchal hegemony, in the topics they dealt with as well as in importance they assigned to political activity as such. Most of the groups took a critical stance toward the state. As Samira Kenawi writes (1995:12), the relation-ship between the women's groups and the state was contradictory: the state was "both enemy and addressee, feared as all-powerful yet called upon to engage in dialogue. The tactics of the women's groups were situated for the most part between avoidance of confrontation and the demand for participation." The line of conflict was drawn between the women's own claim to self-determination and a political voice on the one hand, and the rejection of state imposition on the other. In any case, the conflict was seen, as in other countries of the former Soviet bloc, as one between "us" and "them," i. e. the people versus the party-state apparatus.

Another conflict which differentiated the women's groups in the GDR lies in the fact that some, mainly the Women for Peace groups, criticized the GDR regime as a dictatorship and gave only marginal attention to questions of patriarchal hegemony (Miethe 1999b), while more fem-inistically oriented groups focused debate on the criticism of patriarchal structures.

Most of the women's groups considered specific actions as less important than the simple fact of being together in the group. As noted above, the groups provided an opportunity to discuss issues that were taboo in East German society, or gave lesbians a chance to meet other lesbians. The existence of the groups was a success in itself, and also provided a forum for self-reflection and consciousness-raising processes. Furthermore, these groups acted as an instance of socialization for women who later - in 1989 and the following years - attempted to participate in mixed-gender civil rights groups (Miethe 1999b), and for initiatives that in 1989-1990 led to the establishment of women's civil rights groups, such as the "Independent Women's Federation" (*Unabhängiger Frauenverband,* or *UFV*) (see below).

The more politically critical women used the official channels of protest - writing petitions to state agencies (*Eingaben*) - and more importantly made use of critical church publicity, such as politically motivated services, prayers of supplication, grass-roots Church councils (*Kirche von Unten*), and vigils. Often the groups' actions were witnessed primarily by West German media, and the information was propagated in the GDR through West German TV and radio broadcasts. This uniquely German-German form of communication was only very rarely used purposely by the groups as a means of publicity, partially because they feared the state agencies could then defame their initiatives as "Western agitation."

The existence of all these groups was hardly contingent on material resources. That the women worked and were thus financially independent was a matter of course. Work in women's groups was performed as a rule in leisure time, and was never coupled with the idea of making a paid job out of it; other materials cost little or were obtained in informal ways. Access to the Protestant Church's resources and channels of communication meant access to a relative wealth of possible media.

A wide variety of women's initiatives operated strictly in accordance with non-violent principles. They saw themselves, at least in their theoretical assertions, as generally egalitarian, and were called by one activist as early as 1988 "a kind of seeds for a pluralistic society with a decentralized structure" (Poppe 1988;1990).

In the 1980s there were also several initiatives to set up women's meetings in state-organized cultural centers, or to establish aspects of critical women's studies in the academic sphere. While such initiatives remained isolated events, the Church offered an opportunity for networking on a national level in the context of synods, women's festivals and small "samizdat" publications.

Toward the end of the 1980s even periodicals appeared, such as the church-published women's magazine *Lila Band;* from 1988 on the newsletter of the working group on feminist theology, *Das Netz;* and beginning in 1989 the lesbian group's newsletter, *frau anders* (Hampele 1995:42; Hampele-Ulrich 2000). In this way a small but relatively close-knit network of women's groups had developed by 1989. Although this network did not survive the social upheaval of 1989, it was a substantial prerequisite for the rapid mobilization of so many women in the 1989-1990 period of intense political activity.

THE *WENDE* - THE RISE AND THE FALL OF THE *UFV*

1989 was the year in which the socialist state system finally collapsed with the opening of the border to West Germany in November. When a "Round Table" was organized among government and dissident groups as an interim quasi-governmental body, the "Independent Women's Association" (*Unabhängiger Frauenverband,* or *UFV*) was formed, after the citizen initiatives ignored women's demands to be heard and represented on such issues as abortion rights or the guarantee of minimum gender quotas for party leadership positions. In February 1990 representatives of local women's groups came to Berlin to found a national umbrella organization, the *UFV*.

The *UFV* expressed their wish to sit at the Round Table and to try to influence the formation of the post-socialist society and the impending German unification. The *UFV* united existing and newly created women's initiatives and individuals from various social spheres. In this transitional period preceding the first post-socialist elections of March 1990, the Independent Women's

Federation was the only nationally known feminist political organization. Representatives of this group sat at the Berlin Central Round Table and won two seats in the German Federal Parliament in 1990. Thus the GDR was the only country in Eastern Europe in which an explicitly feminist organization represented women's interests in the process of political transformation (Ferree 1995; Hampele 1993b; Hampele-Ulrich 2000).

The former state-aligned women's organization *DFD* struggled for legitimacy and survival, and was able to achieve stability in the following years mainly in the area of family counseling and women's community centers. After 1990, a kind of dual structure arose as women's initiatives and self-help groups coalesced from the old, official women's organization, on the one hand, and the new, independent women's movement, on the other. This was due to the facts that the *DFD*, with its rather traditionally orientation, appealed to a different clientele than the newly formed *UFV*; that it still had over 60,000 members even after a great drop in membership in 1989-1990;[3] that it had vast fianancial resources; and that, like all associations, it offered jobs financed through government job creation programs.

The membership of the *UFV* is uncertain since it did not develop regular structures and formal membership. Its first meetings in February of 1990 mobilized up to about 3,000 women. After its poor showing in the parliamentary elections, about 25 delegates and staff of the new organization met regularly, representing women's initiatives totalling perhaps 250 to 350 members, although this "base" continually declined. In spite of sufficient funding,[4] it proved impossible in the long run to establish a common organization as an instrument of mobilization. This was mainly due to two factors:

First, after the end of the Round Table period, political activity took place in the parliament and in all-German government commissions. These were institutional levels at which the *UFV* was not a participant. Decisions about administrative structures and projects were subject to local influence, depending on the momentary circumstances and in negotiation with agencies and employment offices: these too were spheres of action in which the young umbrella organization was hardly able to operate, and was thus superfluous. Without an opportunity to influence the rapidly changing social conditions, the new women's organization rapidly lost its attraction.

Second, the *UFV* was to a certain extent the banner at the head of a gathering of women who shared feminist motivations, but who came from very different backgrounds, and who as a whole were understandably not equal to the task of inventing a co-operative, egalitarian form of self-organization with democratic credentials in a very rapidly changing political environment. Although the potential opportunities for women to take political action multiplied, the young organization was unable to reach a consensus on its organizational goal - whether to present candidates for election or to act as an extra-parliamentary lobby, or to work in grass-roots organizing and consciousness-raising. The overwhelming majority of women left this organization during the first two years following the *Wende*, most of them going on to create a heterogeneous, pluralistic women's political infrastructure.

The members of the umbrella organization continued to inform one another about regional initiatives and about the pluralistic, confederated women's political structures being built in the various regions, municipalities and *Länder*. They mobilized women against encroachment upon the existing right to abortion,[5] as well as for the preservation of other beneficial policies for women (such as social benefits or the right to work) in the process of transition from East German law to West German norms and conditions. Forms of action included demonstrations, postcard campaigns and lobbying.

In an alliance with the eastern German Green Party and the civil rights groups, the *UFV* attained seats in the first all-German parliament. Organizationally it did not merge with those parties, however, and therefore came away from later elections for the most part empty-handed. After 1994, the *UFV* was represented only in some municipal councils.

Between 1993 and 1996, the *UFV* organized several all-German women's political conventions intended to advance communications between East and West, and to build political pressure on women's issues. In 1994 the *UFV* was the chief organizer of the nationwide "Women's Strike Day '94." In the same spirit, several post-strike networking meetings were held between representatives of the eastern German UFV and the mostly western German women of the Cologne-Bonn strike committee. While the western German women supported the development of a joint statement of goals and the foundation of a nationwide women's party, the representatives of the *UFV* saw this as a threat to the network-like alliance policy that had been attained during the strike, and they gradually withdrew from this collaboration. Hopes for an all-German initiative were not fulfilled; women from eastern and western Germany could not reach an agreement. The *UFV* was finally disbanded as a national organization in 1998.

At this point there is no publicly effective feminist women's political organization. This is due in part to the dominant, privileged position of parties in the political system (which differs from conditions in the USA), and in part to a correlated, typically German antipathy against organization (the "anti-institutional leaning") in the new social movements, which is particularly marked in the feminist women's movement.

However, it should be noted that each national party represented in the *Bundestag* has its own women's organization. Women have their own associations also in trade unions and in the farmers' organizations. Insterestingly, the post-communist *PDS*,[6] the descendant of the ruling party *SED* which headed the party-state before 1989, has today the highest proportion of women (43.3%) compared to any other national party (Höcker 1995:87). Even though these groups are organizationally distinct and even though their political differences are pronounced, they sometimes cooperate with each other and with the independent women's groups (Ferree and Gamson 1999).

THE COLORFUL SPECTRUM OF WOMEN'S CENTERS

As the short-term, highly politicized mobilization waned, the spectrum present up to then in the women's movement became much more varied. The ensuing mushroom effect resulted in a landscape of initiatives and projects with a colorful spectrum of women's centers, women's shelters and projects similar to those found in western Germany, but with a higher proportion of public funding.

The women's projects deal with a variety of issues. For example, many of them took up the issue of domestic violence. Numerous Women's Shelters were set up in which women and their children found a place of refuge. The shelters offer social and psychological advice as well as help with divorces and housing search. Another popular movement within the movement were self-help initiatives. Among the best known is the "Self-Help Inititative Single Parents" (*Selbsthilfeinitiative Alleinerziehende*, or *SHIA*) from Berlin which was established as early as in Spring of 1990.

Many women's centers exist which focus on such issues as occupation, child-raising, health, women's history as well as such which deal with feminist issues and the use of violence within the family. It has to be noted here that for eastern German women, just like for their counterparts in Poland, the Czech Republic, Hungary or Russia, the term "feminism" has a negative connotation and they therefore do not rely on it for self-definition. This does not hinder them from dealing with feminist issues. Eastern German women utilize the most those services provided by the women's centers which help to integrate them in the labor market. Here we find job training for women as well as computer, foreign language and rhetoric courses.

After 1989 several Women's Archives were established which, just like, for example, the Archive Grey Zone (*Archiv "Grauzone"*) in Berlin, collect documents about the independent women's movement of the GDR. A journal, called Women's View (*Weibblick*), constitutes a new publication put out by eastern German women in which issues, such as East German history or Women in Eastern Europe, are raised to which the western German feminist journals do not pay much attention.

Here we have to note, however, that many women's inititives, projects and publications evade a simplified label "western" or "eastern," since their personnel and issue-range include both. Most of all this applies to eastern Berlin where, because of the closeness to western Berlin, the mixing is the strongest. Most often, however, women from the western side of the city work in women's projects or women's houses in eastern Berlin. Only single cases constitute the opposite movement of the eastern German women to the western side.

To most of the groups and projects named so far, the concept of non-governmental organizations, or NGOs, would actually fit as far as the issues with which they work and their independence from the state structures is concerned. However, in contrast to Poland, this concept does not correspond to the self-definition of the eastern German women's projects. It is used for self-labelling only in exceptional circumstances. This is perhaps accounted for by the fact that in Germany this description is normally used for organizations in the developing countries and recently also in Eastern Europe, but not for groups in one's own country.

The women's initiatives and projects obtained a significant proportion of their resources through job creation measures in eastern Germany, which were funded by the government as a means to combat the rapidly rising unemployment following the collapse of the socialist state and the introduction of the market economy. The fact that they form a segment of the job market therefore characterizes the structure of the women's projects to a much greater extent than in western Germany.[7] Many women earned their living in such projects as long as the public funds were available (until about 1994).

After the state funding had been progressively decreased by the Federal Labor Office, from Spring of 1993 onward, the existence of many such projects was threatened. As Rucht et al. (1997: 158) observed for eastern German projects in general, however, the women's projects returned to more intensive volunteer work, on the one hand, and, on the other hand, had become sufficiently professional to tap other funding sources, thus securing their continued existence. Such funding sources included project grants and institutional subsidies from state agencies and foundations. An increasing number of projects took on the organizational form of co-operatives or independent companies.

The development of a broad spectrum of women's research at the universities after the *Wende* has been dependent similarly on the public funding. The most known new institution of this type is the Central Institute for Women's Studies (*Zentralinstitut für Frauenforschung*, or *ZiF*) at the Humboldt University which started with small groups of women researchers already interested in feminist questions before 1989. The Institute organizes conferences and discussions, brings out a journal (*Bulletin*) and other publications, and runs a women's library. A Gender Studies program established at the same university in 1998 enjoys great popularity among students. At the same time, however, many women's institutes in western Germany were closed, creating a situation of competition for scarce resources, which, understandably, does not further a closer association between eastern and western German feminists.

The women's movement, like any popular movement, is difficult to put into numbers. Rucht et al. (1997:82) estimate that the number of women's projects increased from about 28 groups in 1989 to some 123 groups in 1993 in four different (eastern) German cities which they investigated (Berlin, Leipzig, Halle and Dresden). Although no precise figures are available at present, it can be estimated[8] that 400 women's groups and projects exist in eastern Germany right now. These figures make the women's movement the sector of the eastern German social movement spectrum that developed the most after 1989 (Rucht et al. 1997:84).

This increase in the number of women's projects is related to the fact that many women are active in the eastern German women's movement today who were not active before 1989. This is primarily due to the fact that women's projects suddenly became a job market after 1989, and were able to provide jobs for a number of women who had become unemployed - including women who had not been involved in the women's movement before. This means that there was a shift in the composition of the active group after 1989, and the women who had been active in the independent women's movement under the GDR are in the minority today.

The potential for mobilization has declined further since the high mobilization of women in Spring of 1990. The largest response is generated mainly by the organization of feminist conferences, which reflects the fact that the largest part of the women's movement's audience, in eastern Germany as in western Germany, comes from the college-educated middle class. The all-German Women's Strike Day 1994 mentioned above was prepared with great enthusiasm by an alliance of different women's organizations from unions, parties, the *UFV* and the autonomous women's movement. The response mobilized was nonetheless low (Roth and Ferree 1996).

APPROACHING THE WESTERN STANDARD? VIVE LA DIFFERENCE!

While the current condition of the women's movement in eastern Germany has largely approached that of western Germany, certain clear differences can be observed. The aspects in which similarity has increased include the context structures as well as the issues, the forms of action and the importance of funding:

The Church no longer provides a substitute public. The special relationship between the Protestant Church and the dissident groups has been lost. This development has been detrimental to vitality of the Church in many places, while the women's initiatives have taken advantage of new opportunities for development. Compared to pre-1989, women's organizations associated with the Church have lost their political influence within the women's movement. Whereas before the *Wende* many women's and lesbian groups came together under the auspices of the Protestant Church, even though they were not necessarily Christian, they are no longer dependent on the Church for a gathering place and find their meeting places elsewhere. This change influenced the thematic spectrum in women's groups. Prior to 1989 the strong ties between the Protestant Church and these groups pushed them to confront Christian thinking, the feminist theology and women in the Church. Today these themes are still explored mostly by religious women. The cooperation between the Christian women's groups and the women's groups outside the Church has become pointilistic, a state of affairs which many feminists within the Church find regrettable.

The new social order charges administrative bodies with ensuring equal rights to men and women, a legal mandate already known in the earlier Federal Republic. The *Länder* and municipal authorities have instituted commissioners on women's issues, with different resources and responsibilities in the various *Länder*.

With regard to the issues dealt with, the forms of action and the organizational structure of projects (often associations), and the related, increasingly important question of resources, eastern and western German projects are largely the same. Eastern German women's centers and projects deal with many issues that would not have come up before 1989, such as women's unemployment, abortion rights and social security; or which had been taboo, such as violence against women.

Whereas the issue of material resources had been of secondary importance before 1989, and would not have been decisive for the existence or success of a group, it became crucial in eastern Germany after 1989. Today the existence of many women's projects depends on their ability to find access to resources such as the job creation programs mentioned above.

Since the fall of the GDR, access to public media has become relatively easy; this is a point of similarity with the western German project landscape. As in western Germany, forms of protest today are to a large degree oriented toward publicity, in contrast to the period before 1989. Common forms of protest are small demonstrations, public conferences, information events, newspapers and other publications. Media access can now be taken for granted in eastern Germany, although public interest in such issues is rather marginal. Women's issues are not part of mainstream public reporting, but are now tolerated as part of public discourse, or are dealt with for the sake of "political correctness."

The difference between eastern and western Germany can be seen in the fact that issues of feminist theory - to the extent that such a generalization is admissible - are not accorded the same crucial value in the East that they have in the West. Setting aside the differences in socialization and experience, one reason for this is that eastern German projects as meeting places in a changing everyday environment have inherited the functions of neighborhood and youth work, which have disintegrated. The women's projects perform a certain amount of social work between the previous society and the new, democratic, free-market society. Accordingly, many such initiatives offer childcare and social and legal counseling, for example.

The central line of conflict in socialism between independent, in some cases dissident groups and the state has lost its significance. Within the eastern German women's movement, however, positions rooted in the various experiences in the GDR and its women's movement have survived which are different from those in western Germany. One such position is the attitude, more often taken for granted in eastern Germany, that the state is an instrument responsible for solving problems that affect women (Schenk and Schindler 1995; Miethe 1999b). For this reason too, eastern German feminists have had fewer reservations than many of their western counterparts making use of public funding. Controversial issues in years past have also included the attitudes toward including men (the call for "joint action with men" is heard much more frequently in eastern than in western Germany), the position on demands for employment opportunities for women and the question of child-raising vs. career.

A second difference to western German feminists is the fact that eastern German feminists are more interested in cooperation with men. Through participating in separate actions organized by women and being members of women's groups, her political expectations lay in gender-integrated politics; women and men should work together, even when women do need their own spaces and their own self-concepts.

Naturally the attitudes on the issues mentioned here are homogeneous in neither eastern nor in western Germany. In the German women's movement, however, this probing of the common ground attained, and the debate over the extent to which the differences mentioned above are actually East-West differences, continue to come up again and again. Thus the women's movement in eastern Germany remains sandwiched between the Eastern and Western systems, between socialism and West European liberal democracies.

In spite of all the security measures, the inner German border between the two systems was never hermetically sealed. On the contrary, West influences pervaded the GDR more than the rest of Eastern Europe through the media, personal (including family) contacts and the common language. The fact that the independent women's movement dealt more with feminist issues in the GDR than in the rest of Eastern Europe is due not least to this exchange.

On the other hand, however, the differences that exist today between the women's movements in eastern and western Germany show that in the East certain positions have persisted and further evolved which originated under the specific, East European conditions of the GDR. To understand the women's movement in eastern Germany today it is thus necessary to examine it in the dual context of Western European movements and its contact with Eastern Europe and its socialist past.

NOTES:

1. The originally East German term *real existierender Sozialismus*— "socialism in its actually existing form"—is rendered for the sake of simplicity as "socialism" in this article, and the corresponding adjectival construction as "socialist."
2. The State Security service only counted the Women for Peace groups, since feminist groups were not classified as antagonistic to the socialist state.
3. About one third of the organization's 1.5 million members had resigned by Spring of 1990.
4. The dissident groups had received start-up money from the reform-oriented communist interim government, and received funds mainly in the form of state compensation for election campaign costs, accorded analogously to West Germany's election finance policy.
5. From the GDR's non-penal time-limit model to the earlier Federal Republic's regulations involving social and medical prerequisites and criminal sanctions (Funk 1993; Maleck-Lewy 1995).
6. The full name of the PDS is: The Party of Democratic Socialism (*Partei des Demokratischen Sozialismus*), while that of the *SED*: The Socialist Unity Party (*Sozialistische Einheitspartei*).
7. Such funds have played a role in West Germany as well, but a much smaller one.
8. In each former district of East Germany one can find 10-25 women's projects on the average. In most bigger cities 1-5 projects are found. Together this leads to the estimated 400 groups and projects. These numbers change a lot, since many projects have to finish their work, while new ones constantly pop up.

REFERENCES:

Ferree M. M. 1994. "The Time of Chaos was the Best. Feminist Mobilization and Demobilization in East Germany" *Gender and Society* Vol. 8 No. 4:597-623
Ferree M.M. and W. A. Gamson. 1999. "The Gendering of Abortion Discourse: Assessing Global Feminist Influence in the United States and Germany" in *Social Movements in a Globalizing World*. Edited by D. della Porta, H. Kriesi and D. Rucht. London. MacMillan Press Ltd, pp. 40-56

Funk N. 1993. "Abortion in the German Unification" in *Gender Politics and Post Communism. Reflections from Eastern Europe and the former Soviet Union.* Edited by N. Funk and M. Mueller. New York. Routledge, pp. 194-200

Hampele A. 1993a. "Arbeite mit, plane mit, regiere mit - Zur politischen Partizipation von Frauen in der DDR" in *Frauen in Deutschland 1945 - 1992.* Edited by G. Helwig and H. M. Nickel. Bonn. Bundeszentrale, pp. 281-320

Hampele A. 1993b. "The Organized Women's Movement in the Collapse of the GDR: The Independent Women's Organization (*UFV*)" in *Gender Politics and Post Communism. Reflections from Eastern Europe and the former Soviet Union.* Edited by N. Funk and M. Mueller. London. Routledge, pp. 180-193

Hampele A. 1995. *Der Unabhängige Frauenverband. Organisationslaufbahn eines frauenpolitischen Experiments im deutsch-deutschen Vereinigungsprozeß* (Fallstudie). Dissertation. FU Berlin

Hampele-Ulrich A. 2000. *Der Unabhängige Frauenverband. Ein frauenpolitisches Experiment im deutschen Vereinigungsprozeß.* Berlin. Berliner Debatte Wissenschaftsverlag

Hoecker B. 1995. *Politische Partizipation von Frauen. Kontinuität und Wandel des Geschlechterverhältnisses in der Politik.* Opladen. Leske + Budrich

Kenawi S. 1995. *Frauengruppen in der DDR der 80er Jahre.* Eine Dokumentation. Edited by Senatsverwaltung Arbeit und Frauen. Berlin

Kukutz I. 1995. "Die Bewegung 'Frauen für den Frieden' als Teil der unabhängigen Friedensbewegung der DDR" in *Aufarbeitung von Geschichte und Folgen der SED-Diktatur in Deutschland.* Enquete-Kommission. Frankfurt a.M. Suhrkamp. Nomos. Vol. 7 Nr. 2:1285-1408

Maleck-Lewy E. 1995. "Between Self-determination and State supervision: Women and the Abortion Law in Post-unification Germany" *Social Politics* Vol. 2 Nr. 1:62-75

Miethe I. 1996. "Das Politikverständnis bürgerbewegter Frauen der DDR im Prozeß der deutschen Vereinigung" *Zeitschrift für Frauenforschung* Vol. 14 Nr. 3:87-101

Miethe I. 1999a. *Frauen in der DDR-Opposition. Lebens- und kollektivgeschichtliche Verläufe in einer Frauenfriedensgruppe.* Opladen. Leske + Budrich

Miethe I. 1999b. "From the 'mother of the revolution' to 'fathers of unification' - Concepts of politics among women activists following German unification" *Social Politics* Vol. 6 Nr. 2:1-22

Poppe U. 1988-1990. "Das kritische Potential der Gruppen in Kirche und Gesellschaft" in *Die Legitimität der Freiheit.* Edited by D. Pollack. Frankfurt a.M. Peter Lang, pp. 63-79

Roth S. and M.M. Ferree. 1994. "Sisterhood and Solidarity? Mobilizing for the Women Strike Day in Germany", paper presented at the Meeting of the Eastern Sociological Society held in Boston in March 1994

Rucht D., B. Blattert and D. Rink. 1997. *Soziale Bewegungen auf dem Weg zur Institutionalisierung? Zum Strukturwandel 'alternativer' Gruppen in beiden Teilen Deutschlands.* Frankfurt a. M. Campus

Schenk C. and C. Schindler. 1995. "Frauenbewegung in Ostdeutschland - Innenansichten" in *Gefährtinnen der Macht. Politische Partizipation im vereinigten Deutschland - eine Zwischenbilanz.* Edited by E. Maleck-Lewy and V. Penrose. Berlin. Edition. Sigma, pp. 183-202

2. In the Shadow of the Amicable Gender Relations? - The Czech Republic

Steven Saxonberg

INTRODUCTION

During the period of Communist rule, all women's organizations, except the official Union of Czechoslovak Women, were forbidden in Czechoslovakia. Although women were active in dissident circles, they did not try to establish any underground women's organizations. Instead, they preferred to work for the more general goals of promoting human rights and democracy. Rita Klímová, who became ambassador to the United States in the first post-Communist government, expressed this attitude claiming that "feminism is a flower on democracy" (quoted in Wolchik 1995:19).

Future research will probably show that gender relations were not at all as amicable in the past as commonly portrayed. What is important, however, is not the actual history, but rather the manner in which women's leaders perceive it. If they believe that Czech men and women have a common history of working together against external oppressors, this perception becomes a reality that influences their behavior. Similarly, most Czech citizens believe in the myth of the First Republic being an extremely harmonious, golden era of Czech history. It is considered almost blasphemous to point out that the Sudeten-Germans never really accepted the creation of a Czechoslovak state and that many Slovaks felt their interests were being ignored by the Czech- dominated governments. If one notes that much of the period of the First Republic was during the Great Depression, with all of the class antagonisms that it brought about, then one is promptly dismissed as a "communist." The belief in the harmonious First Republic is a pillar of the Czech political culture. This makes it even more difficult for radical women to gather support for campaigns against "male oppression."

For the citizens of the former Soviet-bloc countries the main conflict ran between the population and the party-state apparatus. Šiklová (1995) argues that Czech men and women have been united many times in recent history in the struggle for national sovereignty. First, Czech men and women struggled against the Habsburg monarchy, which led to the creation of a Czechoslovak state after World War I. Then, they faced German occupation during World War II, the Communist takeover in 1948 and finally, the Soviet invasion in 1968. Since men and women united for the same cause, they did not see each other as enemies. Once the struggle for independence was over, Czech women, rather than having to fight against men on such issues as the right to vote, gained these rights immediately after the founding of Czechoslovakia. Another factor which hindered the creation of independent women's organizations was the fact that the Czechoslovak regime was much more orthodox and repressive than the relatively liberal Polish regime.

THE GROWTH OF WOMEN'S ORGANIZATIONS FROM 1989 TO 1995

After the fall of the communist regime at the end of 1989, the Union of Czechoslovak Women - an official "communist" organization - split into a Czech and a Slovak part. The Czech Union, with around half a million members in 1995, is still the largest women's organization in the country

33

(Gender Studies Center 1995:26). Since 1989 dozens of new women's organizations have emerged. In 1995 the Gender Studies Center in Prague published a book (*Altos and Sopranos*) that listed 30 women's organizations. The Czech Union of Women has encouraged cooperation between the various organizations and tried to establish a national congress of women. These attempts, however, have not been very successful, as most women's groups continue to be sceptical of the Union (Wolchik 1995:10). By the mid-1990s, the Czech Republic had the Czech Union and many small, scattered groups dealing with specific women's issues, but it did not have a cohesive women's *movement* that could exert much influence on society.

Nor has there been much support for the notion of gender equality. Not one of the 30 women's organizations listed in *Altos and Sopranos* has the goal of promoting gender equality and changing traditional gender roles. Two of the groups come at least close. The leader of *ProFem* criticizes the "reigning patriarchalism" and New Humanity (*Nová humanita*) criticizes "relationships of dominance and subordination." *ProFem*, however, has a base of three members, while New Humanity had four members and about 500 activists in 1995. In 1999 New Humanity has gone into "incubation." Furthermore, some women's groups do not even deal with specific women's issues which, however, as I will explain below, is probably related to the fundraising rules. These groups deal with such topics as preventing crime (White Safety Circle), opposition to nuclear power (The Alliance of Women Against Atomic Danger) or need for increased environmental protection (Southern Czech Mothers-Ecology Association, Prague Mothers). Another large group is basically apolitical and concerns itself with specific self-help issues such as putting on art exhibits (The First Women's Art Club), spreading information on AIDS (L-Club Lambda Prague, *Promluv* and Bliss Without Risk), bringing together and providing legal as well as psychological services to divorcees and widows (The Rosa Foundation), providing a babysitting service and nursery school for single mothers (The Club of Single Mothers), publishing books on popular psychology and "serious" literature (Motto Publishers) and providing cultural and social activities to single women (The Women's Educational Club Vesna).

Only 14 of the 30 groups take some sort of stance on the role of women in society. The largest is the Christian Women's Clubs, with about 2,000 members, while the other two conservative christian organizations claim to have altogether around 35 members. They engage in self-help projects that promote the woman's role as a mother. In total, 6 of the 14 organizations are mostly concerned with self-help projects, while only 8 organizations engage in some sort of political lobbying. To be sure, this group has many more members, over 540,000 compared to slightly more than 3,100 members in the 6 self-help organizations. But the Czech Union of Women dominates this field with around 500,000 members. Many of them are probably people who had joined during the Communist era for career purposes and did not bother to leave after 1989. Only around 40,000 members of the Czech Union actually become engaged in political action to influence the position of women within society.

By far the largest organization after the Czech Union of Women is the Movement for the Equal Status of Women in Bohemia and Moravia which claims to have around 35,000 members. Its main goal is to support steps "towards the fulfilment of the enactment of the International Declaration on the Family, Children and Women which was ratified by the Czech government..." (Gender Studies Center 1995:47). As with most Czech women's groups, the Movement clearly opposes Scandinavian types of universalistic social policies. It prefers "differential social policy," i.e. means-tested programs and "keeps its distance from social protectionism" (Gender Studies Center 1995:47). Nevertheless, it also opposes the closing of state-run kindergartens. The Movement is extremely active in lobbying for legislation. It claims to have made suggestions on 60 laws and to have proposed 6 laws. In addition, it has supported individual candidates in local and parliamentary elections. In addition to lobbying activities, the Movement also engages in self-help projects, such as running a home economics school or providing legal and psychological counseling.

Some of the women's groups are directly tied to political parties. This includes the Leftist Women's Club (its 1,000 members are tied to the Left Bloc coalition of Communists and reform-Communists), the Central Committee of the Czech and Moravian Communist Party's Women's Commission (tied to the Communist Party; many of the local organizations merged with the Leftist Women's Club), the Council of National Socialist Women (with around 250 members and supporting the centrist National Socialist Party), and Social Democratic Women (its 723 activists are part of the Social Democratic Party). The Democratic Alternative, with approximately 1,000 members, is a liberal-conservative political lobbying organization that does not directly support any political party.

As already noted, none of the Czech women's organizations openly support gender equality. Many of them openly say that they are *not* feminist. A typical example of their attitude comes from the head of the Leftist Women's Club, Hana Entlerová, who claims that the main issues concerning men and women, have:

> nothing in common with feminism, because full self-realization is the right of men and women equally. At the same time, I am for every woman having complete freedom in deciding whether to do to work or to stay home, whether or not to have children, etc. (Gender Studies Center 1995:66-67).

This statement shows some of the main problems that Western-styled feminism has in the Czech Republic. First, feminism has become such a dirty word that not even women's organizations dare to use it. Second, it is a word that is commonly misunderstood. Entlerová's comment about "full self-realization" being important for men as well as women, shows that even leaders of women's organizations believe that all forms of feminism imply the hatred of men. Third, the statement shows that many women's organizations have as a central demand the right for women to become house-wives, yet they refuse to consider the possibility of eliminating gender roles and encouraging men to also spend time at home with their children. Some women's organizations concentrate on the right of women to stay at home, others on the right of women to work, but *none* of them deal with the issue of eliminating the double burden of work and family by demanding that men share in house-hold duties.

POLITICAL CULTURE AND RESISTANCE TO GENDER EQUALITY

Reasons for the resistance toward the idea of gender equality are closely related to the country's political culture. Czech women's organizations face three different political culture heritages which provide both obstacles *and possibilities* for a future women's movement.

Pre-war political culture
As I have already pointed out, Czech authors on gender issues claim that Czech men and women allied in their struggle against the Habsburg Empire for which women were rewarded in the inter-war period by receiving far more rights than women in other European countries enjoyed.

Seeing men as allies rather than sexual oppressors continued during the subsequent occupation by Nazi Germany and the era of the Soviet domination.

This unwillingness to see men as oppressors makes it more difficult for "radical" women's movements to emerge and it inhibits a critical examination of the power relations within Czech society. What Czech women activists lose in analytical sharpness, they possibly gain by having greater male support for their goals. Women's organizations might have a greater chance of convincing men that they too could gain from greater gender equality. Would they not be better off if their wives earned higher incomes? Wouldn't everyone, except perhaps a few mediocre men, be better off if highly qualified women got the positions they deserved?[1]

Another political tradition left over from the inter-war period is the progressive social legacy. The Social Democrats and the Nationalist Socialist Party participated in most of the interwar governments and pushed through social legislation that was among the most generous in the world at the time (see for example, Deacon 1993). Despite the dominance of the market-liberal politician Václav Klaus in post-1989 Czech politics, support for generous social policies has remained high in the Czech Republic. Because of this social-liberal political culture, such state policies as support for nursery schools, that make it easier for women to work, or generous parental leave benefits, that encourage men to take care of their children, would face less resistance in the Czech Republic than elsewhere.

Communist political culture

The historical legacy of the communist regime presents a greater problem for women activists than the inter-war legacy. First, the very notion of "equality" has come into disrepute because it reminds the population of the rhetoric used by the Communists. The former regime claimed to have created a classless society in which everyone enjoyed equal opportunity. It also claimed to have liberated women by making it possible for them to work. Not only were jobs available to women, they were also provided with nurseries and kindergartens, so that they did not have to stay home.

Of course, women were far from equality with men. There were hardly any women in the top positions in society (Wolchik 1991; see also the appendix of the "National Report" 1994). There was not a single female minister between 1970 and 1989 (Hodný 1991). Nor were there any women in the cabinet, the Politburo or the party's Secretariat. Women were lower paid than men and they still maintained full responsibility for the family. Thus, many women experienced their paying job as a second job rather than liberation (see Scott 1974). Today the "liberation" part of the phrase "woman's liberation" still reminds them of the past regime.

Several scholars have pointed out another reason for opposition to gender equality: the important role which the family played during the period of Communist rule. Since the party-state tried to control all public life, the family became a place where one could retreat from the official rhetoric and seek free expression. Although one could never be certain whether one could trust one's friends and neighbors, one could always trust one's family. Since women were responsible for family matters, their role as mothers often gave them more satisfaction than their role as employees in the public sphere. In Heitlinger's words:

> In contrast to the politically tainted public sphere of work and politics, the individual family was a "free sphere" where people could be their "authentic" selves and resist the instrusion of the all-pervasive communist party-state. As a woman's domain, the family thus provided women with a certain amount of power, authority, and creativity. Women

36

therefore opted for a "cult of motherhood," and children provided an "excuse" for not joining the communist party. (Heitlinger 1996:85)

Even if most women were not happy with the double-burden of having a full-time job and keeping responsibility for the household, they did not support the life as a traditional housewife. Also in this respect there is much continuity with the past. A survey, conducted by the Institute of Sociology at the Czech Academy of Science in 1994, shows that only 11.4% of the women strongly agreed and 15% rather agreed with the statement that "being a housewife is just as satisfying as working for gainful employment" (author's translation, Čermáková & Gatnar, 1994:4). Today even if Czech women would want to return home, most families cannot afford to live on only one salary. The same survey showed that 66.3% of Czech women strongly agreed and another 26.9% rather agreed with the statement that "the majority of women must work today in order to provide financial security for their family" (author's translation, Čermáková & Gatnar, 1994:5). The sociologist, Čermáková (1997:391) concludes that Czech society still has the "gender contract," which emerged during the communist era, in which almost all women worked. As in the past they have lower positions and lower salaries then males, so that they can balance the possibility of both working and having a family.

CZECH EXCEPTIONALISM: 1990-1997

After the fall of the communist regime, the economist Václav Klaus quickly emerged as the dominant Czech politician. As Finance Minister for the federal Czechoslovak government, he worked out the country's economic reforms. Then as Prime Minister of the Czech Republic between 1992 and 1997, Klaus personified the Czech economic transformation and the seeming economic miracle. Although Klaus was intent on the Czech Republic joining NATO and the EU, he still struck a nationalist tone, claiming that the Czech Republic was "more West than the West" (cf. Vachudová, forthcoming). According to his reasoning, the Czech Republic had nothing to learn from the West which is still under the ill-fated influence of the "socialist" ideas. The prime minister, who was infamous for his arrogance, also created an intolerant atmosphere. Anyone who disagreed with him was a "communist" or a "Leftist" (Saxonberg 1999a &1999b).

As long as Klaus was popular and the economic "miracle" had not yet turned into a flop, it was difficult to criticize him and the reigning neo-liberal ideology. If their country was run by an infallible economic guru, what could Czechs learn from the West? So ironically, although most Czechs wanted to join Western organizations, such as NATO and the EU, they were not interested in "Western" ideas.

Saša Marie Lienau (forthcoming), founder of *ProFem*, recalls that in the first years after the "velvet revolution," women's organizations were afraid to criticize "their government." Czech women's organizations and women's activists have also been afraid of "alien" Western feminist ideology. The country was flocked by Westerners, including feminists, who knew little about the country's history or socioeconomic situation and arrogantly demanded that the Czech Republic uncritically follow their advice. Much of the Czech women's reaction, however, expressed the Czech nationalist attitude. Western feminists were ridiculed in the mass media by people, such as the exiled writer Škvorecký, who wrote a series of articles claiming that Western feminists were "openly lesbian" and "radically antimasculine" (Crompton 1997:137). Surprisingly, even somebody who should know better, such as the founder of the Gender Studies Center, Jiřina Šiklová, greatly misrepresented their ideas. For example, she wrote that "many Western feminists believe that Soviet-style socialism had resolved the problem of women's equality in Eastern Europe..." (Šiklová 1998:10). As this author pointed out in a rebuttal, virtually all established Western feminists who wrote about the Soviet-type system, considered it to be patriarchal (Saxonberg 1998).[2] Two leaders of the Czech Union of Women showed a similar lack of knowledge about conditions outside of the Czech Republic. They claim (interviews with Hajná and Malcevová) that their country already has the world's best social legislation, such as the four-year guaranteed maternity leave, so their main goal now is to protect their gains. They were not even aware that 3½ -4 years is now the *norm* for Central Europe.[3]

During the Klaus era it has been difficult to mobilize women around gender issues because there has not been any hot issues to prompt women into the streets (cf. Havelkova 1996). For example, in contrast to Poland or the former GDR, no attempt has been made to restrict the right to abortions. As Heitlinger (1996:81) notes, Czech women were not even concerned about the closing of state-run nursery schools because these had been of poor quality.

PROSPECTS FOR CHANGE

Legacies of Social-Liberalism and High Labor-Market Participation
There are some signs that the prospects for creating a women's movement are improving. First, it is likely that women will become more dissatisfied with their situation now that the Klaus' economic miracle has proven to be temporary and the economy continues to deteriorate. Unemployment is on the rise and is expected to continue as the country dips deeper into recession. Given the social-liberal cultural legacy of the interwar period, Czech women are likely to be supportive of more generous social policies that could improve their situation. Similarly, given the cultural climate of the communist era, during which women became highly educated and became used to financial independence from their male partners, few women are likely to want to leave the workforce for the confines of their homes. Thus, they are likely to support social legislation that enables them to have children but also be able to work.

Even some issues that supposedly inhibit mobilization of women could actually provide possible points of mobilization. For example, it is true that abortions are legal for everyone, but they now cost a lot of money. One defender of the system notes that they *only* cost half of the average monthly wage (Šiklová 1995:41). The fact is that for families with average and below average incomes abortions are becoming increasing difficult.

Similarly, the nursery schools of the past might have been poor and overcrowded, but that does not mean that women will be content to stay at home for much longer periods of time and allow their husbands to provide for the family income. Now that nurseries have become inaccessible, women are expected to stay home for longer periods of time. Parental leave has been extended to four years. Since families are paid a flat rate that amounts to around one-fourth of the average monthly income (calculations based on Josef Trnka, 1998:147 and *Česky statistický úřad* 1997a:14-15), and since men earn more money than their wives in three-fourths of Czech families (Čermáková *et al.* 1995:2), most families conclude that they cannot "afford" to have the man take parental leave. In fact, only around 0.2% of the men make use of their right to do so (calculations based on *Česky statistický úřad* 1997b:35). This means that it will be increasingly more difficult for working mothers to compete with men on the labor market, since they leave the labor market for longer periods of time when having children. Another measure that has lowered the incomes of families is the decision to make child allowance payments means tested (Martin Potucek & Iveta Radicova 1997).

The result of these policies so far, though, has not been a noticeable drop in female labor market participation. Instead, many women have decided to remain at their jobs and delay having children. Consequently, the birth rate has declined by around 30% since 1990 (Calculations based on *Statistická ročenka české republiky '97*, 1997:106). Eventually, many of these women will want to have children, so it is possible that they will begin to complain more about their situation. It is also possible that the new Social Democratic government, which does not share Klaus' market-liberal dogma, might be willing to take steps to improve conditions for families in order to encourage more childbirths.

Ironically, the successes of the Klaus reform could just as likely lead to demands for more gender equality as the failures of his reform. With the transition to the market economy many women are becoming entrepreneurs. The number of female entrepreneurs has increased from 128,000 in 1994 to 159,200 in 1997 (Stastna 1995:26 and *Česky statistický uřad* 1998:308). Many women are now earning high incomes, and within this group many earn more than their husbands. Among the younger generation some women will not think that it is fair for them to also do the majority of household chores.

There already appears to be increasing support for gender equality. A recent survey by the Sociological Institute of the Czech Academy of Sciences (Čermáková *et al.* 1995:2), shows that around one-third of the population disagrees with the statement that "children suffer if the man stays at home with the children while the mother works."

Learning and Increased Cooperation Among Women's Groups

As already noted, political-culture legacies present obstacles, but they also provide possibilities. It is up to individuals to utilize the possibilities and circumvent these obstacles. The disdain for feminist ideology, which comes from the communist political culture, makes it difficult to quickly build a mass movement around general feminist goals. On the other hand, the social-liberal inter-war legacy makes Czechs open to notions of justice and fairness, as well as respect for human rights. When women's organization stress these types of issues, they are often able to get other women's groups to cooperate them. Sometime, they can even get support form the political elite.

A learning process has taken place. Leaders of women's organizations have seen what kinds of issues that can muster support on. Saša Marie Lienau, started *ProFem* as a consulting organization that could help new women's organizations get started. She had spent more than two decades living in West Germany during the communist era which helped her gain experience from the West German women's movement. She notes that although it is still difficult to get women's organizations to cooperate on general women's issues, they can even get Catholic women's organizations to collaborate with them on such issues as violence against women (interview with Lienau). A similar issue which could unite many women's groups was the demand for them to win back a building that had once belonged to a Czech women's association, before it was confiscated by the Nazis and then Communists.

Several steps have been taken recently to strengthen cooperation among women's organizations. On March 6, the Gender Studies Center, *ProFem*, *Promluv* and *La Strada* joined forces to open the Prague Women's Center (Legge 1998). They all have their own offices next to each other and hold seminars and lectures together. An even more significant event is now under way: the founding of a national umbrella organization for Czech women's groups, the Association for Equal Opportunity (*Asociace pro rovné příležitosti*). It was established on 27 November 1998 and has a February 15 deadline for members to join. So far 12 organizations have joined and the association is optimistic (interview with Klimiešova).

A part of the learning process that has gone on is the decline in fear of the former communist organization, the Czech Union of Women. Suspicions are still high against the Union, since it has by far the greatest resources and largest membership of any Czech women's organization. Nevertheless, Czech women's organizations are beginning to realize that something can be gained by cooperating with the mammoth organization, as long as the smaller groups do not lose their identity. The founders of the Association for Equal Opportunity made provisions to insure that no group can dominate the Association. First, each organization only has one vote, regardless of its size. Second, all member organizations are required to inform the Association of all invitations that it receives from abroad for attending conferences, seminars and the like. An organization that does not follow this rule can be excluded from the Association. Consequently, the Czech Union of Women will be forced to share its information with the smaller groups that do not have as many international contacts (interview with Klimešova). This is especially important, given the fact that the Union, because of its size and resources, finds it easier to making contacts with the Western women's organizations. Yet, it is precisely the small organizations that need Western financing in order to be able to attend international conferences.[4] Another factor that perhaps makes Czech women's organizations less fearful of the Union is that the Czech Union's membership has now gone down to around 85,000 members (Lukášová 1998).

Women's organizations are also making headway in influencing politicians on certain issues. Although they did not succeed in getting the pre-war women's building restituted, they have gained sympathy among politicians for such human rights issues as violence against women or the trafficking of women. Czech women's organizations, such as *ProFem* are now involved in discussing laws with parliamentary committees that deal with violence against women. Another group, *La Strada*, which was founded by *ProFem*, campaigns against the trafficking of women. It is now working with the Ministry of the Interior on changing laws to meet European standards (interview with Lienau). Moreover, the chair of the Social Democratic Women, Jana Volfová, was recently elected to parliament. Volfová started a parliamentary subcommittee for equal opportunity and family members. Representatives of women's organizations will sit in the subcommittee.[5]

Increased International Contacts

Now that Klaus is no longer prime minister and his economic policies are generally considered to have been a failure, the era of Czech exceptionalism has come to an end. As a result, Czechs are likely to become more open for foreign influences, including feminist ones. The more open political culture of the intra-war era might win an upper hand against the nationalist-exceptionalist political culture of the Klaus era.

Czech women's organizations have already been forced to take up contacts with Western organizations in order to obtain funding. Except for the Czech Union of Women, all Czech women's organizations have financing problems, and the national government has not been eager to help them.

Regardless of political color, governments have not given women's issues priority. For example, after the fall of Klaus, the interim Tošovský government decided that it should give support to NGOs in order to build up the civil society. The aid was to be financed through receipts of the National Property Fund, which disposes of the money made from selling state assets. The government set up 7 different committees which have equal amounts of money to give to NGOs. However, not one committee is concerned with women's issues (*Vláda české republiky* 1998).

Women's groups must apply for money for specific projects that go under the heading of committee areas such as health, culture, human rights, education and environmental protection. As women's groups, they cannot receive any funds, but they can apply for financial aid, for example, if they want to set up a program to inform people how to avoid getting AIDS.

Czech women's organizations have learned how to utilize the few opportunities that have existed for gaining governmental funding. For example, Klimešová, of the Movement for Equal Rights in the Czech Republic, convinced the foreign ministry to pay her to translate international documents on women's rights into Czech. It was cheaper for the ministry to hire her services than to translate the documents itself (interview with Klimešová). The Czech Union of Women has received governmental funding for running a school in Brno for 16-19 year-old girls and for running a summer camp for children (interview with Hajná).

For the smaller organizations funding has become essential. During the initial transformation period, German and American women's organizations were particularly important as the source of funds. For example, the German Green foundation *Frauen-Anstiftung* provided 100% of *ProFem*'s financing during its first year, 1993 (*ProFem* 1995:16). By 1995 the German organization had increased its funding by nearly 420% and comprised 90% of *ProFem*'s total funding.

In contrast to the mainstream political parties, the Greens have traditionally supported grassroots organizations rather than sister political parties. The Green Party now is beginning to change its strategy. In 1998 the three separate green foundations merged into the Heinrich Böll Foundation (Heinrich Böll Stiftung, 1998:3). According to *ProFem* founder, Saša Marie Lienau, (see interviews), it is now more difficult to get money from the Böll foundation than the *Frauen-Anstiftung*, because the Greens have become more interesting in supporting political parties. In 1997, support from the *Frauen Anstiftung* had already decreased to a level only slightly above the total from 1993 (*ProFem* 1997:12). This spring the Czech women's organizations will have a meeting with the German Greens to discuss what kind of partners their German allies want and what do they expect of the Czech organizations?

In addition to Western political parties and foundations, the EU has become an important source of funding. The PHARE program financed the establishment of *La Strada*, an organization that fights the trafficking of women (*ProFem* 1995:16). The Czech Union of Women has also received funding from PHARE to publish reports on the situation of women in the Czech Republic (*ČSŽ* 1996).

Hana Klimešová (see interviews), of the Movement for Women's Equal Rights, emphasizes the EU's potential lobbying power. At meetings of EU parliamentary groups, Klimešová has told the deputies that the Czech government is only afraid of one thing: the EU. Without pressure from the EU, the government will not take steps to implement the European Union's policies on gender and human rights. Klimešová claims that the EU is now starting to press for such policies. Germany has been especially helpful.

Since Czech women's organizations are so dependent on foreign financing, this lack of equality can lead to tensions at times. Nevertheless, as Czech women activists come more into contact with Western feminists, they also become more influenced by Western ideas. Czech women are likely to become more open to such influences, now that the period of Czech exceptionalism has come to a close. Both Klimiešová and Lienau assert that there is growing support among Czech women's organizations for the notion of gender equality and that the main reason is the growing exposure to the Western discourse. Czech women attend international conferences, while Gender Studies are offered at Czech universities. Although they did not mention it, another source can be the large number of Westerns living in Prague. According to some estimates, as many as 50,000 Americans have been living in the capital, some of whom are bound to be feminist in their orientations.

Similarly, Western men are also more likely than Czech men to do the cooking and wash the dishes. At least among the educated middle-class, there might even be slow change coming about. Czech men will possibly begin to do more of the household chores in order to be able to compete with Western men. Of course, these differences should not be exaggerated. The Czech mass media (including the English language media) loves to point out that Prague has become a haven for Western male chauvinists who can find women that are willing to do all their chores for them. Nevertheless, on the *average* the Western men and women living in Prague are probably more supportive of gender equality than a traditional Czech and should live and argue accordingly.

CONCLUSION: FROM WOMEN'S ORGANIZATIONS TO A WOMEN'S MOVEMENT?

The prospects for building a Czech women's movement are increasing. Women's organizers have gained a decade of experience since the collapse of the communist regime. They have begun to overcome their differences and mistrust, and have started to cooperate more with each other. Women activists have discovered on what kinds of issues they can achieve widespread cooperation. The building of the umbrella organization, The Association for Equal Opportunity, could become a landmark step in uniting Czech women's groups. Women's organizations have also learned how to utilize foreign contacts for funding and national political contacts in order to gain political influence. Their representatives are now involved in discussing legislation on several issues with Czech lawmakers.

Nevertheless, gender equality still appears to be a low priority goal. It is not mentioned once in the Association for Equal Opportunity's "Plan of Action" (Plan of Action:1998), even though one of its founders, Hana Klimešová, claims that gender equality is their main goal (see interviews). Many of the Czech women's organizations, such as the Business and Professional Women's Association, are still only interested in narrow professional questions (interview with Šalanská and APM undated).

Many Czech activists, such as Jiřina Šiklová, have long maintained that Czech feminism and a Czech women's movement will differ from the West. Social movements in different countries always differ from each other, the question is rather whether there will be any important qualitative differences. So far, no uniquely Czech or even East European feminist school of thought has developed. There are, though, important differences in attitudes and probable courses of action.

First, because of the legacy of amicable relationships between men and women, it is unlikely for a radical, confrontationalist sort of feminism to develop in the Czech Republic. Czech women activists are more likely to see men as potential partners in the struggle for equality rather than as exploiters who uphold a patriarchal society. This might actually be an advantage, for even if men are exploiting women, the Czech women's movement is more likely to succeed if it can gain support of a large number of sympathetic men.

Second, for the time being Czech women's organizations do not consider gender equality an important issue. Instead, they are concentrating on such issues as: getting more women elected to political office, fighting indirect discrimination at the workplace and improving law enforcement against violence toward women and the trafficking of women. This does not mean that gender equality will not become an issue. Public opinion and leaders of Czech women's organizations are becoming more positive toward the notion that men should share in household duties. It is already becoming more common today than just a few years ago to see men outside walking the streets of Prague with baby carriages. Czech women appear to turn increasingly critical of the "gender contract" that was set-up during the communist era, when women had jobs, but concentrated on the household work and left the careers to the men.

Third, because of the communist political cultural legacy, Czech women are more sceptical than their Western counterparts of government intervention in favor of greater role equality. They have already experienced a repressive regime that tried to create a new kind of person. There is a widespread belief that changes in gender roles can only come about when women convince men of the need to eliminate gender roles. Here women's organizations have a central role to play.

Even if Czech women's organizations could convince men of the need to stay at home with their children, without changes in governmental policies no real change is likely (see the example of Sweden!). Men would claim that they cannot afford to stay at home and their employers would not let them stay at home. So only if Czech women's organizations do succeed in getting more women elected to political office and women's issues become more prominent on the political agenda and only if successful female politicians and business managers become inspirational role models for young Czech women, then the big question of gender equality will probably eventually come up on the political agenda. How it comes up and what solutions will be offered might differ from the West. Hopefully, we will see some new, more creative Czech proposals. Given the lack of understanding which today's mainstream Czech politicians have for gender issues, it is probably a good strategy for the Czech women's organizations to proceed as cautiously as they are. They need to build up networks of women's organizations and political contacts first, before they have any chance of bringing about radical changes in centuries-old gender roles.

The future in which female entrepreneurs tell their husbands that they cannot be the main breadwinners *and* the main housekeepers might not be all that far off. In politics a day can be like a year. Already, in the past year major steps have been taking in building up umbrella organizations that can help Czech women activists make the leap from leading women's organizations to leading a women's movement.

NOTES:

1. If the most qualified got the best jobs, then productivity would increase and benefit everyone. Finally, if gender roles were eliminated and men also did household chores and helped raise their children, they could gain the cherishing experience of watching their children grow up and having a much closer relationship to their children than traditional patriarchic men (see for example, Saxonberg 1999c).
2. The spokesperson for the Movement for Women's Equal Rights in the Czech Republic, Hana Klimešová (see interviews) , also ridiculed American feminists, noting that in America a "boss is afraid to enter the same elevator as a female employee."
3. Nor were they aware that Sweden and Norway provide much more generous benefits (although for a shorter period) and that these countries encourage men to stay at home by reserving one month of parental leave benefits for the father (one month is also reserved for the mother, and the rest of the period can be split according to the parents wishes). This is not to say that the West has realized the idea of equality. Even in Sweden, more than 90% of the parental leave is taken by women!

4. For example, the organization Change paid the travel costs of 10 women from Eastern Europe to participate in the UN's conference on women held in Beijing in 1995. Without such outside help, few East European women could have made it to the conference. Access to invitations and funds is itself a source of great power: those who know about the invitations can attend the conferences and become the international fac of the Czech Republic.

5. In her turn, Hana Klimešová from the Movement for Women's Equal Rights, is an advisor to Volfová, and thus is able to use the fax machine and other facilities, which are important assets for the impoverished women's organizations (interview with Klimešová).

REFERENCES AND CONSULTED SOURCES:

Čermaková M., H. Maliková and T. Milan. 1995. "Role Mužů a žen v rodině a ve společnosti 1." *Data & Fakta* Nr. 5:1-4

Čermakova M. 1997. "Postavení žen na trhua práce" *Sociologický časopis* Vol. 33 Nr. 4: 389-404

Crompton R. 1997. "Women, Employment and Feminism in the Czech Republic" *Gender, Work and Organization* Vol. 4 Nr. 3:137-148

Deacon B. 1993. "Developments in East European Social Policy" in *New Perspectives on the Welfare State in Europe.* Edited by C. Jones. London. New York. Routledge, pp. 177-197

Eckstein H. 1988. "A Culturalist Theory of Political change" *American Political Science Review* Nr. 3:789-804

Gender Studies Center. 1995. *Altos and Sopranos. (A Pocket Handbook of Women's Organizations).* Prague. Gender Studies Center

Havelkova H. 1996. "Abstract Citizenship? Women and Power in the Czech Republic" *Social Politics.* Vol. 3 Nr. 2-3:243-260

Heitlinger A. 1996. "Framing Feminism in Post-Communist Czech Republic" *Communist and Post-Communist Studies* Vol. 29 Nr. 1:77-93

Hodný M. 1991. *Českoslovenští politici 1918/1991.* Prague. Nakladatelství M. Hodný

Legge M. 1998. "United on Issues, Divided They Stand." *Prague Post.* 18 March (a weekly)

Lienau S.M. forthcoming. "Keine Frauenbewegung, aber bewegte Frauen und (halb-) professionelle Frauenverbände. Die heutige Frauenbewegung in der Tschechischen Republik" (article prepared for a book published by the Heinz-Boeckler-Stiftung)

Lukášová V. 1998. "Statistika ČSŽ—Dnes členská základna" *Prestižní žena.* June (a monthly)

Potucek M. and I. Radicova. 1997. "Splitting Welfare State: the Czech and Slovak Cases" *Social Research* Vol. 64 Nr. 4:1605-1643

Saxonberg S. 1998. "Give Feminism a Chance. A response to Jiřina Šiklová's critique of Western feminism" *The New Presence. The Prague Journal of Central European Affairs.* April (a monthly): 24-25

Saxonberg S. 1999a. "A New Phase in Czech Politics" *Journal of Democracy* Vol. 10 Nr. 1: 96-111

Saxonberg S. 1999b. "Václav Klaus: The Rise and Fall and Re-emergence of a Charismatic Leader" *East European Politics and Society* Vol. 13 Nr. 2:391-418

Saxonberg S. 1999c. "Where Are the Men?" *Electronic New Presence* Nr. 4 in Czech as "Kam se poděli muži" *Britské listy.* 19 January

Scott H. 1974. *Does Socialism Liberate Women?* Boston. Beacon Press

Šiklová J. 1995. "Inhibition Factors of Feminism in the Czech Republic after the 1989 Revolution" in *Women, Work and Society*. Edited by Marie Čermáková. Working Paper 95:4 of the Institute of Sociology. Czech Academy of Sciences, pp. 33-43

Šiklová J. 1998. "Why Western Feminism Isn't Working" *The New Presence. The Prague Journal of Central European Affairs*. January (a monthly): 8-10

Stastna J. 1995. "New Opportunities in the Czech Republic" *Transition* Vol. 1 Nr. 16:24-28

Trnka J. 1998. *Sociální Dávky*. Prague. Linde Nakladetelství

Vachudová M. A. forthcoming. "International Influences on the Czech Republic" draft manuscript for *The Impact of International Factors on Democratic Consolidation in Eastern Europe*. Edited by A. Pravda and J. Zielonka. Florence. European University Institute

Wolchik S. L. 1995. "Women and the Politics of Transition in the Czech and Slovak Republics" in *Women in the Politics of Post- communist Eastern Europe*. Edited by M. Rueschemeyer. Armonk. New York. M.E. Sharpe, pp. 3-27

DOCUMENTS

APM (undated) "About APM" unpublished leaflet by the Asociace Podnikatelek and Manažerek (Business and Professional Women's Association) (put out in Prague)

Čermaková M. and Gartnar L. 1994. *Rodina 1994. Sociologický výzkum sociálních podmínek české rodiny. Základní data z výzkumu zář 1994* (unpublished data collection, from the Institute of Sociology, Czech Academy of Sciences)

Česky statistický uřad. 1997a. *Mzdy zeměstnanců za rok 1996*. Prague. Česky statistický uřad

Český Statistický úřad. 1997b. *Zaměstnanost a nezaměstnanost v České republice podle výsledků výběrového šetření pracovních sil*. Prague. Česky statistický úřad

Česky statistický uřad. 1997. *Statistická ročenka '97*. Prague. Česky statistický uřad

Česky statistický uřad. 1998. *Statistická ročenka '98*. Prague. Česky statistický uřad

ČSŽ (1996) *Postavení žen v České republice a demokratizační procesy v ženském hnutí. Projekt PHARE—Democracy 1995-1996.* Prague. Vydal JOB Publishing

Heinrich Böll Stiftung. 1998. *Nachrichten.* Nr. 2. Impressum. Herausgegeben von der Heinrich-Böll Stiftung Öffentlichkeitsarbeit. Berlin

"National Report of the Czech Republic on the Status of Women in the Czech Republic" paper prepared for Regional Preparatory Session of the Economic Commission for Europe held in Vienna. October 17-21. 1994

Plan of Action to Achieve Equality for Women and Men. 1998. Plan drafted by the Czech Non-Governmental Organisations (a typed mimeograph)

ProFem (undated) *ProFem: středoevropské konzultačři středisko pro ženské projekty* (brochure, put out in Prague)

ProFem. 1995. *Výroční zpráva 1994-1995.* (brochure, put out in Prague)

ProFem. 1997. *Annual Report 1996-97.* (brochure, put out in Prague)

INTERVIEWS

Hajná, Zdeňka	Chairperson for the Czech Union of Women	Prague	January 21, 1999

Klimešova, Hana	Movement for Women's Equal Rights in the Czech Republic and the Czech-German Forum of Women	Prague	January 26, 1999
Lienau, Saša Marie	Head of *ProFem*	Prague	January 18, 1999
Malcevová, Alena	Head of the International Section of the Czech Union of Women	Prague	January 21, 1999
Šalanská, Olga	Director of the Business and Professional Women's Association	Prague	January 19, 1999

3. Continuity in Change: Hungarian Women's Organizations

Andrea Pető

Political scientists often use the red carpet as a metaphor for communism. It covered up the whole society, masking it and giving an impression of homogenity. After the collapse of communism, the red carpet was folded and one found out what it had veiled.[1] As far as different women's organization in Hungary are concerned we find both continuity and change.

After 1989 Hungary increased its drive to be reintegrated into Europe pushing to be admitted to the European Union. Although Hungary had already accepted a United Nations' platform on discrimination against women in 1982, the text itself was first published in Hungary in 1991. In its eagerness to join the European Union and to neutralize the "socialist heritage" of women's emancipation, after 1989 the Hungarian government fulfilled the EU requirement of setting up an institution dealing with "women's issues." This institution was the Secretariat of Women's Policy affiliated with the Ministry of Labor. It was dissolved in 1998, after the victory of right wing conservative political parties, but then reorganized and placed in the framework of the Ministry for Family and Social Issues, mostly because of the pressure from the European Union. This governmental body has the potential to become a powerful and important consultative institution, if the pressure continues from the EU as well as non-governmental organizations, such as the East West Women's Network, Network Women and other international foundations.

The registry of the Women's Secretariat lists more than 350 organizations which claim active involvement in women's issues. The purpose of this chapter is to analyze the present and the future state of these organizations from a historical perspective.

HISTORICAL CONTEXT FOR WOMEN'S ORGANIZATIONS IN HUNGARY

After the storm of Word War II, in the period of "a new beginning" the Hungarian women's organizations, despite their great numbers, did not help Hungarian women to break through the dichotomy of the private and the public sphere.[2] On the contrary, they actually fixed the distinction between the public and the private by confining women to the public sphere. The heterogeneity of civil organizations which continued their activities after WWII produced a colourful picture, but there was one task that was out of question for women: politics. The leader of the Lutheran Girls Association declared during a secret police investigation in Orosháza in June 1947: "Our organization never took a position in a political matter, it is even more true since the members are young girls."[3] She wanted to show that they were harmless to "politics."

In Hungary between 1945-1951 there were 150-200 different women's organizations of every kind. In every medium-size city there was at least one. They had retained their interwar structure (Pető 1997b:268-279). If we narrow our focus to the representation of women in political life during the short period of Hungarian democracy between 1945 and 1947, we can detect two types of women's organizations (Pető 1994-1995:181-207). First, there were the women's branches of different political parties. These performed the roles which men assigned to women in politics. Second, there were women's groups in civic society. In my research on the period between

1945 and 1951, I have not come across a single women's initiative emerging from civil society which had any influence on politics or on women's sections of different political parties (Pető 1998:19-46).

During the 40 years of socialism, the party-state declared itself for equal opportunities to everybody. Yet the actual discrimination of women had its source in state socialism rather than in gender. The bureaucratic, centralized state did not tolerate civil society, there was no room for any autonomous groups. During the communist period there was only one women's organization in Hungary. It was founded in January 1945 as the Hungarian Women's Democratic Alliance (*MNDSZ*). It turned itself into a mass umbrella organization by 1951, forcing other women's organizations to join it (Pető 1998:88-122).

During the "revolution" of 1989 women mobilized just like men did. As in every political, economic and social upheaval they were used as co-soldiers and helpers. But, as soon as the period of dramatic change was over, Hungarian women were pushed back into their "traditional place." After 1989, the rebirth of feminism in Central Europe is generally characterized by the mushrooming of women's organizations different in size and aims. But in Hungary, despite a new law on freedom of assembly, the unfavorable funding rules made a major contribution to the slow but perceptible disappearance of women's organization after 1989. This development does not offer too much hope for changing the existing power structures: the inherited dichotomy between the strong repesentational political system (note the change from the selective to elective systems) and civic organizations.

After the first years of freedom only those women's organizations remained alive which were somehow related to political parties. They mirror the old (inter-war and post-1945) political division between socialists and liberals which reappeared as a cleavage line after the collapse of communism. The Association of Hungarian Women (*Magyar Nők Szövetsége*), as a successor organization of the former mass organization, The Women's Movement, has close ties to the Hungarian Socialist Party. Forum of Women (*Nőforum*), a pool organization of conservative parties, and Feminist Network (*Feminista Hálózat*) receive some support from the liberal parties. The women's organizations affiliated with political parties are acting as a one-way "transmission belt" between women-voters and these parties for which they are supposed to generate loyalty.

The historical structure of women's mobilization in Hungary is thus replicated today in that the main division line is between these semi-private organizations which are strongly affiliated with political parties, and which keep their NGO status to open up sources for funding, and those organizations which mobilize women around a few new issues. If these issues are not considered important or relevant for their policy making by political parties, then these NGOs can only hope to get funding from state sources, as happened with NGOs working with women and domestic violence.

Hungarian women's organizations in 2000 are characterized by their dichotomous profiles: lay or religious, local or national, welfare service or professional. The religious women's organizations mostly have an ameliorative profile. Some are organized around goals determined by a small group of local people, others in a top-down fashion, from the national level towards local branches. The professional women's organizations are interest protection groups of women in the same profession, such as medical doctors or policewomen. Their membership statistics are not public. Because of the continuous struggle for outside funding, each and every organization has avital interest in keeping its membership figures secret.

Since 1989 several NGOs organized by women are concerned with environmental issues, such as the organizations "Clean Water," "Air," "Green Women," "Women for Lake Balaton." The second new issue are Roma human rights as well as Roma women. The third issue is the consequences of the collapse of the state health system which not only left many social groups without social security coverage (most of the Roma population, in fact), but also failed to provide service for patients with special diseases, such as the Down syndrome, or chronic illnesses. Traditionally women are the caretakers in the family, so several women's organizations, such as, for example, "Hold by Hand," formed to help women to perform their roles. The fourth issue is women victimized by violence. "Esther" targets victims of sexual violence. "White Cross" takes care of women who were subjected to criminal violence. While it is relatively easy to get funding for "helping services," even if they are performed by women, the problematic question of funding becomes even more complicated when human rights issues are at stake.

It should not be ignored that personal relationships and networks have increasingly become important in shaping gender relations in Hungarian politics. Leaders of influential women's organizations have always been connected through family ties to male politicians. However, the visibility of the wives of major politicians varies by party. Wives have barely been seen in the Socialist Party since 1989. However, a few female socialist politicians are visible in their own right as a consequence of "socialist emancipation." This party contrasts sharply with the Smallholders' Party in which the wife of the Leader - a former operetta star - tried to solve a crisis of confidence created by her husband within the party. When in 1992 various party factions were formulating their programs for the Smallholders' Party prior to registering, she submitted a registration request for a new party using the name of her husband. Since a personal name cannot serve as a name for a political party, the registration request was rejected. However, after the power struggle was over, the wife not only served as the Head of the Women's Section of the Party, but also as its Vice President. Although this is an extreme example, in today's Hungary it is not just acceptable, but somehow required that the partners of distinguished politicians take part in "public life." Before 1989 even the marital status of politicians was a state secret. Today the wife of the President of Hungary, for example, is frequently seen taking part in receptions and organizing charity activities, a common "feminine" activity for other wives as well (Zimber 1994). After 1998 wives of leading politicians enriched their roles by promoting religious charities.

FEMINISM AS A MOBILIZATION FORCE

The feminist movement was born in Hungary at the turn of the century, along with a new educated middle-class (Pető 1997c:182-187). This class fought for women's access to professions which were previously the domain of men and it raised the question of equality as well. The Association of Female Clerical Workers, the forerunner of the Feminist Association (1904), demanded equal rights with men. Some educated middle-class women echoed it. The feminist movement, banned in 1951 and then re-established in Hungary after 1989, claims that gender equality is tied to the desires of middle-class women. Yet, "at the same time, a group of highly educated, self respecting, well-to-do women with a lot of leisure time, which is the basis of the Scandinavian and American upper middle class feminism, is missing in Hungary." (Tamás quoted in Corrin 1994:211) This may be true inasmuch as after 1989 there were no influential interest groups outside party politics. Therefore, women's interests have been subordinated to a dominant parliamentary political discourse with middle-class women staying satisfied with their political representation in the existing political system.

At the present, the Hungarian feminist movement is confined to a very narrow social spectrum. It is mostly made up of women intellectuals, sociologists, economists, journalists, and a few historians in their mid-thirties and mid-forties, based in university centres. Since 1989 women researchers have pioneered such fundamental issues as housing, employment, economic and sexual rights, (self)perception of women, body image, sexuality or media presentation from a gender point of view. Since generations of women grew up without experiencing any real opportunities to engage in political activity, and since they matched their lives to the demands and expectations of state socialism, political activism of women during the first decades of the twenty-first century must be cautious and tolerant, but persistent.

TRANSITION: LOSERS OR WINNERS. WOMEN IN BUSINESS

A small group of women entered the new phase of democratic transition with comparative advantages: they were the influential group of women in business characterized by high level of educational and organizational experience. The different organizations of women in business with their small but exclusive leadership might serve as a power centre for women's organizations in the future. In the world of business, women, as leaders, are still strangers.[4] According to recent research (conducted by males), the leadership styles of men and women are markedly different. The research also points out that "...female subordinates often use special tactics to take part in leadership; although they remain in the background they may exercise their personal influence on the male leaders." (Schleicher 1992:42)

During the 1990s transformation of the Hungarian elite, half of new leaders were women: by 1994 two-thirds.[5] But the women's own perception of this change in status is not what one might expect. Most women feel that they have more duties and thus experience more stress and nervousness as a result of social change. Only 4.1% polled in 1996 declared that they live better now than they did before moving to a leadership position.[6] Competing in an environment that is alien, hostile, and less than rewarding, is still a painful reality for these women. One may hope that when the reserves of authoritarian power and battle-oriented "male leadership" are over, the twenty-first century will be more receptive to a new land of "feminine leadership."

EAST MEETS WEST?

When the first feminist "political tourists" came to Hungary after 1989, they were surprised not to find the kind of feminist sisters they expected. Moreover, they were shocked by the negative connotation of the word "feminist" and the vehement non-identification with this term by Hungarian women fluent in foreign languages (Rueschemeyer 1994; Feischmidt, Magyari-Vince and Zentai 1997).

Why was there no feminism in Hungary in 1989? It depends on how we define feminism. If it is defined as a sensitivity towards "female related issues," then traces of feminism can be found before 1990 in certain intellectual circles, mostly among dissenters. On the other hand, the Soviet bloc countries were closed, intellectually and linguistically, from the rest of the world and certainly from the West. Before 1990, very few translations were published in Hungarian. Only those who could read foreign languages had access to feminist writings. Crucial alternative sources of information, such as Radio Free Europe and Voice of America, were probably not the best media by which to spread liberal feminist ideas in Eastern Europe. Although there was a "state feminist" women's movement in Hungary before the collapse of the socialist state, it would be an oversimplification to identify "feminism" with it. It shared many of the characteristics of the political system: it was centralized, bureaucratic, inefficient and conformist. Nevertheless, it has to be acknowledged that it employed some enthusiastic workers who wanted to be feminists and wished to act in favor of women within the existing governmental framework.

During East-West dialogues, it often occurs that radically different problems are articulated by women from the East and the West, and yet all identify themselves as feminists (Adamik 1993:207-212; Tóth 1993:213-223). The "Women of the East" are mostly concerned with police corruption, environmental problems, limited access to information, losses in social services and a lack of affordable housing. The absence of the rule of law is an issue that particularly affects them. In the "West," or rather in that segment of the Western feminist discourse which has found its way to Hungary, debate is stirred by reproductive rights, economic inequality and domestic violence (Schepple 1995:69). Misunderstandings arise between these positions because they speak two different languages: the language of social politics and the language of rights. The women of the West follow the liberal tradition of 1776, articulating their demands in legal terminology. The women of Central Europe still have to become familiar with the possibilities and limitations of fighting for women's legal rights.

In countries which underwent the "state feminist" period, "women" do not exist as a historical subject and they are not publicly acknowledged as a collective. The "Past of their Own" has been stolen from them by totalitarianism. The rich network of women's organizations was destroyed by 1951 by the communists either because these associations were religious and the atheist power did not want them to exist, or because they were tied to the pre-1945 conservative right-wing regime, or because their ideas and goals were incomprehensible to the new political power as it happened in the case of the Feminist Association. The socialist heroines of the communist period were fake. General and universal suffrage arrived to this region as a "present" handed in by the armed Soviets. They brought no real democratization even after 1945. Therefore, searching for women as a subject in Hungary will always necessarily fail. The results of the previous three democratic elections (1990, 1994, 1998) proved that the less a party advocates a women's program, the stronger its electoral appeal to the voters.

In the former Soviet bloc a revolutionary elite which will revolutionize the rest of the population constitutes a familiar concept with negative connotations. Enlightening speeches therefore will not raise feminist consciousness. In a region with a totalitarian past, such speeches are also dangerous. In the long run, however, it is probably true that: "The rise of feminism on a significant social scale is a product of the experience of the masculinism inherent in civil society; it depends crucially on the creation of social distance between men and women, on a perceived imbalance of social power and sense of worth. In these terms, the development of feminism in Eastern Europe is simply a matter of time." (Watson 1993:83) Hungarian society faces the task of building a new political system, one that acknowledges inequalities and develops a new body of social knowledge which recognizes gender distinctions as a part of human dignity and freedom.

NOTES

1. See more on this in Pető 1997a.
2. For the full list of Hungarian women's organizations 1945-1951, see Pető 1998:180-183.
3. Hungarian National Archive (*Magyar Országos levéltár*) XIX-b-1-c. 5633. 321.
4. A well-based case study researching the motives of women entering politics after 1989 is missing in Hungary. For an attempt to compare the lifecycles of 15 male and female politicians in top governmental positions, see Koncz 1996.
5. Whatever they do on the job, women are less likely to use personal influence in getting their first job. If they are in leading positions, they probably gained them by taking out an advertisement. And if we compare career paths, we see that women climb from one step to the other, while men sometimes jump over steps (Koncz 1993:35). The values held and characteristics preferred by male and female top managers do not seem to differ. This throws into the question the feminist hope that female top managers might employ a "feminine" leadership style, based on mutual love and co-operation. It appears that female managers have to fight against the prejudice of their male colleagues as well as that of their "sisters." In comparison with their male colleagues, women reach the "glass ceiling" earlier. Women are more likely than men to have been appointed to the highest managerial positions, to make matters worse. Their performance is not approved of either in the workplace or within the family.
6. Figures from the survey of the SEED Foundation quoted in Dobszay 1996:97.

REFERENCES

Adamik M. 1993. "Feminism and Hungary" in *Gender Politics and Post Communism. Reflections from Eastern Europe and the Former Soviet Union.* Edited by N. Funk and M. Muller. New York. Routledge, pp. 207-212

Corrin C. 1994. *Magyar Women, Hungarian Women's Lives. 1960s-1990s.* New York. St. Martin Press

Dobszay J. 1996. "Nehéz napok. A nők és a munka" (Difficult Days: Women and Labour). *Heti Vilag Gazdasag* June 8:96-97

Feischmidt M., E. Magyari-Vince and V. Zentai. eds. 1994. *Women and Men in East European Transition.* Cluj-Napoca. EFES

Funk N. and M. Müller. 1993. *Gender Politics and Post Communism. Reflections from Eastern Europe and the Former Soviet Union.* New York. Routledge

Koncz K. 1993. "Nők a rendszerváltásban" (Women in Transition) *Társadalmi Szemle* 12:24-37

Koncz K. 1996. "Nők a felső vezetésben. Politikusok önmagukról és a nőkről" (Women at the Higher Level of Leadership. Politicians on Themselves and on Women) *Társadalmi Szemle* 2:53-63

Pető A. 1994-1995. *As the Storm Approached. Last Years of the Hungarian Women's Movements before the Stalinist Takeover.* Budapest. CEU History Department Yearbook, pp. 181-207

Pető A. 1997a. "Hungarian Women in Politics" in *Transitions, Environments, Translations: The Meanings of Feminism in Contemporary Politics.* Edited by J. Scott, C. Kaplan and D. Keats. New York. Routledge, pp. 153-161

Pető A. 1997b. "'Minden tekintetben derék nők.' A nők politikai szerepei és a nőegyesületek akét világháború közötti Magyarországon" (Proper Women in all Meaning. Political Roles of Women and Women's Associations in the Interwar Hungary) in *Szerep és alkotás* (Role and Production). Edited by B. Nagy and M.S. Sárdi. Debrecen. Csokonai, pp. 268-279

Pető A. 1997c. "These goals have approached Us. Hungarian Women after 1945" in *The Democratic and Social Progress. Plans and the Reality 1942-1945*. Edited by S. Gábor and J. Jemnitz. Budapest. Magyar Lajos Foundation, pp. 182-187

Pető A. 1998. *Nőhistóriák. A politizáló nők történetéből. 1945-1951*. (Women' Stories. From Women Making Politics. 1945-1951). Budapest. Seneca

Rueschmeyer M. ed. 1994. *Women in the Politics of Post Communist Eastern Europe*. New York. Sharpe

Scheppele K.L. 1995. "Women's Rights in Eastern Europe" *East European Constitutional Review* Vol. 4 Nr 4:68-70

Schleicher I. 1992. "Nők a vezetésben" (Women in Leadership). *Vezetéstudomány* 1:41-44

Tóth O. 1993. "No Envy, No Pity" in *Gender Politics and Post Communism. Reflections from Eastern Europe and the Former Soviet Union*. Edited by N. Funk and M.Muller. New York. Routledge, pp. 213-223

Watson P. 1993. "The Rise of Masculinism in Eastern Europe" *New Left Review* Vol. 198:1-83

Zimber S. 1994. *És akkor miniszterné lettem. Interjúkötet*. Budapest. 150év Lapkiadó KFT

DOCUMENTS

Hungarian National Archive (*Magyar Országos levéltár*) XIX-b-1-c. 5633. 321. (refers to an archival unit which consists of unnumbered documents on women's associations)

PART II

RELIGIOUS MOVEMENTS

4. Features of New Religious Movements in Eastern Germany

Klaus Hartmann

EASTERN GERMANY AS A NEW OPPORTUNITY

When the Berlin wall fell in November 1989 the citizens of East Germany began to cross the geographical border between the East and the West. In doing so, they also started to step over social, political, and economic borders. They gained access to a world full of new life opportunities. They freed themselves from the so-called socialist regime which repressed any orientation other than the socialist one, just as it repressed any kind of religious life.

While the East Germans were still euphorically looking westwards checking out their new opportunities, there were others in the West who already began to move eastwards. These people did not bring along only new material goods, but also novel spiritual offers. The Iron Curtain had prevented many inhabitants of the Soviet bloc from coming into contact with non-socialist political systems and ideas. One of its consequences was that new religious movements from the West could hardly gain influence in the GDR.[1]

With the fall of the Berlin wall the representatives of the new religious movements in the West saw their big chance in the East. They expected that with the breakdown of socialism the entire belief system would collapse. They expected to find a spiritual and intellectual vacuum which they would be able to fill out with their religious ideas.

This generally shared expectations were based on two premises. First, one supposed that due to longlasting repression by the East German party-state, headed by the *SED*, East Germans became psychologically oriented to hierarchical orders and closed structures. New religious movements offered precisely such orders and structures. The weekly (West) German magazine *Der Spiegel* (1990:97) so formulated this assumption in one of its headlines: "Out of the *SED* youth organization *FDJ*, up into the next religious group." Secondly, it was assumed that the institutional change brought about by German reunification would cause intensified feelings of uncertainty and put pressure on people to reorientate their life plans and biographies. New religious movements were supposed to answer the new needs by offering re-training in conjunction with personal counselling. This way they could harness people's needs to their semi-public programs and missionary aims.[2]

Moreover, the vision of big success of the new religious movements was grounded in the special religious situation in East Germany. In the four decades of the socialist regime the Protestant (*Evangelisch*) and the Catholic Church had lost about two thirds of their membership. At the time when the GDR was founded 81% of the population still belonged to the Protestant and 11% to the Catholic Church. By the time of the collapse of the East German regime in 1989-1990, however, their numbers were reduced by two-thirds. Little more than 25% of the population were members of the Protestant Church, about 4% belonged to the Catholic Church (Pollack 1994:373-445). Thus, to new religious movements eastern Germany looked like an open, accessible pool of potential followers. The conditions for successful missionary activities seemed to be just perfect.

The religious arena was hardly occupied in a sense that Christianity did not dominate the field with its definition of legitimate religious beliefs.[3]

With the downfall of the socialist regimes and the new freedom of religious beliefs, Protestant Church officials as well as many observers came up with specific expectations concerning the future Protestant Church. While in East Germany church members were exposed to many disadvantages and repression, church leaders now hoped that with the disappearance of repression church membership would increase again. Moreover, early in the 1980s the Protestant Church as well as initiatives and organizations at its base played a major role in the process of political change in the GDR. This Church and the party-state made a pact in 1978 to the effect that in exchange for more religious tolerance, the Church would support the East German state. From then on it increasingly came to serve as a protective umbrella for the lay and religious dissenters, even though it also worked to restrain dissent. Dissenters took up such issues as the militarization of the society, gender, environment, exploitation of the developing countries and the role of the Church in society (Pollack und Rink 1997). They established a plethora of groups which together amounted to the women's, environmental, peace and the Third World movements. Dissent organized within this Church finally culminated in the "silent revolution" of 1989. While calling it a "Protestant revolution" (Neubert 1990) certainly overestimates the role of the Protestant Church in the downfall of the regime (Pollack 1993), this Church and Protestantism as such gained increased general respect. This nourished the assumption that the Protestant Church would gain ground in eastern Germany.

To say it right away: both predictions failed. After the downfall of the East German regime neither did new religious movements spread out in eastern Germany nor did membership in the Protestant Church increase significantly. On the contrary, the expected openness of East Germans towards spiritual ideas of new religions as well as the extra bonus for the confessional churches did not materialize. This leads us to raise the question: Why did the social change not bring mobilizing effects in the field of religion? Was the opportunity structure for new religious movements perhaps not as appropriate as assumed?

In the following, I will first sketch some tendencies in the development of new religious movements in eastern Germany and then discuss their possible explanations. I will shed light on the older initiatives and organizations at the base of the Protestant Church as well as the official Christian churches only insofar as this information contributes to a better understanding of this development. Fully understanding the present situation of new religions movements in eastern Germany requires a look at the situation before the "big change."

RELIGIOUS MOVEMENTS IN THE GDR

Because of the central role of the *SED*, its monopolistic power position and the primacy of politics it instituted in East German society shortly after World War II, the relationship between religion and the *SED*-state was in principle political. This relationship was fundamentally influenced by the political and ideological demands of the party-state leadership and changed along with different strategies the *SED* adopted to increase its legitimacy. In the founding phase of the GDR in the fifties, the dominant strategy of the *SED* was to exclude religious movements and the Church from society as much as possible. In 1950, after a spectacular show trial, Jehovah's Witnesses were banned; in 1951 Christian Science. The same happened to other groups like the Pentecostals. The *SED* wished to gain legitimacy and loyalty for the "new society" by systematically creating a uniform socialist ideology. In its view, religious ideas were associated with the selfish individualism of bourgeois capitalist society. The *SED* defined religion as an opposition to its ideological philosophy and goal of developing a so-called "socialist personality" (Müller 1997).

Thus the Protestant Church was faced with the policy of exclusion which led to a conflict mainly in the field of education. The struggle about how young people should interpret their life peaked in 1954 when the state introduced a kind of youth consecration (*Jugendweihe*) as an alternative to traditional Christian confirmation ceremony (Urban and Weinzen 1984; Pollack 1994:129-136). The state, however, did not count only on open confrontation and prohibition of religious movements. Its goal was to limit religion to the private sphere and exclude it completely from public discourse.

With its policy of exclusion the *SED* also tried to destroy the traditional relations and networks among religious groups which crossed the inner German border and connected these networks to the Western world. The *SED*'s policy ensured that most of the 35 or so registered smaller religious groups in the GDR had tremendous difficulties in maintaining contact with the West. This directly affected the religious lives of their members since their church centers were often located in the West. Famous preachers were not granted permission to travel to the GDR. Religious communities in East Germany were deprived of access to special spiritual places. For example, the religious life of the Mormons centers on a temple but until 1985 none existed in the GDR.

In this repressive context some religious groups declared themselves independent from their mother church. They did not want to take the risk of state atrocities. For example, the Johannical Church (*Evangelisch-Johannische Kirche*) formed its own church leadership in 1964. The Protestant Church also was facing this problem. In 1969 the eight territorial Protestant churches of the GDR separated themselves from the Protestant churches of West Germany and formed their own federation, the *Bund der Evangelischen Kirche in der DDR (BEK)*. From then on the East German Protestant Church called itself "Church in Socialism."

In East Germany the attitude of the of the party-state towards religious movements changed as the relationship between the Church and the state became less confrontational since the end of the seventies. The concessions of the party-state which granted more religious plurality were due to inner political as well as foreign policy demands. The case of the Church of Jesus Christ of Latter-day Saints well illustrates this point. The Mormons, who in 1969 had separated themselves from their leadership in West Berlin, were allowed to built their own temple in Freiberg (Saxony) with the financial support of their mother church in the United States. It was the first temple of the Mormons in a socialist country as well as in Germany. It cost about 5.5 million DM (about 3 million dollars). Though the party-state long hesitated because it feared that with the construction of the temple Mormon missionary activities would increase, it finally gave its permission. Increasing economic problems forced the East German government to look for new means of gaining access to foreign currency. Also, cautious government support to the Mormons was meant as a slap in the face of the Protestant Church and the dissent groups organizing under its auspices since the late 1970s. The building of the temple was used by the party to demonstrate that it is well possible for religious people to get along with the socialist state in a "constructive" manner. The party press organ, *Neues Deutschland (29.10.1988)*, so contrasted the Mormons with the Protestant Church and its members: "The Saints of Latter-day are never drop-outs, but optimistic and positive in their thoughts and activities. (...) The Church is fundamentally not a place for somebody looking for a platform or a roof for political opposition. (...) Thus the young men feel committed to do their compulsory military service."[4] Ultimately for the *SED* leadership the building of the temple was a success in foreign affairs too. It could demonstrate its openmindedness and tolerance to the world (Fincke 1994: 255-257).

More than 100,000 people visited the temple of the Mormons during the first two opening weeks, alhtough they had to stand in line hour after hour. Yet the Mormons did not succeed in their mission, the number of their followers did not increase at all. General interest taken in the temple was not of religious nature but rather indicated that after decades of homogenizing secular mobilization drives people came to regard religious movements as alternatives to the offical doctrine of the party-state.

In general the East German party-state leadership was quite successful in its repressive effort to control society. Apart from the New Apostolic Church, which was with about 85,000 members the biggest congregation, no religious group gained followers prior to 1989, although officially the party-state allowed any new religious group. Before the "big change" the GDR counted altogether around 215,000 members of religious groups. Including friends and sympathizers in the calculations gave an estimated number of about 500,000 people (Fincke 1994:217)

RE-FORMING THE RELIGIOUS FIELD AFTER THE "BIG CHANGE"

Along with the "big change" in 1989-1990 not only did the political, economic, and social situation change rapidly in eastern Germany, so did the religious situation (Obst 1991:197-204). No later than in 1989 hitherto banned religious groups as the Christian Science were permitted by the state again. On November 9, Scientologists were already standing at the border control stations of the Berlin wall, passing out their Dianetic books to the East Germans who were entering the West. It only took a short time until one saw Krishna monks just as other movements in small provincial towns of eastern Germany. Some even claimed the "big change" to have been induced by their leaders' intervention or God's pleasure at their endeavours. The Unification Church proclaimed "Moonism" as a third way beyond socialism and capitalism. All in all, freedom of religion, of mission and of travelling led to a "free religious market."

After the "big change" the numbers of new religious movements increased, especially in the south of East Germany, a rural area, which traditionally has been open to religious life. Unfortunately, we have no reliable statistics concerning this increase (but see note 6, and Pickel 2000 and Pollack 2000). Nowadays, one can distinguish three different features of New Religious Movements,[5] (NRMs), in eastern Germany:

First, there are some, but very few NRMs which had a continuous legal status during the GDR regime, as for instance the Mormons. They are mostly small residual groups, not connected to their mother churches in the West anymore. These groups appear as closed circles, very much concentrating on themselves. It is difficult to get access to these groups from outside. Reunification between these groups and the western groups turned out to be rather difficult.

Second, there are the old NRMs which had been legal in East Germany until the party-state prohibited their religious activities, as for instance the Jehovah's Witnesses and the Christian Science. No later than 1989 these groups resumed their missionary activities. In their missionary activities they stressed their past persecution by the GDR-regime. Jehovah's Witnesses have scored some successes using this missionary strategy. They claim to be the only true "persecuted" Christians and point out that all other Christian churches have lost their credibility due to their co-operation with the socialist state.

Third, there are the new NRMs which for the first time appeared officially only after 1989. During the *SED*-regime some were hiding in small circles. Among these NRMs one can find Christian groups such as the Universal Life (*Universelles Leben*) as well as non Christian movements like ISKCON (the International Society for Krishna Consciousness), the Unification Church, the Osho movement, Transcendental Meditation (TM), the Church of Scientology and others. Quite soon after the fall of the Berlin wall these groups surfaced in the city centres of all bigger towns in eastern Germany. They offered performances, vegetarian food and literature to the passers-by. But within just a short time the followers of Krishna already had to close their most important temple in eastern Germany, the "Vedish culture centre" in Weimar, because it did not attract enough people. Similar was the development of TM; in 1993 they offered quite a lot of programs and courses at adult education colleges, but by now most of them have been cancelled due to lack of interest (Fincke 1996:61).[6]

Not only the religious movements, but also the Protestant Church has had to deal with new pluralism and liberalism. This Church lost its position as a special site where dissenters could meet within the repressive *SED*- regime. It had to take on the challenge of rethinking and redefining its task in a new plural society. Just as the Protestant Church in western Germany, the Protestant Church in eastern Germany put into practice the diversity model of a church offering a variety of services in order to meet different needs of different people.

Furthermore the Protestant Church was faced with the fact that the dissenters, human rights groups, peace groups, women's groups, ecology and Third World groups all left the Church in order to take part in the new political order. Some joined the New Forum and, later on, the political party, the so-called *Bündnis 90*, to which it gave rise (Pollack 1995:35-39).

Generally speaking, in the first years after reunification the Protestant Church saw a considerable loss of church members in eastern Germany. It lost 11,172 members in 1989 and three years later it lost 106,745 members (Hartmann and Pollack 1997:27-28). Moreover, in eastern Germany 48.9% of the respondents stated they do not believe in God, while in western Germany only 10.2% did so (Pollack 2000:32; Pickel 2000). Not just the former activists found new political structures to participate in and so left the Church, also earlier inactive church members gave up their church memberships for various reasons. For instance, with the imported tax system of the Federal Republic, after 1989 they had to pay church taxes with every pay check.

To note a contrary trend, it is worthwhile to take notice of a small, often overlooked, movement of new members registering in the Protestant Church in eastern Germany. For example, in 1991 this Church lost 82,761 of its members, but in the same year gained 23,980 new members.[7] Among such new members one finds individuals who did not belong to the Church earlier as well as individuals who renewed the church membership which they had cancelled during the *SED*-regime (Hartmann and Pollack 1998).

AN ATTEMPT AT EXPLANATION

In this closing section, I will sketch some explanations for the unexpected phenomenon that new religious movements have not attained a strong hold in eastern Germany so far. One reason for their failure could be that most of the religious groups chose the wrong strategy of mobilization. Their mother churches are located somewhere in western Germany or in the United States, so most of them simply sent missionaries from western to eastern Germany. This turned out to be a severe, tactical mistake since the conflicts which errupted between the "Wessis" and the "Ossis" in the process of reunification turned into a barrier also for the western missionary activities. The missionaries had to face all kind of prejudices against the West and its representatives coming to the East. They were accused of displaying a "know-all" attitude, (that is, presuming to know everything better than the eastern Germans and telling these eastern dummies what they should and should not do). For the new religious movements their advantage of having something new to offer soon turned out to be a disadvantage. Eastern Germans associated these offers with western arrogance with which they already felt fed up.

Moreover, at the beginning of their missionary activities the religious groups did not know whom to target as their customer groups. They opted for general mail shots or performing in public places. Such activities turned out to be too unfocused to secure gains in followers. By now, they target specific social groups as clients. For instance, TM is concentrating on people trying to make their own careers in the process of economic change. Scientologists focus on property and investment consultants.

However, an explanation of strategic errors does not shed light on the whole phenomenon. If one looks carefully, the failure of new religious movements turns out to be not just a matter of strategic problems which can be solved by improving communication strategies. One also needs to realize that social change within eastern German society first produced social differentiation necessary to create ground for new religious movements.

Moreover, one can ask whether the view that eastern Germany was the perfect field for new religious movements was really based on good arguments. After the downfall of the *SED*-regime with its authoritarian structure East Germans were expected to be looking desperately for new hierarchical structures which new religious movements offered. This argument follows the idea that there is a close parallel between the structure of a society completely controlled by the state and people's mentality. However, life course research on people's biographies has shown that the assumed correlation between totalitarian political conditions and specific personality structures has to be questioned (Huinink and Mayer 1995:152-155). The *SED*-regime was less successful than it claimed in shaping "socialist personalities." One could at least argue that the specific phenomenon of the so-called East German mentality tells us much more about a specific technique of adjustment to the political structures of the *SED*-regime than it explains the longlasting effects of a totalitarian regime on people's personalities in all their complex dimensions.[8]

Another way of explaining the unexpected failure of new religious movements is to look at the "Western" functions of the new religious movements and to ask whether they are needed in eastern Germany.[9] Quite often these new religious movements have the role of expressing opposition to established religious structures. Some of the Christian movements, like the Pentecostals, are based on the idea that only they offer true Christianity. In other words they need a religious society to which they are the counterpart. They need a traditional Christian background in order to radicalize Christianity through their specific interpretation. So one could argue that because of secularization of eastern Germany after forty years of the *SED*-regime, the religious background needed for radicalizing, new religious movements was missing. This was the main reason for the missionary failure of the new religious movements.

However, one can ask further whether new religious movements could not create an opposition to something else in eastern Germany besides traditional religion. Taking into consideration "East German mentality" again, it is said that people socialized in East Germany tend to share the values of the petite bourgeoisie such as merit, orderliness, tidiness and need for security (Pollack 1997:296-297). East German people prefer a sharp distinction between the private and the public sphere. In this respect new religious movements could offer a counter-idea of community to replace that of the bourgeois family, of expressive search for identity to replace that for privacy. Even if secularized eastern Germany did not provide a religious background which could be opposed, there is this bourgeois cultural background new religious movements could question.

Combining these considerations together with Inglehardt's idea (1977) that post-material values need a high level of material satisfaction, one could argue that East Germans have been following their material desires. In the context of high unemployment figures and high employment insecurities, they have been oriented to meeting their material needs rather than following post-material ideas offered by the new religious movements (Barker 1997:45; Pollack 1997:297). The cultural opposition offered by the new religious movements simply does not meet their preferences.

This explanation is most instructive. However, for further research it seems to be necessary to take into consideration that new religious movements are not a mass but rather a niche phenomenon. Future opportunities for new religious movements depend on the on-going formation of social milieus. The appeal of new movements strongly depends on one's individual position in society, for instance, whether one regards oneself as a winner or loser of German reunification. Hence, possible oppositional ideas, which new religious movements will create, are likely to be as diverse as individual biographies for which they aim to provide meaning. For this reason further research on opportunities of new religious movements in eastern Germany needs to take into consideration both the functional and the subjective dimension of religiosity.

NOTES:

1. For the variety of "New Religious Movements" in the West, see Barker 1993; for the process of their transfer to the East, see Barker 1997.
2. Strong warnings were brought up especially by Protestant Church Officials (Gandow 1990). "A new invasion of soul-hunters" was foreseen. This was also the title of a conference organized by the Konrad Adenauer Foundation in Leipzig in 1991.
3. The opportunity structure for religious movements depends on the field in which the discourse is taking place and the discourse participants (Bourdieu 1992).
4. In the Protestant Church there was a critical debate about compulsory military service. Some dissenters refused to do it and even more protested against the militarization of the East German state.
5. For a broad definition of "New Religious Movements," see Barker 1993:233.
6. It is impossible to present reliable statistics concerning these groups and their members. In contrast to the East German period of time, nowadays there is no obligatory registration or census of these groups. Figures on NRMs vary depending on one's definition of the NRMs. Any statistics of membership supplied by the groups themselves varies broadly depending on who is counted as a member. Some groups, for instance, Transcendental Meditation, count any person who attended one of their courses as a member.
7. This indicates that it is necessary to distinguish between the total numbers of religious movements and individual religious orientations (Hartmann and Pollack 1998).
8. For an example of a religious biography in the former GDR, see the case study of Hartmann and Pollack 1998:38

9. For theoretical grounds of the concept of "New *Religious* Movements" and the differentiation between those and "New *Social* Movements," see Eiben and Viehöver 1993; Hannigan 1990; 1991; 1993; Beckford 1985; Stark and Bainbridge 1985.

REFERENCES:

Barker E. 1993 "Neue religiöse Bewegungen. Religiöser Pluralismus in der westlichen Welt" Sonderheft 33 der *Kölner Zeitschrift für Soziologie und Sozialpsychologie*:231-248
Barker E. 1997. "But Who's Going to Win? National and Minority Religions in Post-Communist Society" in *New Religious Phenomena in Central and Eastern Europe*. Edited by I. Borowik and G. Babinski. Kraków. Nomos, pp. 25-62
Beckford J. A. 1985. *Cult Controversies. The Societal Response to the New Religious Movements*. London. Tavistock
Bourdieu P. 1992. "Die Auflösung des Religiösen" in *Rede und Antwort*. Pierre Bourdieu. Frankfurt a.M. Suhrkamp, pp. 231-237
Eiben J. and W. Viehöver. 1993. "Religion und soziale Bewegungen" *Forschungsjournal Neue Soziale Bewegungen* 6 Jg. Heft 3-4:51-75
Fincke A. 1994. "Zwischen Widerstand, Ergebenheit und diplomatischen Lavieren. Sekten und Sondergemeinschaften in der DDR" *Materialdienst der Evangelischen Zentrale für Weltanschauungsfragen* 57 Jg. Heft 8-9:217-228; 250-259
Fincke A. 1996. "Invasion der Seelenfänger? Sekten und religiöse Randgruppen finden in den neuen Bundesländern weniger Zuspruch als befürchtet" *Psychologie Heute*. Heft 8: 58-63.
Gandow Th. 1990. "Jugendreligionen und Sekten auf dem Vormarsch in die DDR" *Materialdienst der Evangelischen Zentrale für Weltanschauungsfragen* 53 Jg. Heft 9:221-233
Hannigan J. 1990. "Apples and Oranges or Varieties of the same Fruit? The New Religious Movements and the New Social Movements compared" *Review of Religious Research* 31 Jg. Nr. 3:46-258
Hannigan J. 1991. "Social Movement Theory and the Sociology of Religion: Toward a New Synthesis" *Sociological Analysis*, pp. 311-331
Hannigan J. 1993. "New Social Movement Theory and the Sociology of Religion: Synergies and Syntheses" in *A Future for Religion? New Paradigms for Social Analysis*. Edited by W. H. Swatos. London. Sage, pp. 1-18
Hartmann K. and D. Pollack. 1997. *Motive zum Kircheneintritt in einer ostdeutschen Großstadt*. Heidelberg. Forschungsstätte der Evangelischen Studiengemeinschaft
Hartmann K. and D. Pollack. 1998. *Gegen den Strom. Kircheneintritte in Ostdeutschland nach der Wende*. Opladen. Leske + Budrich
Huinink J. and K.U. Mayer. 1993. "Lebensverläufe im Wandel der DDR-Gesellschaft" in *Der Zusammenbruch der DDR*. Edited by H. Joas and M. Kohli. Frankfurt a. M. Suhrkamp, pp. 151-171
Inglehart R. 1977. *The Silent Revolution: Changing Values and Political Styles Among Western Publics*. Princeton. Princeton University Press
Müller M. E. 1997. *Zwischen Ritual und Alltag. Der Traum von einer sozialistischen Persönlichkeit*. Frankfurt a.M./New York. Campus
Neubert E. 1990. "Eine protestantische Revolution" *Deutschland Archiv*, 23 Jg. Heft 5:704-713

Obst H. 1991. "Auf dem Weg in den weltanschaulichen Pluralismus. Zur geistig-religiösen Lage in den neuen Bundesländern." *Materialdienst der Evangelischen Zentrale für Weltanschauungsfragen,* 54 Jg. Heft 7:193-205

Pickel, G. 2000. "Konfessionslose in Ost- und Westdeutschland - ähnlich oder anders?" in *Religiöser und kirchlicher Wandel in Ostdeutschland 1989-1999.* Edited by D. Pollack and G. Pickel. Opladen. Leske + Budrich, pp. 206-235

Pollack D. 1993. "Religion und gesellschaftlicher Wandel. Zur Rolle der evangelischen Kirche im Prozeß des gesellschaftlichen Umbruchs in der DDR" in *Der Zusammenbruch der DDR.* Edited by H. Joas and M. Kohli. Frankfurt a.M. Suhrkamp, pp. 246-266

Pollack D. 1994. *Kirche in der Organisationsgesellschaft. Zum Wandel der gesellschaftlichen Lage der evangelischen Kirche in der DDR.* Berlin. Kohlhammer

Pollack D. 1995. "Was ist aus den Bürgerbewegungen und Oppositionsgruppen der DDR geworden?" *Aus Politik und Zeitgeschichte,* B 40-41:34-45

Pollack D. 1997. "New Religious Movements in East Germany" in *New Religious Phenomena in Central and Eastern Europe.* Edited by I. Borowik and G. Babinski. Kraków. Nomos, pp. 293-300

Pollack D. 2000. "Der Wandel der religiös-kirchlichen Lage in Ostdeutschland nach 1989. Ein Überblick." in *Religiöser und kirchlicher Wandel in Ostdeutschland 1989-1999.* Edited by D. Pollack and G. Pickel. Opladen. Leske + Budrich, pp. 18-47

Pollack D. and D. Rink, eds. 1997. *Zwischen Verweigerung und Opposition. Politischer Protest in der DDR 1970-1989.* Frankfurt a.M. Campus

Stark R. and W.S. Bainbridge. 1985. *The Future of Religion.* Berkeley. University of California Press

Urban D. and H.W. Weinzen. 1984. *Jugend ohne Bekenntnis? 30 Jahre Konfirmation und Jugendweihe im anderen Deutschland 1954-1984.* Berlin. Wichern-Verlag

5. Religious Revival in Poland.
New Religious Movements and the Roman Catholic Church

Paweł Załęcki

INTRODUCTION

To understand the form and growth of various religious movements in Poland after 1989, one has to keep in mind the unconventional religious development in this country in the past 20 years. Generally speaking the domestic policies of the communist state were relatively liberal, even towards religion, in the 1970s. The activity of the foremost Zen Buddhist group began in the early 1970s (Doktór 1995) and at the end of the decade many other oriental and occult groups were established. However, it was only in the 1980s that the appropriate government agencies started registering religious movements and associations (Urban 1998). This hastened the process of their institutionalization.

The fall of the communist regime in 1989 and transformations of the socio-cultural situation resulted in the redefinition of the role of the Polish spontaneous social movements. With growing opportunities for public social activities, with an increasing chance to mobilize resources, many new social movements emerged and developed. Most of them were the New Religious Movements (NRMs). The NRMs enjoyed a remarkable percentual increase in their membership. In the Central European countries various non-traditional cult groups attracted several tens of thousands of people in each country, more in Russia. These proportions expressed in cardinal numbers, however, are not big. Traditional churches are usually in a better position in the new missionary conditions and circumstances. Such was also the case after the downfall of the communist order with its official aggressively atheistic ideology.

The comparative statistical research carried out in Central Europe showed a lower percentage of traditional forms of religiosity there than that in Western Europe - a result of the past communist rule. Poland is an exception here. The comparative data in the European Values Systems Studies (EVSS) collected in 1990 also proved an exceptional position of Poland in Central Europe. In Poland people who are not members of any denomination constitute 3.7%, whereas in East Germany, the Czech Republic and Bulgaria this proportion was 60% (Doktór 1997). In Poland the NRMs and their dynamics is broadly commented on in public, both in mass media and in the parliamentary debates. This social phenomenon is seen as a specific challenge to the dominance of Catholicism in this country.

However it should be remembered that, a widespread view to the contrary, Poles' religious beliefs cannot be classified as typical pro-church faith in a literal meaning of this word. The Roman Catholic Church is the biggest religious organization in Poland. It has been closely connected with both the statehood and the culture of this country for over one thousand years (966 - Christianization of Poland). Some 93-94% of Poles declare their affiliation with the Catholic Church. Almost always, however, the relationship between the Poles and the Catholic Church takes the form of a traditional participation in its rituals. The dominant group among Polish Catholics are so-called "passive churchgoers" (72.4%), another biggest group are "marginal members of the Church" (13.0%). "The people of the Church," that is those who participate actively in the life of the Church, also in its non-confessional activities, take the third position only (11.0%) (Marody 1994).

THE NEW RELIGIOUS MOVEMENTS

Almost all New Religious Movements found in Poland, even those of oriental origin, arrived from the Western countries. Only few NRMs have no agencies or "headquarters" abroad (see appendix for some detailed examples). The best known New Religious Movements that started in Poland due to a missionary activity of their representatives from the West or the USA are: (1) Science of Identity Institute "Chaitanya Mission" (in Poland since 1988, registered in 1990, ca. 1,000 followers); (2) International Society for Krishna Consciousness, ISKCON (in Poland since 1976, registered in 1988 as Society for Krishna Consciousness-Bhakti Yoga; in 1991 change of the name, ca 12,000 followers and ca 500 persons after the religious initiation); (3) The Family (The Children of God, The Family of Love - in Poland present since 1974, ca. 150 followers); (4) Bahá'í Faith (in Poland since 1989, registration in 1992, ca. 500 followers); (5) Unification Church (in Poland since 1980, registration in 1990, ca. 500 followers).

The following groups are recognized as movements of native Polish origin: "New Jerusalem" (established in early 1980s, ca. 30 followers), "Panunistic Religious Association: Disciples of the Holy Ghost" (registration in 1988), "The God's and Lamb's Sea of the Apostles in Spirit and Truth, Alpha and the Omega, the First and the Last, the Beginning and the End" (established in 1947), "Church of Healing through the Holy Ghost - Heaven" (ca. 60 followers, including children), "The Ausran Clan" (established in 1954, several dozen followers), "The Native Church of Poland" (registration in 1995, ca. 500 followers), "Association of the Native Faith" (registration in 1996, ca. 100 followers), "I Believe in Man's Good (registration in 1992, ca. 20 followers)" and some New Religious Movements acting within the Roman Catholic Church in Poland.[1]

On May 17, 1989, the bill on the freedom of belief and worship was introduced in Poland. It started a mass registration of religious movements and communities. Until this law was voted through, hardly 30 religious groups were active in Poland. Twenty-three of them were registered in the 1980s (apart from those of Christian origin, there were five Buddhist groups, three that drew on the tradition of Hinduism, and two that refer to the Rosicrucian and Muslim traditions). Some of the movements registered in May 1989 used to work informally earlier. However, many of them (particularly most of the Western imports) started their activity at the beginning of the 1990s. At the beginning of the 1990s the growth rate and development of cults quickened. Some authors argue (Urban 1998:95) that in spite of their great variety – in terms of provenience, views and structure – most of the New Religious Movements registered in Poland can be categorized as:[2] (1) religious groups that have existed in Poland for a longer time and those, which having had no formal legal status before, emerged as offshoots of some mother group; (2) new religious communities, which separated from their mother movement in the course of system transformation; (3) Christian movements which were formed as agendas of the Western missionary organizations; (4) independent congregations and denominations of a Protestant provenience; (5) neo-pagan movements (old-Slavic included); (6) religious movements connected with the eastern religious traditions; (7) groups associated with the so-called "new religions."

The fundamentalist and Protestant NRMs offer courses on the Bible and focus on healing. The NRMs of the Asian origin profit from the growing interest in meditation, vegetarianism and Eastern philosophies. Some NRMs stress psychotherapy and specific parapsychological concepts, while others attempt to revive old Slavic beliefs. It has to be emphasized that conversions are very few in Poland. They are motivated not by economic or social factors, but instead by the individual search for alternative ethical systems or self-realization.

The rapid increase in the number of NRMs in the early 1990s has by now subsided. In 1999 we have more than 300 various religious groupings. Actually, the number of these groupings does not change dramatically, although some decrease in the number of the NRMs is noticeable. A statement of one of the highest spiritual leaders of the International Society for Krishna Consciousness in Poland well captures the past and current trends: "When the system transformation started in Poland in 1989, the Movement developed very fast. People were interested and joined... It can be said there was a real Krishna Movement boom. And now, after these 8-9 years, we can notice that this interest has diminished and the number of followers is not growing that rapidly. In fact quantity seems to have been replaced by quality."[3] This is perhaps true for many other NRMs which, having achieved stability, still strive for new members.

THE LIGHT LIFE MOVEMENT AND THE ROMAN CATHOLIC CHURCH

Overall the NRMs have only a small number of followers. Considering the denominational structure of Polish society (the dominance of the Catholic Church and of Catholics), they are and will probably remain peripheral phenomena.

The biggest and the most influential Polish religious movements are found within the Roman Catholic Church. The most prosperous NRM of this sort is the "Light-Life Movement." This movement, called LIGHT-LIFE (Światło-Życie) or OASES, emerged in the 1950s as one of the manifestations of the religious revival in Poland. Its name refers to Greek words ΦΩΣ-ΖΩΗ which constitutes the Movement's symbol.

The history of the Movement is very interesting. In the 1950s, besides the processes of industrialization, urbanization and modernization that nearly everywhere resulted in the "decline of the sacrum," the active policy of the atheist communist State aimed to eliminate religion from the public sphere. It attempted to confine religious life to the private sphere as part and parcel of its overall goal of gaining total control over the political, cultural and religious domains. In spite of the new social and political system in post-war Poland and the secularization policy of communist authorities, the Catholic Church began to build up religious life and restructure the church authorities. The Episcopate of Poland used to consist of 20 bishops compared to more than 100 of them nowadays.

At the beginning - after the Second World War - the state authorities showed remarkable restraint in their declarations and attitudes towards the church. With no major obstacles, the church carried out its religious work and functioned as a relatively independent social institution largely unaffected by the political system. Soon it adopted a rather unfriendly attitude towards the state. Having launched an intensive Stalinization process in many fields of social life, the Polish Workers' Party (Polish United Workers' Party since December 1949) started an open war against the church and religion itself. In 1953 the church was accused of a hostile policy towards Poland stimulated by the Vatican and Western political centres. The state authorities started slandering bishops and expelling them from their dioceses. The work of church schools and associations was restricted, church press and publications were censored. Though avoiding open anti-socialist declarations and promoting political neutrality, the church appeared to be the main, well-organized institutional centre opposing the expansionary politics of the communist party-state.

October 1956 witnessed a shift of power within this state and the process of liberalization in political life. In December 1956 the Minor Agreement was signed between the Church and party-state representatives. It considerably improved church-state relations. Catholics regained their weekly, *Tygodnik Powszechny,* which had been banned. They also gained representation in parliament, a couple of brand new monthlies, and permission to set up their organizations, such as, for example, *KIKs,* the Clubs of Catholic Intelligentsia. The Agreement marked a return to more religious tolerance. The relationship between the Polish party-state and the Polish Catholic Church remained strained until the 1970s, however, when the Catholic Church began to thrive in the general liberalized context. The unexpected repressive events of 1976 led to the development of both lay and church-affiliated oppositional groups. Many Catholic priests sheltered oppositional activities even against the opposition of the bishops. When a mass movement *Solidarność* emerged in 1980, the Catholic Church played an important advisory role. It also functioned as the prime intermediary between *Solidarność* and the party-state. After general Jaruzelski introduced the state of emergency in the end of 1981, the Church curtailed some of its own oppositional and opposition-sheltering activities. Nevertheless, in the 1980s as well as earlier it represented to some people a way out of the intolerable reality created by the party-state. For others, however, not the Church as such, but rather one of several Catholic movements provided a venue of spiritual revival.

In the years 1962-1965, the Second Vatican Oecumenical Council met. The Polish church before this Council is called a "folk church" because of strong tradition and authoritarianism which resulted in obedience, uniformity of actions and attitudes. The cult was dominated by folk forms of worship. The Vatican Council was followed by essential changes in the church. Laicat grew in importance, the liturgy was reformed and Latin replaced by the national language. Service became a dialogue between a priest and parishers. Traditional folk religious practices began to diminish. This religious revival resulted in new forms of religious associations and movements. One of them was "Light-Life Movement," which developed fully in the 1980s. It emerged as an informal, spontaneous social group centred around Rev. Franciszek Blachnicki (1921-1987). From 1950s on, the Movement has continuously stressed its strong ties with the institution of the Roman Catholic Church.

From its very inception, the Light-Life Movement was meant to fulfil the following functions: i. to transform the individual, spiritual life of its own members as well as their immediate social milieu, ii. to build a "new community" of "new people" who would create and share a "new culture," centred around the ideas of Jesus Christ, iii. to "give witness" to the wider social environment through the correspondence between the actual lifestyle of its members and their own ideas and principles, iv. to transform the parishes into "communities of communes," "communities of 'new-born'" people, both laymen and clergy, who would take full responsibility for the perfection and dissemination or religious lifestyle, v. to transform the whole society through the dissemination of the "new culture."[4]

The Light-Life Movement did not have its own resources. The Movement's communities,

"Oases," which were organized by local priests, were allowed to use the material and financial resources of Roman Catholic parishes. They used church buildings in which communities met. The Church gave them money to organize religious retreats during vacations. Even more important was access to the symbolic and organizational resources of the church: its religious doctrine and cult or the legacy of the Scripture as well as the leadership and authority structures, the theologically educated leaders and various institutions, operating under the "church's umbrella."

People were recruited to the Movement by means of private, informal contacts of old members with their acquaintances and friends, the promotion of religious lifestyles held during outdoor evangelization organized by the communities, the Church's catechization held in schools and the occasional participation of "non-members" in the community activities. Religious conversion is a central route to membership. Evangelization is also present but only within some of the Movement's communities. It is relied on to attract new members.

It is impossible to estimate an exact number of Light-Life's members. Table 1 indicates estimated data on the number of permanent members of the Movement (according to the Movement's official data). The practice or "counting" the members shows a tendency toward lower values and does not include some communities.

TABLE 1:

THE ESTIMATED NUMBER OF PERMANENT MEMBERS OF THE OASES MOVEMENT
BETWEEN 1969 AND 1988*

1969 - 700 persons	1976 - 20,000 persons	1984 - 64,000 persons
1970 - 1,000	1978 - 30,000	1985 - 70,000
1971 - 1,500	1979 - 30,000	1986 - 76,000
1972 - 3,500	1980 - 40,000	1987 - 77,000
1973 - 6,000	1981 - 45,000	1988 - 77,000
1974 - 9,500	1982 - 50,000	
1975 - 14,000	1983 - 53,000	

SOURCE: Information received by the author from the central archives of Oases. See also Doktór, Kowalczewska, Werbanowska 1991:133-146 for some figures.
*No precise data are available since 1989. My estimate is that the Ligh-Life movement's size was 90,000-100,000 members in the 1990s.

The shared religious rituals held within the Light-Life consist of formal rituals that are universal within the Roman Catholic Church. More movement-specific religious rituals include religious conversion. The leader of the whole community is the "moderator" and the formal leader of a whole Movement is the "national moderator."

Among significant *internal* activities of Light-Life's communities we find meeting groups,[5] diaconate groups, summer spiritual camps, spiritual teaching, education and religious rituals. The largest meeting group is called the Great Prayer Meeting, the Prayer Gathering or the General Meeting. Its participants are all members of the community and very often - because of its open status - people from outside (non-members). It is usually organized once a week. Its main function is to connect "supernatural reality" to "everyday reality."[6]

The second kind of meeting group is the Small Group. It consists of 3-9 persons, often of the same sex, with the same prescribed level of religious initiation. It is one of the most important means of social control within the community, being at the same time the social setting for the socialization processes. The leader of every Group is called the "animator."[7]

The most significant *external activities* of the Light-Life Movement cover such actions as contacts with other, mostly Catholic, religious groups, missions and evangelizations, Christian conferences, charity actions and work for the well-being of local parishes. The most significant external activities of the charismatic current, nearly totally absent in the traditional current, are the outdoor, street evangelization, permanent and temporary missions outside the country.

In the second half of the 1980s political and cultural life in Poland underwent deep transformations. The spiritual, self-educational and evangelizing character of the Light-Life was influenced by the changes in social milieu. However, even some time earlier, the Movement was becoming more and more amorphic. It split into two currents in the second half of the 1980s. The first can be called the "lithurgic-biblical" current and the second - the "charismatic-evangelizing-ecumenical" current. They differ mostly in terms of their own goals and their attitudes towards the social reality around them.

The "lithurgic-biblical" current can he roughly described as "traditional" and "dominating" within the Light-Life Movement. The communities subscribing to it seem to focus on personal and communal self-improvement. These communities and their functions can also be described as "pro-members" oriented. When they engage in any activities aimed at the outside world, they made a special effort to avoid any social conflicts.

Communities subscribing to the "charismatic" current willingly engage in the activities aimed at the outside world, even if they may result in conflicts. The specificity of this current lies in the charismatic and ecumenical dimension, almost totally absent in the first one. The religious practices of the charismatic current differ also from the universal religious practices held within the Catholic Church. However, many of them, such as glossolalia, prophecy, Baptism in the Holy Spirit are comparable to the everyday practices of many other religious Christian groups and movements.

The final factor that helps distinguish between these two currents is their attitude towards "self-sufficiency." The charismatic current engages in various activities driving it to a kind of material and financial "operational" independence from the institutional church. This current becomes autonomous in the field of its "economic capital" but not in the field of "symbolic capital."

At the present time, in the lithurgic-biblical current, we can observe only a small increase of the number of new members, while at the same time many members are leaving it. This is due mainly to the highly defined personality standards within this current and, at the same time, by the absence of psychological and social mechanisms reducing the negative effects of failures in living up to these standards. The traditional current clearly exercises a much stronger pressure on self-improvement compared to the charismatic. Its members develop strong feelings of own sinfulness and imperfection. Since total realization of accepted values and ideas is impossible, many people become frustrated and have abandoned the Movement. People older than 25 also leave the Movement because of a strong attachment to their work and/or family duties. Another reason for their leaving can be found in the formal structure of this current. In the entire movement we can distinguish three main age groupings. There are the Oasis of God's Children (children 7-14 years old), the Youth Oasis (15-25) - alternatively Oasis of the University Students - and the Family Oasis (parents and their young children). The organizational gap causes the problem of placing people over the age of 25 who are neither university students nor married.

The inflow of new members to the charismatic current is both permanent and significant. The guarantee of the fulfilment of the defined, shared tasks and ideas is placed and assigned not to self-improvement but to a personal relationship with God. The charismatic current is not confined to children. As a movement it covers the children, parents, university students, single adults and whole families. The withdrawals of the regular members are rare. An interesting regularity is perceived - some members of the traditional current move their "significant participation" to the charismatic current. Reverse mobility does not take place.

The Light-Life has developed within the framework of the Roman Catholic Church, being one of its parts. From the very beginning, in its ideals and in its social practice, it drove towards overt spontaneity, and the manifestation of this is the emergence of the new ways of religious expression. Out of necessity, it had to function, during the first three decades of its existence, within the unfriendly, anti-religious political system. From the point of view of this system, the Movement's activities were not authorized, even illegal. The Movement was able to operate only due to the resources supplied by the institutional church. This situation gave the church a chance to control the Movement. In its initial stage of development, only very small tensions in the relations between the Movement and the institutional church occurred. They had a rather lo-cal character: some parish priests did not like the independent and spontaneous activity of the lay persons.

The systemic transformation in Poland created new opportunities for the emergence of new forms of public, including religious, activities. The spontaneous aspect of the movement gained new opportunities of stronger expression. For the traditional current this situation of increased "external" political freedom has not been particularly important. It has remained unchanged. The charismatic current, however, began to take advantage of this new situation, paying particular attention to the development and autonomy of its own resources.

This gain in autonomy has not affected its choice of symbolic resources. On the contrary, its symbolic and ideological dependency on the Roman Catholic Church strengthens its definition as well as its self-definition as a Roman Catholic social movement.

The church hierarchy, however, is clearly split in its evaluation of its new activities. During several National Conferences of the Polish Episcopate, especially in 1994, the "problematic questions" of several charismatic communities of the Light-Life Movement were discussed and, at the beginning of 1995 a local bishop excluded three charismatic Light-Life's communities from the Movement. He defined them as Catholic religious communities, autonomous from the Movement.

The Movement itself is also split. Some leaders of the charismatic current consider the possibility of an official withdrawal from the Movement to create independent structures. In the 1990s an increasing economic and structural autonomy of the charismatic current became significant in many of its communities. The gradual withdrawal of many charismatic communities from the Light-Life Movement is ongoing. The possibility of the withdrawal from the Roman Catholic Church, however, is not being considered.

CONCLUSION

Taking into consideration a remarkable number of the Light-Life followers, we can say that the Movement accounts for much of the growth of the NRM-sector in the Polish society (see Załęcki 1997). The research on its two currents and the way they change suggests several points. First, we can note some stability in the religious attitudes of those Poles who do not belong to the traditional structures of the Roman Catholic Church. Now that transformation processes are over in Poland, they are no longer a source of increases in the NRMs or the number of their followers. Religious movements respond to the changed context in different ways. Many of them, though, have not ceased to attract and recruit new members and to extend their spiritual formation. They still constitute a specific challenge for religious movements that develop within the Catholic Church.

NOTES:

1. In Poland the Catholic movements are much more numerous than others within the NRMs. Sometimes they have between a couple to several tens of thousands of members. The best known movements of this kind are: The Light-Life Movement (also knows as Oases), The Revival in Holly Spirit Movement, The New Teachings Movement, the Fokolarini Movement, the Faith and Light Movement, the Maitri Movement, the Communities of Christian Life Movement, the Family of Families Movement.

2. I mean here the registered religious groups, of which there are about 130. It is estimated that the number of all NRMs in Poland is twice or three times as big as the number of those registered.

3. A recording from the private collection of the author.

4. It should be added that the last two functions have actually been conceptualized and fulfilled only by *some* of the communities that have identified themselves with the Movement.

5. The gathering of leaders, the Animators' Meeting - apart from its religious activities - considers the members' efforts to recognize the community's needs, prepares the spiritual teachings and solves other community's problems (including financial ones). The diaconate groups are the task-oriented small groupings. They cope with technical, financial, musical (instruments), vocal and other functions. The major role of the summer spiritual camps is reinforcing a deeper involvement with a strong orientation on the community's lifestyle. It also becomes the important symbolic focus centre of the communities' activity.

6. The main activities include singing of religious songs, saying various, more or less public prayers, spiritual teaching and giving witness to the personal faith. The social functions of that meeting are focusing on "super natural reality" and reinforcing a religious definition of every day existence - both for the individual and the group.

7. The Small Group has a very informal, face-to-face character. It is to secure stability and development of each individual's personality. Main activities of such a group are closely related to the activities held in the General Meeting. Because of the small number of participants in such a group, it becomes a place of not only common prayer but also of personal, mutual sharing of the individual experiences, problems, enjoyments, successes, etc. High level of mutual trust and defining others as brothers and sisters results in the feeling of a high level of security in interpersonal contacts.

REFERENCES:

Doktór T. 1995. "Buddhism in Poland" in *The Future of Religion. East and West*. Edited by I. Borowik and P. Jabłoński. Kraków. Nomos Publishing House, pp. 117-126

Doktór T. 1997. "Nowe Ruchy Religijne w Europie Wschodniej" *Przegląd Religioznawczy* Nr. 4:51-71

Doktór T., J. Kowalczewska and J. Werbanowska. 1991. "Uczestnictwo w nowych ruchach religijnych a poczucie sensu życia i poziomu niepokoju" *Euhemer - Przegląd Religioznawczy* Nr. 4:133-146

Marody M. 1994. "Polak-katolik w Europie" *Odra* Nr. 2:2-10

Urban K. 1998. "Z problematyki legalizacji nowych związków religijnych w Polsce w latach 1977-1997" *Nomos. Kwartalnik religioznawczy* Nr. 22-23:87-106

Załęcki P. 1997. *Wspólnota religijna jako grupa pierwotna*. Kraków. Nomos

Country: *POLAND*	Movement Type: *Religious*
How Many Organisations?	*9*
Organisation Name(s): if several, list the names of the most important organisations	*Science of Identity Institute ,,Chaitanya Mission"*
When did the movement emerge?	*1977 in Hawaii, in Poland present from 1988, registered in 1990*
Number of Active Members: Past, Now Number of Members Per Organisation:	*1990 : ca 550 1998: ca 1000*
Issues/Themes:	1. *practise of bhakti yoga* 2. *spiritual development* 3. *problems of modern human being and society, ecological and environmental issues, dangerous religious sects (sic!)* 4. *vegetarianism*
Organisational Structure:	*decentralised, no community life accept few supervisors of local organisations*
Range of Protest Forms: Innovations?	*'open letters' to public people and academics working on NRMs and sects* 1. *showing the similarities between bhaki yoga and Christianity* 2. *public lectures* 3. *publishing ,,Haribol Polska" magazine, books, brochures, audio types* 4. *2 hours of everyday meditation*
Frequent Symbols:	*symbols of the Hindu origin*
Recourse to Violence/: Conflict Lines:	-----
Mobilising Power:	
Access to Government/Business/Unions:	
Public Resonance:	*negative media coverage, some institutional opponents (e.g. Movement for the Defence of Individual and Family, Republican League)*
Source(s) of Financial Resources:	*members' contributions, sale of Movement's publications*
Allied Movements:	*member of World Vaishnava Association (WVA)*
Additional Information:	

Country: *POLAND*	Movement Type: *Religious*
How Many Organisations?	*4*
Organisation Name(s): if several, list the names of the most important organisations	*LECTORIUM ROSICRUCIANUM. Internation School of Golden Rosicrucianum*
When did the movement emerge?	*1924 in Holand; In Poland: 1983, registered in 1986*
Number of Active Members: Past, Now Number of Members Per Organisation:	*1989: ca 90 1992: ca 140 (Disciples)*
Issues/Themes:	*1. propagation of Movements' Gnostic ideas* *2. lectures and spiritual schools* *3. publications* *4. spiritual development*
Organisational Structure:	*formalised and centralised*
Range of Protest Forms: Innovations?	*1. Two ways of appurtenance: (a) loose membership, (b) active discipleship* *2. To be a member you have to accomplish a special, introductory course* *3. To be a disciple you have to accomplish 1 or 2 years of spiritual studies* *4. No drugs, alcohol and tobacco . Disciples are vegetarians* *5. Disciples must take a part in School's meetings (3 times a month)*
Frequent Symbols:	*rose and cross, „circle-triangle-square"- graphical - see below*
Recourse to Violence:	
Mobilising Power:	
Access to Government/Business/Unions:	
Public Resonance:	*mainly impassive or negative*
Source(s) of Financial Resources:	*members' contribution and gifts, no economic activities*
Allied Movements:	*LECTORIUM ROSICRUCIANUM. In a branch of the Internation School of Gold Rosicrucianum*
Additional Information:	*Movement of Christian and Gnostic origin*

Country: *POLAND*	Movement Type: *Religious*
How Many Organisations?	*6 main centres (5 Temples)*
Organisation Name(s): if several, list the names of the most important organisations	*International Society for Krishna Consciousness, ISKCON*
When did the movement emerge?	*1966 in USA; in Poland present from 1974, registered in 1988 as Society for Krishna Consciousness-Bhakti Yoga; in 1991 change of the name*
Number of Active Members: Past, Now Number of Members Per Organisation:	*1988: ca 800 and ca 300 persons after the religiously initiated, 1989: ca 3000, 1997: 12,000 and ca 500 persons after the religious initiation (according to Movement's information)*
Issues/Themes:	*1. religious activities in Wishnu tradition,* *2. vegetarianism* *3. propagation of movement's ideas (including outdoors missionary activities)*
Organisational Structure:	*decentralised but all organisations have mutual connections and contacts*
Range of Protest Forms: Innovations?	*Peaceful demonstrations during missionary activities,* *1. vegetarianism* *2. no alcohol, no drugs, no tobacco, no cafe, no tea, no cacao, no gambling* *3. sexual intercourse allowed only for pregnancy in formal marriage* *4. straight regulations of almost all spheres of members' life* *5. vegetarian restaurants,*
Frequent Symbols:	*symbols of the Hindu origin*
Recourse to Violence\Conflict Lines:	*----*
Mobilising Power:	*charity action: „Food - The Heart's Gift", Hare Krishna's Festivals, street presentations, organisation of meetings with spiritual teachers*
Access to Government/Business/Unions:	
Public Resonance:	*negative media coverage, some institutional opponents*
Source(s) of Financial Resources:	*members' contributions, sale of Movement's publications and products*
Allied Movements:	
Additional Information:	

Country: *POLAND*	Movement Type: *Religious*
How Many Organisations? Organisation Name(s): if several, list the names of the most important organisations	*The Family (The Children of God, The Family of Love)*
When did the movement emerge?	*1968 in USA, 1974 in Poland*
Number of Active Members: Past, Now Number of Members Per Organisation:	*1997 : 150*
Issues/Themes:	*propagation of counter-culture Movements' ideas*
Organisational Structure:	*centralised locally, decentralised globally - local (national) organisations have broad autonomy, authoritarian leaderships and strong social control*
Range of Protest Forms: Innovations?	*Mail-Campaigns directed mainly to scholars and academics working on NRMs* 1. *'Flirty fishing' as a way of acquiring money, new members and adherents (essentially abandoned)* 2. *'sharing of spouses' - sex is allowed among all adult, established members* 3. *they leave their hitherto environment (family, work, school)* 4. *receiving new, personal name of biblical origin*
Frequent Symbols:	*graphical - see below, symbols of the Christian origin*
Recourse to Violence\Conflict Lines:	----------
Mobilising Power:	
Access to Government/Business/Unions:	
Public Resonance:	*strong negative media coverage, some institutional opponents*
Source(s) of Financial Resources:	*members' contributions (tenth part of members' income), financial help from Western Family's Organisations*
Allied Movements:	
Additional Information:	

Country: *POLAND*	Movement Type: *Religious*
How Many Organisations?	*9 (regional centres)*
Organisation Name(s): if several, list the names of the most important organisations	*Bhá'í Faith*
When did the movement emerge?	*XIX Century in Persia, 1989 in Poland , registration in 1992*
Number of Active Members: Past, Now Number of Members Per Organisation:	*1989: several dozen 1998: ca 500*
Issues/Themes:	*propagation of movements' ideas, especially the idea of being the fulfilment of foregoing religions and the idea of unity of human beings*
Organisational Structure:	*centralised*
Range of Protest Forms: Innovations?	 *Religion without rituals, no drugs, no alcohol, no tobacco*
Frequent Symbols:	
Recourse to Violence:	-----------
Mobilising Power:	
Access to Government/Business/Unions:	
Public Resonance:	*mainly impassive*
Source(s) of Financial Resources:	
Allied Movements:	
Additional Information:	*group of Islamic origin*

Country: *POLAND*	Movement Type: *Religious*
How Many Organisations? Organisation Name(s): if several, list the names of the most important organisations	*The New Jerusalem (hitherto: The City of Christ - New Jerusalem)*
When did the movement emerge?	*1978, registered in 1980*
Number of Active Members: Past, Now Number of Members Per Organisation:	*1990: ca 1000 1997: 30 (including 15 teachers), ca 200 candidates for members*
Issues/Themes:	*propagation of Movement's ideas proclaiming the vision of modern Church without dogmas, temples, rituals, public prayers*
Organisational Structure:	*community structure*
Range of Protest Forms: Innovations?	*1. self-healing 2. propagation of healthy lifestyle*
Frequent Symbols:	*,,The Throne of God"*
Recourse to Violence:	---------
Mobilising Power:	
Access to Government/Business/Unions:	
Public Resonance:	*mainly impassive*
Source(s) of Financial Resources:	*members' contribution*
Allied Movements:	
Additional Information:	*group of Christian origin*

PART III

ENVIRONMENTAL MOVEMENTS

6. The New Subversives - Czech Environmentalists after 1989

Petr Jehlička

INTRODUCTION

Between the 1980s and late 1990s the Czech environmental movement has developed from two official national conservationist groups, which were recognized by the communist regime and which in their activities overlapped with more independent initiatives, into a complex network of diverse groups. Early in the last decade the standing of the environmental movement shifted from champions of democracy and esteemed reformers to elements dangerous to democracy. A cosy arrangement by which the movement was essentially integrated in the state environmental administration disappeared overnight when environmentalists were purged from state institutions following the 1992 general elections. The second half of the 1990s witnessed further diversification of the Czech environmental movement, its professionalisation and also moderation of the means it employs to pursue its goals. Environmentalists also refocused from "small" to "big ecology" - today this movement addresses the whole range of environmental issues. Most recently, to many observers they have once again taken up the role of pioneers of civil society.

BRONTOSAURUS HAS SURVIVED: THE CZECH ENVIRONMENTAL MOVEMENT BEFORE NOVEMBER 1989

Apart from about 2,000 dissidents concerned mainly with human rights - signatories of *Charta 77* - who posed outright political challenge to the undemocratic regime, the only other outlet of serious protest against some practices of the communist regime, was what would, using the contemporary vocabulary, be referred to as the environmental movement. However, the term has to be used with caution. First of all, throughout the 1970s and most of the 1980s, there were hardly any groups other than nature conservationists. Second, as Tickle and Vavroušek (1998) point out, these groups were still tied, albeit often loosely, to the state apparatus. Third, until the second half of the 1980s, activities of all existing environmental organizations were related to what the communist aparatchiks labeled "small ecology" as opposed to "big ecology." Unlike "big ecology," that is decision making processes on strategic and politically charged issues that were reserved for the Communist Party and state administration, "small ecology" meant activities which from the Communist Party's view were harmless and non-political. At least initially, in the early 1970s, the regime saw little danger to its legitimacy in citizen' participation in nature conservation. Hence, environmental organizations were typically engaged in cleaning water streams of rubbish, looking after protected areas, disseminating knowledge on functioning of ecosystems and educating young people in ecology in strictly scientific terms. A leading Czech sociologist Hana Librová similarly assesses the situation a decade later:

The goals pursued by humble and devoted activity of nature protectors were, on close

81

inspection, in a fundamental contradiction to the government's orientation on extensive economic growth that was later replaced by the effort to maintain the status quo of citizens' consumption at any cost, including devastation of the environment and natural resources...At a practical level and measured by actual results of [Czech nature protectors'] work, their activity was foolish. Czech nature protectors were seeking to save individual plants, register ant-hills and prevent amphibians from being run-over by cars when they migrated across a road. At the same time, government policy was capable of turning vast tracts of the country into desert by a single stroke of the pen (Librová in Vaněk 1996: 42-43).

It is estimated that in the late 1980s the membership of a single organization - the Czech Union of Nature Protectors (*Český svaz ochránců přírody; ČSOP*), which was the largest Czech environmental group, was about 26,000 (Kundrata 1992). This is a figure that far exceeds the most optimistic estimates of the combined membership of Czech environmental groups in 2000. At present *ČSOP* has, after recovering from a major membership crisis of the early 1990s, 8,000 members out of whom about 3,000 are children and young people below the age of eighteen. The standing of *ČSOP* in the context of Czech environmental movement has changed too. While the Union, or more precisely, some of its several local branches, was by far the most important actor of the Czech environmental movement in the 1980s, it has been keeping a low profile in the course of the 1990s in comparison with more media oriented environmental non-governmental organizations (NGOs) that concentrated on campaigning and political lobbying. It has been only recently when the Union, under the new and young leadership, adopted a more active and in the Czech context innovative approach to nature conservation. For instance, in 1999 *ČSOP* started a pilot project aimed at testing the feasibility of land trusts as means of effective protection of small territorial units that would engage local people in nature conservation.

The first Czech environmental organization officially established after the 1948 communist coup was Yew (*Tis*). It formed in 1969 when the Association for Nature Conservation broke away from the National Museum Society. *Tis* occasionally went beyond the usual nature conservation activities of the time. According to Vaněk (1996:34) in 1971 *Tis* sent a letter to the president of Czechoslovakia criticizing the government's intention to build a hydropower plant in a landscape protected area and its members read extracts from Rachel Carson's book "Silent Spring" on the Czechoslovak Radio. *Tis* eventually succumbed to the pressure of the Communist authorities that demanded that this organization beyond its direct control would "voluntarily" disband itself. *Tis* officially ceased its activities in December 1979.

However, by the government decision the Ministry of Culture of the Czech Republic was delegated a task to establish a new conservationist organization that would replace *Tis*. The new, officially sanctioned organization - *ČSOP* - was established already in September 1979. The *ČSOP's* official task was "to develop ideo-educational and propagandistic activities aimed at winning masses for nature conservation and protection of the environment along the Communist Party line" (Vaněk 1996:41). The top hierarchy of *ČSOP* was composed of *nomenklatura* cadres. Many *Tis* members, unaware of the official goals with which *ČSOP* was charged by the authorities, joined the new organization. In fact, they had no choice if they wanted to continue their conservationist work.

Before 1989 the movement as a whole was still predominantly marked by technocratic and scientific, and hence partial solutions that centred on locally manifested environmental pollution threatening human health. As Kundrata (1992) pointed out "one has to take into consideration the fact that since the 1950s, at least 90 per cent of university graduates received a highly specialized education not based on a holistic or global approach." For a small but growing circle of groups and individual activists, however, environmental issues had their causes in economic and political conditions.

Several groups in ČSOP, especially in the latter half of the 1980s, became engaged in activities that transcended the field of small ecology and that led to cooperation with some independent (and illegal) groups. The case in point here is the publication of the "ecological bulletin" *Nika* which was the official magazine of the Prague City Committee of ČSOP and which, in the course of the whole 1980s, dared to enter into a direct confrontation with the Communist Party's line over some environmentally controversial projects. *Nika* printed not only articles by its staff editors and occasionally under false names articles by "ecological dissidents," but also by members of the Ecological Section of the Biological Society of the Czechoslovak Academy of Sciences.

The only legal environmental organization that perceived and approached environmental problems explicitly as "big ecology" issues was the Ecological Section (*Ekologická sekce*) of the Biological Society of the Czechoslovak Academy of Sciences. This professional organization of environmentalists evolved from a group of friends and colleagues, most of whom held jobs in various institutes of the Academy of Sciences and was in a close contact with some dissidents from *Charta 77*.[1] In its peak in 1989, the membership of the Section reached 400. As most members of the Section worked as researchers in the Academy of Sciences, they enjoyed privileged access to environmental data, most of which were treated by the regime as top secret information. The Section's activities largely consisted of organizing seminars and lectures that were open to the public. It also prepared a number of expert reports commissioned by various government institutions. However, the Section's single act that had a significant impact on the politicization of the environment in communist Czechoslovakia was the leaking of the "Report on the State of the Environment in Czechoslovakia"[2] to *Charta 77* in 1983 and its publication by the Western press in 1984.

The fact that the material was published in the *Charta 77*'s *samizdat* periodical *Infoch* left the communist authorities relatively complacent due to its limited impact on the public. However, its appearance in *Le Monde, Tageszeitung* and *Die Zeit* as well in the Radio Free Europe broadcast infuriated the authorities. The casualties among the Section's members were limited though. Only the distributor of the original 20 copies of the Report Jaroslav Stoklasa was forced to change his employment and move from Prague to České Budějovice (Vaněk 1996:69). Moreover, the progressive group within the Communist Party was put on a defensive.[3] The Report certainly facilitated an increased international pressure on the Czechoslovak government to embrace the environment as a legitimate issue and in this way helped to strengthen the position of Czech environmentalists *vis-a-vis* the communist authorities. From the mid-1980s a number of Western delegations raised the issue of environmental pollution in communist Czechoslovakia and thus contributed to gradual transformation of the environment into an international issue.

The feature, in which another major environmental group of the 1970s and 1980s - *Hnutí Brontosaurus* (Movement Brontosaurus) - resembled ČSOP, was the cleavage between its top level that was controlled by *nomenklatura* cadres of the Socialist Union of Youth (*Socialistický svaz mládeže, SSM*) and its most attractive activities conducted by ordinary members. Each group of *Brontosaurus* volunteers was formally part of a local *SSM* branch (Bouzková 1999). However, in reality, this relationship can be best described as "arms-length" (Tickle and Vavroušek 1998).

Brontosaurus's roots date to 1973 when several young people, members of *SSM* in the Academy of Sciences' Institute of Landscape Ecology in Prague, who were influenced by ideas of the 1972 UN Conference on Human Environment, started a campaign under the slogan "Brontosaurus has not survived..." aimed at ecological education (Bouzková 1999). *Brontosaurus* could count on almost 10,000 volunteers in its heyday (Kundrata 1992).[4]

Brontosaurus was engaged in a range of activities, the most popular of which were summer camps that started in 1975. Participants worked there as volunteers for two weeks, yet the demand highly exceeded the number of available places. Only about a tenth of applicants were allowed to participate. *Brontosaurus* also organized photographic and cartoon competitions about environmental problems. This loose movement also managed to extend its activities to the international level. In the mid 1980s a *Brontosaurus* group from Charles University in Prague linked with *ELTE* club in Budapest, *Ekotrend* from Banská Bystrica in Slovakia and *Polski klub ekologiczny* (*PKE*) in Cracow and established the first truly international East European environmental organization. In 1989, but still under the reign of the Communist Party, *Brontosaurus* organized a mass gathering of young people in the Šumava mountains to which the central committee of *SSM* invited a Czech emigrant and then German Green Party MP Milan Horacek, as a guest speaker. People from the Ecological Section and even some *Charta 77* signatories also took part in this event. The fall of the communist regime was in the offing.....

After November 1989 *Brontosaurus* broke off its bonds with *SSM* and established itself as an independent organization. Unlike in the 1980s, the organization is almost absent from the media coverage, but it has carried on with its traditional activities aimed at environmental education of young people mainly at summer camps. As a member of the *Brontosaurus* leadership concluded his recent article, *Brontosaurus* may have lost some of its influence in society, but not necessarily its relevance (Vnenk 1999).

Several independent environmental groups were founded in the final year of the old regime. The first was Prague Mothers (*Pražské matky*) established during a smog alert by women alarmed about the health of their children in winter 1988/89. The second group, established in September 1989, that gradually evolved from a *ČSOP* local branch took the name Children of the Earth (*Děti Země*) and from its inception aspired to be a Czech branch of Friends of the Earth. However, it was another group emerging in 1989 that later on became the Czech member of this international organization. This was Rainbow Movement (*Hnutí Duha*) founded in Brno by secondary school students in summer 1989. All three groups have experienced a dynamic development in the 1990s and the last two have become the backbone of today's Czech environmental movement.

In the final year of the communist period, these groups, and *Pražské matky* in particular, on several occasions dared to take their protest against the neglect of environmental deterioration to the public domain. Thus the environmental protests became part of a new wider phenomenon in communist Czechoslovakia - open confrontation with the communist power in the form of mass demonstrations. As Slocock (1996) noticed, groups such as the Ecological Section and *ČSOP* provided the framework for critical evaluation of the communist regime's environmental performance which eventually led many individuals into more overt forms of involvement in dissident movements. Environmental political mobilization was an important part of the wider movement that in November 1989 eventually brought down the communist regime in Czechoslovakia.

The Velvet Revolution

Although the extension of the phrase "green velvet revolution," appropriately coined by Podoba (1998) for the course of revolutionary events in Slovakia, to the Czech environmentalists' role in the November 1989 would be a little far-fetched, "it is also clear that [Czech] environmentalists played a significant role in the growth, organization and politics of the new 'official' opposition" (Tickle and Vavroušek 1998).

It often escaped commentators' attention that several demonstrations centred on unbearable smog situations that regularly occurred in Northern Bohemia each autumn, took place a week before the Prague student march of 17 November 1989. A 16-year old apprentice put up posters around the North Bohemian town of Teplice that called on fellow citizens to gather on 11 November and protests against "the inhuman attitude of leading figures of the political apparatus" (Vaněk 1996: 131). Between 800-1,000 people protested against air pollution wearing masks and demanded clean air and healthy environment for their children. Demonstrations in Teplice continued for the subsequent three days and had a domino effect across Northern Bohemia. Similar demonstrations were called and prepared in five other North Bohemian cities for the period between 15 and 21 November.

However, before these demonstrations could reach the full scale, events in Prague led to the almost instant collapse of the regime in the country. Here too, environmentalists took an active part in the revolution. The single person who became probably the most influential figure was the co-chair of the Ecological Section (*Ekologická sekce*) Josef Vavroušek who "quickly assumed a prominent role within the Civic Forum, chairing the 'Programme Commission' responsible for strategic policy development" (Tickle and Vavroušek 1998). He made sure that environment figured among the most important issues which Civic Forum wanted to address. In the wake of the November revolutionary days a number of environmental groups emerged. However, it was the Green Party that almost instantly became the main manifestation of popular Czech environmentalism.

The Rise and Fall of the Green Party

The high degree of political mobilization connected with the formation of the Green Party has by now fallen into near oblivion. However, it was the Green Party rather than environmental groups that immediately after the November 1989 political upheaval became the champion of the environmental cause in the Czech Republic. Founded as the first political party after the demise of the old regime - only four days after the pivotal student demonstration on 17 November 1989 - it attracted wide support and ranked high in pre-electoral opinion polls in 1990. Its press release claimed that the party had 5,200 members and 11,000 signatures supporting its legalization (Jehlička and Kostelecký 1995). The intriguing fact, that was little noticed at the time though, was that the Prague founding circle secured an office space including the equipment necessary to run a newly established party so quickly. This was a time when other nascent political parties had no resources at all. It is now established that the origin of the Green Party in Prague was connected to the Communist regime's secret police. Local groups that later formed the Green party consisted of people who were unknown to environmental activists involved in the pre-November 1989 environmental movement.

The initially massive popularity of the Green Party was reflected both in the media coverage and in results of opinion polls. For instance *Mladá fronta* daily reported at the end of January that the Green Party had 15,000 members in the Czech Republic. A month later, during the founding congress of the Green Party, the same newspaper put the number of its members at 80,000 nationwide. As far as the opinion polls were concerned, the Greens maintained a stable 11 per cent support from February until the run-up to the first free general elections. However, in the parliamentary elections of June 1990 the party did not manage to overcome the five per cent electoral threshold to enter the Czech or the federal Czechoslovak parliament. As funding derived from the electoral performance is the main source of income for most Czech political parties, the Greens' financial decline was a logical consequence. The lowest point in the short history of the Green Party came with the 1996 general election in the Czech Republic, when the party did not secure enough financial means to field its candidates.

The Czech Green Party stood for what was under the communist regime regarded to be a radical environmental agenda. Its typical features were strong emphasis on local pollution of air, water and soil and articulation of environmental demands with public health claims (van der Heijden 1999). The Czech Greens found their electoral support primarily in industrial areas particularly affected by environmental pollution. This is the opposite pattern to that found in some West European countries such as Germany and Britain, where areas most devastated by "old" industrialization manifest relatively low environmental concern, whether it is indicated by membership in environmental NGOs (Cowell and Jehlička 1995) or by the vote for green parties (Jehlička 1994).

A research project on the Czech Greens conducted in 1992 and 1993 showed that the belief that the Green Party's activity contributed to the improvement of people's health was the second most important factor for joining the party thus confirming that in the Czech Republic environmental problems were generally understood as human health related issues (Jehlička 1998). The leading figures in the Green Party were former medical or veterinary doctors and polytechnic graduates.[5] As such, this party had little resemblance to West European Green Parties of the time. It embodied a value orientation that Eckersley (1995) calls human welfare ecology that was associated with the rise of Green Parties in Western Europe in the 1970s.

The murky origin of the Prague branch of the Party, the absence of publicly known and credible people in the ranks of the Greens, and an unanimous refusal of rest of the environmental movement, whether traditional nature conservationist organizations or new campaigning groups, severely undermined the credibility of the Green Party. Its chances in the political arena were further undermined by the fact that all political parties, left and right, by the time of the first general elections adopted most of the Green Party's agenda aimed at cleaning up the environment as a pre-condition for reducing risks to human health.

THE ENVIRONMENTAL MOVEMENT BETWEEN 1989 AND 1995: FROM CHAMPIONS OF DEMOCRATIZATION TO EXTREMISTS SUBVERTING DEMOCRACY

The first effect of the arrival of democracy on the environmental movement was a massive brain drain to newly founded state environmental institutions. It is no wonder then that a remarkable feature of the first "enthusiastic" period after 1989 (November 1989 - mid-1991; see Jehlička and Kára [1994] for more details) was the close relationship between state officials and activists from non-governmental environmental groups. The Czech Ministry of the Environment (MoE), for instance, both initiated the Green Parliament composed of representatives of almost all environmental groups in 1990 and granted it a status of a consultative body.

Fagin (1994:489-490) so summarized the situation following the departure of leading activists from environmental movement to the state administration:

After the revolution of November 1989 the new administration was composed of dissidents and activists many of whom had been involved with ecological groups. The degree of overlap between the new political regime and NGOs was particularly evident in the Ministry of the Environment at the federal and republican levels: Josef Vavroušek, the federal Minister, and Bedřich Moldan, Czech Environment Minister had both been members of the Ecological Section of the Biological Society which was part of the Czechoslovak Academy of Sciences.... Others such as Dr Jaroslav Stoklasa, responsible for compiling data on the state of the environment in the early 1980s, were now working within the Ministry.

In the middle of the 1990s Slocock (1996) described the Czech environmental network as a compact and relatively cohesive network with its roots in professional environmentalist organizations tolerated under the former regime, such as the Ecological Section and voluntary organizations like ČSOP. Although many former activists turned officials were later removed from the top posts, this network remained almost intact throughout the 1990s. For the most part of the decade ČSOP enjoyed a privileged access to the Ministry of the Environment and its funds earmarked for support of environmental NGOs. The Society for Sustainable Living (Společnost pro trvale udržitelný život, STUŽ) formed by Josef Vavroušek in 1992 that in some respect, mainly by its membership and type of activity (seminars, public discussions, publishing reports) resembled Ecological Section, also exerted, due to its personal contacts, a considerable degree of influence on the MoE and became an important part of the Czech environmental policy network.

Apart from this network with its roots in a more distant past, the Czech environmental movement of the early 1990s consisted of new groups, such as Hnutí Duha and Děti Země, that were founded shortly before the November 1989 upheaval and that quickly adopted Western campaigning know-how. This type of activity, by standards of Czech political culture entirely unconventional, encountered hostility in all quarters of the society and turned out to be counterproductive. Furthermore, due to their financial dependence on Western sources (foundations, partner organizations), these groups could easily be portrayed by their opponents as pawns in hands of foreign interests and their activity as a foreign intervention into domestic affairs.

Borrowing the term from Patočka (1999:16) the activities of most movement organizations established around 1990 and operating at the national level, could be described, with some degree of simplification, as "student happenings" that were designed to draw the attention of the general public to various environmental issues. However, following the 1992 general elections, Czech NGOs, or at least those with the more radical agenda, gradually came to realize that it did not suffice to bring problems to light and that their methods should reflect their effort to achieve concrete changes. As by 1992 the cosy relationship between the environmental movement and the state administration was over, some groups and most notably Hnutí Duha and later also Greenpeace (that was established in Czechoslovakia in March 1992), began to employ a repertoire of activities that fell in a broad category of "civil disobedience." As this was the time of the growing influence of Western environmental NGOs on their Central and Eastern European counterparts, Czech environmental groups were restructuring their activities towards campaigning that also included direct actions.

Two determined campaigns featuring direct actions defined the Czech environmental movement of the first half of the 1990s and at the same time significantly contributed to the alienation of the movement from large sections of the general public unaccustomed to confrontation as a strategy of environmental groups. Annual blockades of the construction site of the nuclear power plant Temelín, anyway rather of symbolic value due to the low number of participants, were part of the anti-nuclear campaign. They were in many ways counterproductive. Most media and citizens regarded these blockades as emotional and completely irrational actions. In as technocratic society as the Czech one that highly values scientific but value-free rationality and hard data this was a profoundly damaging accusation. While the Czech government first turned on and then turned off the Temelín plant in October 2000 and the Czech environmental movement still campaigns against this plant, another major battle of the early 1990s was quickly resolved. Several NGOs, initially Greenpeace and later a few others including *Hnutí Duha*, joined forces to save a North Bohemian village, Libkovice. As so often during the former regime, but this time under the new democratic government the village was to be erased from the surface since it was located on brown coal deposits. The inhabit-ants of the village were forced to leave their houses. The environmental movement cooperated with those Libkovice citizens who refused to be evicted and tried to save the village by all sorts of means ranging from photograph exhibitions to tying themselves to buckets and bulldozer blades. Eventually they lost the battle as all Libkovice citizens were moved out and most buildings were pulled down.[6] Most importantly, even this confrontational campaign alienated the Czech public.

The short period between 1990 and 1992 when attempts were made for integrated pollution control and when more advanced principles such as the principle of prevention were employed, was followed, starting with June 1992 when the second general elections were held, by a new period during which many progressive features were abandoned. What was previously seen as a necessary first step towards fundamental improvement of the state of the environment - clean-up and installation of end-of-pipe technologies - suddenly became the ultimate goal of pollution control policy. The Ministry of the Environment lost many of its newly gained competencies and environment again became a discrete policy area.

To document an almost anecdotal dimension of the U-turn of Czech environmental policy in the course of the 1990s it suffices to say that the notion of sustainable development became completely banned from official government documents despite the fact that it frequently appears in Czech environmental legislation that was passed just a few years earlier. To the right-wing government of the new prime minister Václav Klaus and to him personally, integrated environmental policy presented a glaring example of a much loathed state interventionism in the free functioning of market forces based on newly introduced private ownership.[7] This anti-environmental crusade was endorsed by the majority of the media.

The anti-environmental campaign culminated in 1995. Similarly to the Communist controlled media in the mid-1980s accusing environmentalist of being threats to the progress of society, in February 1995 Czech environmentalists appeared on a list of subversive elements which was drafted by the state intelligence services. Apart from environmentalists, other groups on the list of subversive elements were skinheads and Communists. Typically, it was the new campaigning groups that were included in the list: Greenpeace, *Děti Země*, *Hnutí Duha* and *Animal SOS*. In addition to the accusation of being a threat to the well-being of society that was reminiscent of the past, this time environmentalists were also portrayed as a threat to democracy. Thus, over only slightly more than five years environmentalists went through a paradoxical transformation from being one of the major proponents of democracy to one of its major threats (Fagin and Jehlička 1998). After a massive wave of protests both from foreign and domestic bodies and individuals, state authorities were forced to remove environmental organizations from this list.

Given how small and weak Czech environmental NGOs were at the time of this campaign, its intensity and scale was striking. In 1994 and 1995 Fagin (1996) carried out research based on interviews with staff of the main offices of several environmental groups in the Czech Republic. He found out that Greenpeace in large towns and regions relied on an average of between 10 and 20 activists, the majority of whom were students or people under 25 (Fagin 1996:141). This means that the total number of Greenpeace supporters was unlikely to exceed five hundred. Of *Děti Země*, Fagin (1996:152) says:

> Membership of *Děti Země* increased from 60 in 1989 to approximately 600 in 1994, of which approximately 80 are active. The 90 per cent of members who play a passive role in the organization pay subscriptions and receive regular information about current campaigns and activities. The vast majority of members are students, and people under 25.

Another proof of the very weak position of these environmental NGOs, directly stemming from their tiny membership, was their financial insecurity and dependence on external sources, mainly on Western foundations. For instance, in 1994 Greenpeace Czechoslovakia had a budget of 220,000 USD, out of which the contribution of Czech and Slovak members was less than two per cent. The rest was a transfer of money from Greenpeace International (Šálek 1994). *Děti Země* did better, as their income from membership fees was 12 per cent in 1994, 37 per cent coming from services offered by the organization and only 40 per cent of their annual income was covered by Western foundations. The rest (11 per cent) were grants from the Ministry of the Environment on specific projects (Fagin 1996:155).

By the mid-1990s (and after six or seven years of existence) the new NGOs still had a small membership and very little support in society which was, beyond student circles, confined to several dozen intellectuals (writers, actors, journalists, actors and academics). Their activities were seriously hampered by lack of financial means, for most of which they depended on Western donors. At the same time, however, they were becoming professional organizations adopting organizational structures and campaigning methods developed by Western NGOs.

The backlash of the establishment against environmental groups coupled by little response to their activities by society certainly shook their confidence.[8] In any case, apparently the lesson taken by the Czech environmental movement as whole was that it should adopt more moderate behavior, especially as far as the means by which they pursued their goals were concerned. As a result, direct actions were almost abandoned as most activists believed that they gave rise to the majority of bad press these groups received.

THE SECOND HALF OF THE 1990S: THE STRUGGLE FOR RECOGNITION AND FINANCIAL SECURITY

Preparation of reports by hired experts, lobbying in the parliament, close cooperation with sympathetic journalists and a better use of the existing laws became increasingly favoured methods of NGOs' activities in the second half of the 1990s. This change gradually started to deliver results. Environmental NGOs and their activities now enjoy much more positive coverage in the media and some leading activists became popular participants in TV and radio debates. It is obviously difficult to establish to what extent this is the result of the intentional self-moderation effort and to what extent it is the result of the learning process on the side of journalists. There is also a small but growing circle of usually young politicians who are sympathetic to the environmental movement. The two major national NGOs, *Hnutí Duha* (now the Czech branch of Friends of the Earth) and *Děti Země* also transformed themselves into well organized and relatively effective organizations. The environmental movement as whole has gone, although to various extent, through three major shifts (Jancar-Webster 1998):

- the shift to democratic institutions;
- the shift from protest to policy-making;
- the shift to professionalism and expert knowledge.

In my view these shifts have two more dimensions:

- the shift to diversification and specialization of the environmental movement accompanied by increased ability of communication and mutual support;
- the shift towards a more global perception of environmental problems and their complex nature embedded in social, economic and political practices.

Unlike Hungary or until recently also Slovakia, there are groups in the Czech Republic that operate at the national level (*Děti Země* and *Hnutí Duha*), that combine what used to be called in the past "big" and "small ecology." Labor within these groups is divided between the center of these groups that usually focuses on political lobbying, publication of newsletters and magazines, and cooperation. Cooperation involves experts, such as scientists and lawyers as well as their foreign counterparts and local branches (that usually enjoy a large degree of autonomy) that deal with locally or regionally significant environmental issues. Greenpeace also operates at the national level, but does not fit the same category of NGOs as it does not have local chapters. All three organizations lead long-term and quite sophisticated campaigns on specific issues, such as energy, forestry, protection of landscape, quarrying of minerals and the like. The campaigning skills and ability of Czech environmental movement to exert significant influence was best documented in 1999 by the largest campaign to date that focused on the question of the continuation or halting of the construction of Temelín nuclear power plant. Although environmentalists lost this battle, very few people expected the advocates in the government of the plant to win by a very narrow margin. The government's vote was 11 in favour of continuation of the construction against 8 who opposed it (for more details see Axelrod 1999).

There are other groups that are present in certain areas of the country that lead campaigns focused on all sorts of regionally significant issues. Typical examples of this type of organizations are Friends of Nature (*Přátelé přírody*) in Ústí nad Labem who concentrate on protection of the Elbe river valley, and Old Protectors of the Jizerské Mountains (*Staří ochránci Jizerských hor*) in Liberec whose main concern is the replacement of the spruce monoculture in the mountains with a biologically more diverse forest. Another NGO of this type is South Bohemian Mothers (*Jihočeské matky*) who have been relentlessly fighting the construction of the nuclear power plant Temelín throughout the 1990s.

However, there is also a growing number of environmental organizations specializing in education. These groups run "houses of eco-education." They provide teaching for school classes or other groups of children. At least one example of an "ecological institute" exists in the Czech Republic. This is *Veronica* in Brno, which is formally still part of the *ČSOP* but developed in a unique establishment that could be described as the institute of applied ecology. *Veronica* publishes a periodical aimed at nature conservation, carries out applied research centred on landscape ecology and provides consultancy on household ecology to the general public. *STUŽ*, with its privileged access to state environmental institutions despite its quite radical views, is a rather unusual environmental group.

What has remained unchanged though, despite the above described major transformations, is the dependency of Czech environmental groups on foreign sources of funding. It has been only very recently that NGOs realized that they have to look for an alternative source of funding, because most Western foundations that provided finances for NGOs in Central Europe in the past decade considerably reduced the amount of funding or completely withdrew from the region. An alternative, domestic source of money in the shape of a special fund that was set up several years ago during the process of privatization in order to provide funding for non-profit activities, failed to benefit environmental groups. Out of six categories of potential beneficiaries of this fund that was disbursed in 1999, environmental groups were the least successful applicants. As a consequence, most of the groups have recently launched campaigns aimed at recruiting as many people as possible as their regular fee-paying subscribers. Greenpeace claims to have tripled the number of their supporters over a year period so that is now between 4,000 and 5,000, whereas *Hnutí Duha* estimates the size of its fee-paying membership at 500 and the number of supporters of *Děti Země* slightly exceeds three hundred.

Environmental groups' ability to open the increasingly closed political system and effectively challenge it via legal proceedings and the use of EIA law has recently made them the most visible and influential part of civil society. However, while the major mainstream environmental groups have become increasingly content with their higher status and degree of recognition in the society, a more radical current of activism mixing environmental, social and political issues under the banner of movement against globalization, has emerged outside the established circles of semi-institutionalized NGOs. Two major manifestations of this more radical movement were Global and Local Street Parties that took place in Prague in the past two years and that attracted far more young people than anybody had expected.

CONCLUSION

Between the late 1980s and early 1990s the Czech environmental movement as a whole quickly moved its attention from targeting pollution that has in the meantime become a problem universally recognized by all quarters of the society, in part due to its role in bringing down the former regime, to much more controversial issues such as lifestyle and consumption patterns. The movement also started to identify some economic interests that are behind environmental damage.

By and large, Czech environmental groups initially failed to realize that they function not only in a society that is not used to public participation, but which is also deeply technocratic. In such a context, environmental groups' objectives and methods easily appear as irrational and emotionally laden. This poses a fundamental barrier for further expansion of the environmental movement in

Czech society. At the turn of the century, the Czech environmental movement finds itself in a paradoxical situation. Its cognitive and policy-making capacity does not match its ability to build a sufficiently large social support. On the one hand, the skills and knowledge of most groups and individuals and their ability to influence the course of events have increased impressively over the last decade. On the other hand, the movement has failed to generate more than several dozen committed activists and several thousand supporters which means that for the foreseeable future its ability to maintain the scale of its activities is in great danger, given the withdrawal of much of the foreign sources of funding from the country.

NOTES

1. The Ecological Section initially focused on ecology in purely scientific terms, but most participants realized that these environmental issues are inextricably economic and social issues (Václav Mezřický quoted in Vaněk 1996). Due to personal contacts of its leading personalities, this group found a shelter in the Academy of Sciences. The Section officially started its activity within the Biological Society in March 1979.
2. The Report was commissioned by the Czechoslovak prime minister Lubomír Štrougal who was by the then standards regarded as a moderate reformer. The Report provided a descriptive overview of the state of the components of the environment (air, water, landscape, forests and agriculture) and was critical of the adverse effects of environmental degradation on public health.
3. The leak of the document hit the more progressive factions in the Communist Party, however difficult it is to speak of progressive groups among Czechoslovak Communists. The Report was published in the West at a time when conservative forces in the Communist Party came up with a thesis "Ecologists - enemies of socialism" (Vaněk 1996:70).
4. The origin of *Brontosaurus* illustrates its "split" character that was maintained during its existence throughout the communist regime. As Vaněk (1996:36) reminds us, the initial motivation for this activity was a difficult situation in which the Institute found itself at the time. The Institute faced criticism for too little political involvement, meaning in the contemporary jargon, too few members of the Communist Party and *SSM* among its employees. The director of the Institute suggested that an *SSM* branch should be established that would deal with environmental issues. The Czech central committee of *SSM* declared 1974 the Year of Environmental Protection and "Action Brontosaurus" became the flagship of it. The media owned by *SSM* joined the Action which became very popular and brought the attention of many young people to the environment. It was so successful that the central committee of *SSM* decided to continue this sort of activity and officially founded *Hnutí Brontosaurus* as an integral part of *SSM* in 1975.
5. Other features distinguishing Czech Green Party members from their West European counterparts were much lower proportion of Czech Greens holding university degrees, much higher percentage of manual workers and a small proportion of post-materialists among them. As far as Greens with university level of education are concerned, the Czech group was dominated by graduates holding degrees in sciences and engineering (together 77 per cent) while in the Western Europe and in particular in the UK, this group is a minority among the Green Party members who have university education (Jehlička 1998 and 1999).
6. However, the movement could celebrate a moral victory, although it was a very sour victory. A few years later it turned out that, as most experts and all environmental movement organizations which

took part in this confrontation had argued, the destruction of the village was completely unnecessary. The edge of the open cast mine has never reached the former village due to unfavorable mining conditions underneath.

7. In his social anthropological study of the post-communist transformation of the Czech society, Holy (1996:158) points out that the link between free market and democracy is in Czech society construed differently than it is usually done in the West. In Western conceptualization, the market guarantees individual freedom of economic choice as democratic pluralism guarantees individual freedom of political choice. In the Czech conceptualization, it is not so much freedom in the sense of exercise of choice as freedom in the sense of an unconstrained expression of human nature that is linked to the concept of the market. If private property is construed as part of human nature, only a free market economy based on private ownership of the means of production offers people real freedom, for, in contrast to the planned economy, it does not constrain their natural propensity toward it.

8. Little success of NGOs' campaigns was blamed by many activists on too radical views or poor ability of NGOs to present their proposals to the media and the general public in a coherent and convincing way. For example, this topic became a subject of a polemic between two leading activists that appeared in the *Hnutí Duha's* monthly *Poslední generace* (Patočka 1995; Piňos 1995).

REFERENCES

Axelrod R. 1999. "Democracy and Nuclear Power in the Czech Republic" in *The Global Environment. Institutions, Law, and Policy*. Edited by N. J. Vig and R. S. Axelrod. London. Earthscan, pp. 279-299

Bouzková S. 1999. "Hnutí Brontosaurus" (Movement Brontosaurus). *Sedmá generace* Vol. 8 Nr. 11:19-20

Cowell R. and P. Jehlička. 1995. "Backyard and biosphere: the spatial distribution of support for English and Welsh environmental organisations" *Area* Vol. 27 Nr. 2:110-117

Eckersley R. 1995. *Environmentalism and political theory. Towards an ecocentric approach.* London. UCL Press

Fagin A. 1994. "Environment And Transition in the Czech Republic" *Environmental Politics* Vol. 3 Nr. 3:479-494

Fagin A. 1996. "The Transition to Democracy in the Czech Republic - An Alternative Perspective and Assessment." PhD thesis. University of Manchester

Fagin A. and P. Jehlička. 1998. "The Czech Republic: Sustainable Development - A Doomed Process?" in *Dilemmas of Transition: The Environment, Democracy and Economic Reform in East Central Europe*. Edited by S. Baker and P. Jehlička. London. Frank Cass, pp. 113-128

Holy L. 1996. *The Little Czech and the Great Czech Nation. National identity and the post-communist social transformation.* Cambridge. Cambridge University Press

Jancar-Webster B. 1998. "Environmental Movement and Social Change in the Transition Countries" in *Dilemmas of Transition. The Environment, Democracy and Economic Reform in East Central Europe*. Edited by S. Baker and P. Jehlička. London. Frank Cass, pp. 69-90

Jehlička P. 1994. "Environmentalism in Europe: an East - West Comparison" in *A New Europe: Social Change and Political Transformation*. Edited by C. Rootes and H. Davis. London. UCL Press, pp. 112-131

Jehlička P. 1998. "A Comparative Investigation into the Dynamics of Environmental Politics in

Western and Eastern Europe 1988 - 1993 with Special Reference to the Czech Republic." PhD thesis. Cambridge University

Jehlička P. 1999. "The Development of Czech Environmental Policy 1990-1995. A Sociological Account" *Czech Sociological Review* Vol. 7 Nr. 1:37-50

Jehlička P. and J. Kára. 1994. "Ups and Downs of Czech Environmental Awareness and Policy: Identifying Trends and Influences" in *Protecting the Periphery: Environmental Policy in Peripheral Regions of the European Union*. Special issue of *Regional Politics and Policy* Vol. 4 Nr. 1:153-170

Jehlička P. and T. Kostelecký. 1995. "Czechoslovakia: Greens in a post-Communist society" in *The Green Challenge. The Development of Green Parties in Europe*. Edited by D. Richardson and C. Rootes. London. Routledge, pp. 208-231

Kundrata M. 1992. "Czechoslovakia" in *Civil Society and the Environment in Central and Eastern Europe*. Edited by D. Fisher, C. Davis, C. Juras, and V. Pavlovic. London, Ecological Studies Institute; Bonn, Institute für Europäische Umweltpolitik; Belgrade, ECO-Centre, pp. 31-50

Patočka J. 1995. "Jak se nám daří?" (How are we doing?) *Poslední generace* Vol. 4 Nr.7: 18-20

Patočka J. 1999. "Duha deset let na cestě: lidé a křižovatky" (Duha ten years on the road: people and crossroads) *Sedmá generace* Vol. 8 Nr. 10:15-23

Piňos J. 1995. "Proč se nám nedaří?" (Why aren't we doing well?) *Poslední generace*Vol. 4 Nr. 7:15-17

Podoba J. 1998. "Rejecting Green Velvet: Transition, Environment and Nationalism in Slovakia" in *Dilemmas of Transition: The Environment, Democracy and Economic Reform in East Central Europe*. Edited by S. Baker and P. Jehlička. London. Frank Cass, pp. 129-144

Šálek M. 1994. "Vy Češi sníte ničivý sen o energetickém ráji" (You Czechs have a destructive dream of an energy paradise) Interview with Matti Wuori. *Respekt* Vol. 5 Nr. 6:10

Slocock B. 1996. "The Paradoxes of Environmental Policy in Eastern Europe: The Dynamics of Policy-Making in the Czech Republic" *Environmental Politics* Vol. 5 Nr. 3:501-521

Tickle A. and J. Vavroušek. 1998. "Environmental politics in the former Czechoslovakia" in *Environment and Society in Eastern Europe*. Edited by A. Tickle and I. Welsh. Harlow. Longman, pp. 114-145

Van der Heijden H.-A. 1999. "Environmental Movements, Ecological Modernisation and Political Opportunity Structures" in *Environmental Movements: Local, National and Global*. Edited by C. Rootes. Special Issue of *Environmental Politics* Vol. 8 Nr. 1:199-221

Vaněk M. 1996. *Nedalo se tady dýchat* (It was impossible to breathe here). Ústav pro soudobé dějiny AV ČR. Praha. Maxdorf

Vlašín M. 1999. "Bylo nebylo - dávno tomu aneb staříčký ochranář vzpomíná" (Once upon a time - a veteran conservationist reminesces) *Sedmá generace* Vol. 8 Nr. 11:21-22

Vnenk P. 1999. Vliv není totéž co význam (Influence is not the same as relevance). *Sedmá generace* Vol. 8 Nr. 10:32

7. Grassroots and Global Visions: Slovakia's Post-socialist Environmental Movement*

Edward Snajdr

The environmental movement in Slovakia has been marked by significant changes in structure and strategy since the collapse of communism in 1989. In addition to the emergence of new forms of activism and issues, a variety of environmental organizations, associations and political parties with different aims, goals and activities comprise the post-socialist movement. Strategically, environmentalism[1] in Slovakia has moved from an anti-regime, counter-cultural volunteer movement focused on protest to a patch-work of civic organizations attempting to establish an environmental policy agenda for the transition. Structurally, the movement has changed from a nationally configured umbrella conservation union during communism to a diverse collection of small but highly active independent non-governmental organizations (NGOs). Accompanying these changes, activists face the difficult task of maintaining campaigns for effective environmental action on a variety of levels.

This chapter describes the diversity of Slovakia's post-socialist green movement focusing in particular on what Slovaks call the Third Sector and what has been described as a civil archipelago (Butora and Butorova 1999:88), a loose network of NGOs and civic initiatives that functions independently of the state and whose participants have tried to work together as a broad-based social movement. I will focus on three distinct currents of ecological activism that have developed during the transition: grassroots mobilization, radical activism and environmental policy formulation and advocacy. While the efforts of individual activists and NGOs may intersect with these currents, I argue that each current involves a different aspect of environmentalism resulting in a unique relationship with Slovakia's nascent democracy and the broader political and social context of the transition from communism.

ORIGINS, REVOLUTION AND FACTIONS

Before 1989, Slovakia's greens were commonly known as *ochranári* (literally, nature protectors) or conservationists, and *ochranár stvo* or conservation provided the foundation for the growth and mobilization of ecological activism under communism. Ecological activism, in turn, provided many Slovaks with an unexpected opportunity to challenge the regime prior to the Velvet Revolution. Under the communist system, unlike other civic groups, conservationists enjoyed a unique position of organizational freedom and independence. While the Slovak Union of Nature and Landscape Protectors (*Slovenský zväz ochrancov prírody a krajiny*, hereafter *SZOPK* or the Union) was the only environmental organization allowed by the Communist Party, it required no party affiliation and moreover remained independent of the National Front.[2] *SZOPK* was a countrywide, all-volunteer organization that provided its members with a legitimate vehicle for pursuing small-scale civic activities oriented toward the preservation of nature.

Unlike other local *SZOPK* organizations devoted to traditional nature activities, the Bratislava *ochranári* combined the preservation of historical landscapes with a broader environmental agenda.

In addition to their weekend renovation brigades and summer reconstruction projects, Bratislava activists began to write in the mid-1980s about large dam projects, problems related to nuclear energy, air and water pollution and Slovakia's social environment in their monthly magazine, Nature Protection (*Ochránca Přírody*). The growing political confidence of the Bratislava group reached a climax in 1987 when its members published Bratislava Aloud (*Bratislava/nahlas*), an unofficial report on the dismal state of the environment and openly critiqued the regime's lack of responsibility concerning the country's mounting pollution problems. After *Bratislava/nahlas SZOPK*'s membership increased rapidly and attracted Slovakia's small dissident community, many of whom joined the organization and began to publish articles and editorials about not only the environment but also social problems and censorship.

At the time of the Velvet Revolution in 1989, *SZOPK* activists enjoyed widespread popularity and unity, becoming one of the first groups to speak out against the regime in Slovakia. Consequently, environmentalists played a visible role during the mass demonstrations and strikes leading up to communism's fall.

The unity enjoyed by environmental activists in 1989 however did not last long after the collapse of the regime. Slovakia moved quickly from a stagnant arena monopolized by a single party to a transition filled with newly liberated interest groups, a growing market economy and increasingly heated identity issues, in particular *vis-à-vis* their fellow Czechs and neighboring Hungarians. In this new period, the environmental movement suffered a loss of exposure and popularity as its activists attempted to pursue more effective roles in a society increasingly preoccupied with economic reform and revitalized national identity. Not surprisingly, in this context, the movement's first setback came after many of its representatives tried to form an ineffective and fractuious Green party (*Strana zelených, SZ*), which split twice in the first half of the 1990s.[3]

Since the most available candidate for environmental activism outside the formal political arena was *SZOPK*, the Union maintained its role as the leading environmental organization in the first two years after the Revolution. In 1990, in addition to forging contacts with other NGOs in Western Europe and around the globe, the Union launched a campaign against the construction of the Gabcikovo hydroelectric plant on the Danube River. This high-profile action, however, including a month-long demonstration at the dam site, was met with fierce opposition from government officials who supported the dam's completion as part of a wave of renewed national pride in the face of pressure from Hungary to abandon the project.[4]

NEW NGOS IN A NEW NATION

After the collapse of the regime and the beginning of painful economic reforms, *SZOPK*'s state funding was severely reduced. At the same time, many local groups began to disengage from their affiliation with the Union and sought independent status. On the foundation of these small, local groups from the communist period, activists began to form new NGOs. These NGOs can be categorized as generating three major currents of environmentalism: grassroots mobilization, radical activism and policy formulation and advocacy. Grassroots mobilization includes activists who consider it important to work with existing legislation to achieve an immediate, desired outcome. Their focus remains at the local community level involving only those individuals whose lives are directly affected by an environmental issue. Radical activist groups are similar to many Western environmental organizations in that they employ public tactics such as demonstrations and information campaigns that provoke a response from observers or at least serve to heighten awareness of an issue among the members of a society. Such organizations are primarily interested in education as a vital part of the political process. Finally, environmental policy advocates are focused on broad and systemic change as well as lobbying for legislation that can effectively solve a wide range of environmental problems. Together, these currents comprise the environmental element of the civic Third Sector in Slovakia. Many activists in fact straddle one or more of these identities despite the limitations of their particular organizations and it is not uncommon that these different types of organizations work together to achieve a common goal. I will describe each type of organization below and follow with a discussion of how these groups interact as an aggregate movement.

CULTIVATING GRASS ROOTS

One of the most important dimensions to post-socialist environmental activism in Slovakia has been the need to mobilize local communities around a green agenda and to educate the public as to their civic rights under the new system. This aspect of post-socialist environmentalism parallels the historical development of grassroots activism in the US and Europe twenty years ealier. *SZOPK* provided an organizational tradition upon which such activism could develop and several independent NGOs have grown out of this pre-1989 umbrella organization.

One of the most effective NGOs built on the remnants of the old Union is the Dubnica Environmental Group (*Danubica environmentalná skupina, DES*). What began as a small *SZOPK* organization in the town of Dubnica in western Slovakia has developed into a highly active proponent of grassroots consciouness within the local community focused on reducing the problem of solid waste disposal. DES first revitalized its organization with a "Milk in Bottles" campaign that urged residents to purchase milk packaged in glass. Despite the fact that milk sold in paper cartons carried the Green label, suggesting to the consumer that it was safe for the environment, DES effectively argued that the glass bottling process already used by local producers was more ecological. To mobilize town residents, DES activists set up information tables in the town's square, posted fliers and sought out local media for their campaign. In addition to this project, DES has embarked on other campaigns related to recycling old textiles and the promotion of local garden produce in place of manufactured canned goods. While their efforts are extremely small in scale, limited to one town and surrounding communities, this type of environmental activism provides the organization with immediate results and has promoted a positive public image in addition to its short-term goals.

Through its activism, the Dubnica Environmental Group has touched on not only a major environmental issue, but also an important social and economic reality in transition Slovakia. Rising prices have hit shrinking Slovak wages and the influx of competitive products from the West and elsewhere have challenged local manufacturers. DES offers an increasingly financially strapped public with a positive lifestyle model of reduced consumption in a growing consumer world. The organization does not attempt to reach beyond its sphere of influence and uses its small active membership (numbering between ten and twelve) as effectively as possible. Its major aim is to change local behavior at the grassroots rather than alter an entire system.

While DES focuses on the environmental aspects of a transition marked by a growing consumerist ideal, the Center for Environmental Public Advocacy (*Centrum pre podporu miestneha aktivizmu, CEPA*), in central Slovakia, is oriented toward educating communities about their rights under current Slovak law. Even though Slovaks now enjoy political freedom after the collapse of the regime, many citizens remain relatively unaware of their civic powers as a community. In effect, CEPA members work as organizers, educators and lobbyists for people affected by environmental problems. Its activists establish relationships with isolated villagers, in particular, the elderly, who might not be aware of the potential legal power they have recourse to under the new system. The Center works to encourage, essentially grow, local grassroots awareness of environmental and social problems and to facilitate ways in which affected communities can solve them. Like DES, CEPA was also created in 1993 from one of the Bratislava basic organizations of *SZOPK* and is now a small collection of activists (five members) that since 1994 CEPA has gained an affiliation with Friends of the Earth International.

A recent and representative campaign waged by the Center was its fight to defend the residents of Dubakovo. This tiny village near Zvolen experienced massive out-migration due to a government decision during socialism to construct a dam at the village site. Even after the regime collapsed and inspite of the fact that the dam was never built, a government policy of banning structural improvements and new construction continued to affect the village, reducing its population to 120 elderly residents with no public transport, health care facilities or cultural center. One of the Center's leading activists explains,

> CEPA has been helping the citizens of Dubakovo understand their rights in the decision making process and has also connected them with other communities suffering from similar experiences. CEPA, representing local residents, challenged the governmental and corporate policies which led to Dubakovo's downfall in Slovakia's Constitutional Court in August of 1996. In December 1997 the Court decided that the construction ban …was an unconstitutional restriction of basic human rights (Zamkovsky 1998).

CEPA activists hope that the Dubakovo case establishes a precedent for other communities affected by state policies and big works projects like power plants and hydroelectric dams.

In eastern Slovakia, another *SZOPK* affilliated NGO has emerged that may set an important trend in the arena of grassroots mobilization. People and Water (*Ľudia a voda*) began as a local *SZOPK* group focused on offering alternatives to government large-scale dam construction in the Ticy Potok region. The organization combines voluntarism through environmental camps with local government campaigns to educate residents about alternative water systems. Working with local mayors in villages affected by large dam projects, *Ľudia a voda* successfully lobbied the state government to accept a pilot project of small-scale dam networks and to respect new environmental legislation calling for an EIA (Environmental Impact Assessment) process requiring the consideration of construction alternatives. Like CEPA, *Ľudia a voda* represents grassroots mobilization through NGO action that is not only aimed at resource management and environmental consciousness but also encourages public education concerning civic and community rights within the democratic process.

YOUNG RADICALS

In addition to NGOs focused on building grassroots awareness and action, transition Slovakia has witnessed the emergence of more radical environmental activism. Unlike their smaller and more

98

localized cousins, radical organizations have younger members and are more connected with parallel NGOs of a similar nature in Western countries or around the globe. Of these new groups, young activist groups are the most visible and perhaps the most cooperative with each other.

Two NGOs form the core of young urban activism: Greenpeace and For Mother Earth (*Za matku zem*). Greenpeace arrived in Bratislava in the summer of 1993 and *Za matku zem* was formed a year-and-a-half later by former Greenpeace activists who had left the organization because it was limited by its international office to issues of nuclear energy. In addition to these groups are Freedom for Animals (*Sloboda zvierat*), Children of the Earth (*Deti zeme*), and Free Alternative (*Slobodná alternativa*), a human rights organization.

The key tactic for these activists is the public demonstration. Gathering in prominently visible places, these activists often dress in masks and carry colorful banners, shouting slogans and urging the public to join them in protest. For example, in the summer of 1994, Greenpeace activists hung a banner off of one of the cooling towers of the Mochovce Nuclear Power Plant. In December of that year, young activists marched through the streets of Bratislava, blocking trams in a campaign to convince the public to stop purchasing products that contain freon. In the winter of 1995, a group of young demonstrators paraded through the city wearing only a banner proclaiming "I'd rather go naked than wear fur" as part of an animal rights campaign led by *Sloboda zvierat*. In the spring of 1995, *Za matku zem* joined in an international anti-nuclear demonstration with activists from Austria, linking Vienna and Bratislava with a banner containing signatures gathered in both countries. At such spectacles, the Slovak police, always standing guard near by, often quickly break up these demonstrations on the grounds of disturbing the public.

These young radicals have learned to use a wide range of tools for increasing the effectiveness of their activism. Submitting press releases, compiling expert studies and distributing leaflets in remote villages are as important to young Greens as are the highly colorful and symbolic demonstrations through which they first introduced themselves to the public.[5]

In addition to tackling issues within their home country, young Greens have cooperated with environmental groups in neighboring countries on the anti-nuclear energy campaign. In the spring of 1995, members of Greenpeace and *Za matku zem* joined a group of protestors from other Central and East European countries in a demonstration at the European Bank for Reconstruction and Development (EBRD) to halt the bank's review of a loan to the Slovak government and Electricite de France for the completion of the Mochovce plant. When France detonated nuclear explosives in the Pacific Ocean in the summer of 1995, Slovak activists from *Za matku zem* and Greenpeace quickly responded by chaining themselves to the French embassy in Bratislava. They prevented embassy workers from entering the building and attracted nationwide media coverage, and issued a statement of protest to the French government.

This globally oriented activism became a hallmark for a new green agenda within Slovakia's environmental community. Young activists have begun to encourage their older counterparts to join them in their global environmental campaigns. For example, in the summer of 1995, a group of international activists passed through Slovakia in a protest march against nuclear energy. *Za matku zem* linked up with the Walk for a Nuclear Free World by guiding the group of fifty activists through Slovakia over a three- week period. During this time, *Za matku zem* arranged for visits to nuclear power plants, schools, dam sites, and discussions with other Slovak environmental groups.

While young radical activists represent a growing trend within the environmental movement, their involvement in civic issues goes beyond ecology to include other civic problems facing Slovak youths. Of note has been recent and close cooperation between activists from *Za matku zem*, Greenpeace and Children of the Earth (*Deti zeme*) with anti-fascist youth groups and animal rights leaders over the broader issue of civil service laws.

A SLOVAK "CLUB OF ROME"

The Society for Sustainable Living (*Spoločnosť pre trvalo udržateľný život, STUŽ*) was established shortly after the breakup of Czechoslovakia in 1992 by a collection of activists formerly involved in the conservation Union. The goal of this organization is to provide a comprehensive forum for environmental groups in both the Slovak and Czech Republics.

STUŽ built itself as an organization around the concept of sustainability. "Sustainable development" is a term that found widespread popularity among international environmental organizations after appeared in the Bruntland Commisssion's 1987 report "Our Common Future." This phrase provided the narrative base for the 1992 Earth Summit in Rio. But the members of *STUŽ* felt that the term "development" recalled the large project policies of the former regime. In its place they formulated the notion of sustainable living and thus the name of the organization.

STUŽ has pursued several projects since its inception in 1992 despite its limitations on funding, resources and personnel. In additon to holding semi-annual membership meetings at the national level and various regional conferences, *STUŽ* continued to lobby the new Slovak government and parliament, devise a comprehensive energy policy for transition Slovakia, and create models of sustainable living. This last undertaking parallels the notion of "bioregion" or "biocorridor," a concept embraced by Western deep ecologists, such as members of the Wilderness Society. But *STUŽ*'s bioregion in the White Carpathian Mountains also includes a "cultural region" as an attempt conceptually to integrate the natural ecosystem with the local human population and building on the conservation ideas of the Bratislava *ochranári* from the socialist period.

Slovakia, like many European countries, does not possess large expanses of land uninhabited by humans. Thus, the construction and maintenance of bio-corridors of protected wilderness areas are problematic and highly political. According to *STUŽ*, the idea of a region that meets the requirements of sustainability must be formulated with human settlements in mind. Locating an ecological niche is one of the organization's primary goals.

One problem emerging from the establishment of this Slovak "Club of Rome" is that other activists who are engaged in more direct action campaigns see *STUŽ* as a cumbersome think-tank, even a vestige of socialism involving long meetings and detailed reports, that are ineffective in solving more immediate ecological and social problems. The umbrella nature and network-building orientation of *STUŽ*, however, make it the most effective NGO for unifying other groups towards a consistent environmental policy in Slovakia. *STUŽ* holds monthly meetings and, using limited resources, tries to maintain avenues of communication on a national level between local environmental groups working on a variety of campaigns.

FUTURE PROSPECTS

Will the appearance of more radical environmental groups in Slovakia, such as the young greens, help more mainstream organizations interested in working at the local level and in small communities or on the larger, systemic level of government policy? Kamieniecki (1994:333) suggests that the emergence of radicalism may "make business leaders and government more likely to cooperate with more mainstream environmental groups." Yet despite their diversity, NGOs in Slovakia have had considerable difficulty gaining access to and response from government officials and suffer a distorted image in the public's mind. Slovak environmentalism has often been viewed as a collective movement by politicians and the public. This problem is partly the result of the movement's public history. During communism, green activists from a variety of backgrounds and professions, mobilized under one, decentralized branch of a nation-wide organization. As one of the only groups in Slovakia to become political under the regime, the public associated environmental activism with *SZOPK* members and the *ochranár* assumed a political identity. This association between *ochranár* and politics carried over into the transition in mind but not really in kind. The notion that all *ochranári* belonged together was a slogan for the Union in its early days before the Revolution, and it became a social category within Slovak society after the appearance of *Bratislava/ nahlas*. An *ochranár* challenged authority, lived alternatively, and went against the current of conformity. As a result, the press and the public tended to lump different post-socialist organizations into this vestigal category of late socialism thus blurring the distinctions and differences among them.

Consequently, it has been the case that some activists, moving from issue to issue and organization to organization, have carried with them a public identity that they are unable to change. For example, the head of Greenpeace in Slovakia, who had led the banner hanging at Mochovce in 1994, was often met with charges from by-standers of "anti-Slovak" sentiments. At a demonstration against the plant in 1995, one by-stander asked, "You were against Gabcivkovo and now you are against Mochovce...what are you for?" Prior to her role as the head of Greenpeace, she had been closely involved in the failed Stop Gabcikovo campaign as a Union activist and her reputation followed her into other campaigns.

Regardless of whether the new NGOs are capable of maintaining a positive image in the public's mind, the most pressing problem that all Slovak environmental organizations face is their own sustainability. Funding activism remains a continuing and increasingly difficult struggle for most groups. In the first years of the transition, foreign funding was often readily available in the form of grants, equipment and Peace Corps volunteers. International foundations and governments provided start up resources, such as money for office space, phone lines, fax machines and computers. The two most important sources of funding for environmental groups in Slovakia in the first half of the 1990s was the Environmental Partnership for Central Europe and the Regional Environmental Center of Central and Eastern Europe. The Environmental Partnership's program, which included funding from several private sources and was directly managed (until 1997) by the German Marshall Fund of the United States, continues to provide grant opportunities for NGOs willing to plan clearly organized projects and campaigns. These resources are now managed and disbursed by in-country officers. Whether the investments made at the local level can produce effective long-term results remains to be seen. Other funders for environmental groups include the PHARE Democracy Network out of Brussels, the Open Society Fund, USAID programs and ProSlovakia, a funding program provided by the Slovak government.

Given the variety of environmental groups in Slovakia, it is clearly problematic to classify them as belonging to one, uniform social movement. While such a notion is certainly a desire of the activists themselves, it is important to keep in mind the different currents described above. If the fundamental feature of all of these orgnizations is a commitment to social change, regardless of age group, social status or education, then one might suggest using Scott's (1996) conception of social movement to characterize Slovak environmentalism. It is perhaps too early to suggest that environmentalism, considered as such, will enjoy renewed support by the post-Meciar government despite the fact that many former *SZOPK* activists have re-entered politics. Butora and Butora (1999) suggest that Slovakia's "democratic awakening" or "second velvet revolution" has only just begun with the fall of Vladimir Meciar's populist government, finally allowing for the unfettered development of Slovak civil society. Whether *STUŽ* can in fact serve as an effective coordinating vehicle for all environmental NGOs as part of this invigorated Third Sector remains to be seen. Perhaps more important is the question should there even be more centralization to a diverse set of groups that have just emerged from a highly centralized past? Regardless of its disunity and diversity, the environmental movement in Slovakia, thus far, has continued to develop at the grassroots level in the spirit of a green global vision.

NOTES

* Field research for this chapter was carried out in the Slovak Republic in 1994 and 1995 and was supported in part by grants from the National Science Foundation, Fulbright-IIE and the International Research and Exchanges Board (Title VIII). The author would like to thank the Woodrow Wilson International Center for Scholars for funds granted in 1998 which were used in part to write this chapter.

1. It is difficult to give a uniform definition of the term "environmentalist" as it is used so commonly in the West. In Slovakia only a few activists actually use this term to describe themselves and the nature of their work. "Environmentalista" as a label only appeared in Slovak public discourse after 1993. While in Slovak "aktivista" is the self-chosen moniker of young greens, I use the term "activist" more generally to refer to those individuals involved in some type of activity geared toward protecting the natural or social environment.

2. The National Front was the euphemism for co-opted and controlled "independent" organizations and political parties under the communist system.

3. See Frankland 1994, and Jehlička and Kostelecký 1991 for an overview of the Green Party in Slovakia.

4. Much to the Union's dismay, the newly-formed Green Party, which like other parliamentary parties had been caught up in the impending split of Czechoslovakia, offered little support for the anti-dam campaign. As continued protests appeared to be ineffective and construction proceeded in spite of a decision pending at the International Court of Justice, *SZOPK* decided to pare down its protest efforts. After the failure of the Stop Gabcikovo campaign, the Union backed off from confrontational and politically controversial issues, returning to a more traditional role as a resource and organizational center for environmental education and volunteer conservation. For a more thorough account of the development of the Gabcikovo-Nagymaros dam controversy, see Fleischer 1993, Fisher 1993 and Fitzmaurice 1996.

5. For a more detailed discussion of young activists and their tactics see Snajdr 1998b.

REFERENCES

Butora M. and Z. Butorova. 1999. "Slovakia's Democratic Awakening" *Journal of Democracy.* January:80-95

Fisher S. 1993. "The Gabcikovo-Nagymaros Dam Controversy" *RFE/RL Research Report* Vol. 2 Nr. 37:7-12

Fitzmaurice J. 1996. *Damming the Danube.* Boulder. Westview Press

Frankland E.G. 1995. "Green Revolutions?: The Role of Green Parties in Eastern Europe's Transition 1989-1994" *East European Quarterly* Vol. 24 Nr.3:315-345

Fleischer T. "Jaws on the Danube: water management, regime change and the movement against the Middle Danube Hydroelectric Dam" *International Journal of Urban and Regional Research* Vol. 17 Nr.3:429-443

Jehlicka P. and T. Kostelecký. 1992. "The Development of the Czecho-Slovak Green Party Since the 1990 Elections" *Environmental Politics* Vol. 1 Nr. 1:72-94

Kamieniecki S., S. D. Coleman and R. O. Vos. 1995. "The Effectiveness of Radical Environmentalists" in *Ecological Resistance Movements.* Edited by B. Raymond Taylor. Albany. State University of New York Press, pp. 315-333

Scott A. 1990. *Ideology and the New Social Movements.* London. Unwin Hyman

Snajdr E. 1998a. "Green Mask, Green Mirror: Environment, Culture and Politics in Slovakia's Transition from Socialism 1985-1995" Doctoral Dissertation. University of Pittsburgh

Snajdr E. 1998b. "The Children of the Greens: New Ecological Activism in Post-Socialist Slovakia" *Problems of Post-Communism* Vol. 45 Nr. 1:54-62

Zamkovsky J. 1998. "New Life for Dubakovo." Link. Amsterdam. *Friends of the Earth International* 83:19

8. Green Future - in Hungary?

Katy Pickvance with Luca Gabor

THE GROWTH OF INTEREST IN GREEN ISSUES

After World War II the badly developed economy in Hungary needed rapid modernisation. Communist ideology maintained that industry, especially heavy industry, was the most important part of a modern economy and thus after the communist takeover in 1948 a huge industrialization process took place (Peto and Szakacs 1985). This process, combined with the increased use of chemicals in the agricultural collectives, created a severe environmental situation. The pattern of industrial and agricultural "development" the socialist camp followed was the same one that the developed world had already taken.

The recognition of the damage caused by these processes first started in most developed countries in the 1970s (Richardson 1995). Important questions, such as that of consumption, economic growth and the limits of in the supply of natural resources were raised. They were followed by calls for mass mobilization to think these questions over as well as calls for responsible responses (Limits of Growth and Blueprint of Survival 1972).

The environmental situation in the "East bloc" differed from that in the "West" for two major reasons. Firstly, consumption "fatigue" which led to the development of "postmaterialist" values in the "West" could not occur, as living standards were much lower than in the "West." Secondly, information concerning the environmental damage, caused by the industrial and agricultural development, was not published in the controlled Eastern European press.

However, some socialist countries were less isolated than others. Hungary was one of the Soviet bloc countries with the most open political system and received a freer information flow from Western societies. As a result, green ideas reached the country not long after they had gained popularity in countries like Germany and Austria. Thus even before the regime change people started to be aware of the environmental damage caused by socialist policies. Public opinion surveys, however, were not done on the subject in the 1970s. The first one which assessed the situation was conducted in 1985, still years before the regime change of 1989. This survey found that 80% of the Hungarian population were aware of environmental problems and were very concerned about them (Kulcsar and Dobossy 1988). Their main concerns were over air and water pollution, industrial and nuclear waste, and the decreased extent and quality of forests.

The solution to these problems was seen, however, differently by Hungarians, compared with their West European counterparts. In the above quoted survey Dobossy and Kulcsar (1988) found that people in Hungary believed that only a government could or should do something about solving the problem of the environment. The idea of mass organization to influence authorities did not occur to people in Hungary in the mid 1980s. This was understandable given the political context.

Although Hungary was one of the most liberal Soviet bloc countries - since the 1970s the political approach was a lot more liberal compared to other socialist countries-, it stilll had a centrally controlled regime. Critical voices were tolerated, but those few social movements which appeared were tracked down by the police and neutralized (Pickvance 1998).

Thus even the first environmental movements only appeared at a later stage, after 1984. The earliest movements emerged simultaneously in large cities and small villages. Their emergence was the strongest sign of the growing political thaw. The reason environmental movements were among the first to appear was because environmental issues were not viewed as a potential threat to the regime. They were tolerated to a much larger extent in the mid-1980s than openly political movements. These were considered to be a potential threat to the regime and were cracked down on. This led to a situation in which before the regime change environmental issues attracted politically minded people who either blamed the regime for the lack of responsible policies or joined green movements to express their discontent without running the risk of a direct confrontation with the regime. Consequently, from the mid-1980s there was a sudden upsurge of green groups. By the time the regime changed and the law legalizing free associations was passed by the first non-communist government (elected in March 1989) dozens of environmental groups existed. By the early 1990s their number grew to several hundreds, according to Szirmai (1997). They varied in size and locality. Their concerns ranged from local to national or even global issues.

They had, however, several characteristics in common. They went through a stage, just before and soon after the regime change, when mass demonstrations were a frequently used method to express views and put pressure on the authorities. After a short period, however, a "demonstration fatigue" occurred in Hungary, as a result of which it became increasingly difficult to mobilize large numbers of people to demonstrate, at least for a while.

Uniquely, Hungarian politicians, especially those in charge of environmental issues, not only did not condemn mass demonstrations but regretted their disappearance from the political scene. The politicians even blamed the green movements for not trying harder to mobilize mass demonstrations which could help them when lobbying for environmental causes within the government.

Another general characteristic of Hungarian environmental movements is that they are reluctant to unite under a federal organization. The many groups which exist all over Hungary enjoy a continuous flow of information. They communicate mainly via annual conferences or other meetings but are not willing to unite under an organizational umbrella or any other hierarchical structure. The many attempts to create such structures all failed.

The concrete reasons for the green groups coming into existence vary but they all had a particular objective at the outset. These included diverting road traffic, closing down a particular factory, preventing new projects being built on unsuitable sites. Some were triggered by specific events and others by a general concern about the state of the environment. The pattern, however, was similar in many cases. First, they mobilized forces for or against a concrete goal. Then they widened their interest and took up problems which were outside their original scope but became important as the struggle evolved. This also became part of a conscious survival strategy to maintain the movement after achieving their immediate task. As Zald and Ash (1987) argued, when a movement achieves success by realizing its initial goal, this can lead to the movement's end.

Hungarian examples also support West-based arguments. A movement against a proposed nuclear damp site in a small, picturesque village, called Ofalu, near the city of Pecs, in the southwest, is an example of a local movement triggered by a concrete event and which came to an end after accomplishing its objective (Juhasz et al. 1993). The Ofalu movement achieved tremendous success against all the odds by stopping the government from building the planned project but the movement did not survive this success.

Next I will analyze three concrete examples - Green Future, the Danube Circle and the Air

Group - in considerable detail in order to show a contrary trend and also to illustrate the wider spectrum of environmental movements in Hungary. The Danube Circle, a large scale, nationwide movement, a reaction to the proposed dam on the Danube, resembles Green Future, a movement in an industrial suburb on the outskirts of Budapest which started off with concrete concerns, in that both later grew into movements with general environmental concerns. They contrast with other movements which came into existence as a reaction to a generally growing concern about the state of the environment such as Reflex, in the city of Gyor (western Hungary) or the Air Group, in Budapest.

THE DANUBE CIRCLE

The Danube Circle is the best known environmental group in Hungary and also gained an international reputation (Waller 1992; Fleischer 1993). It became a national movement well supported by many in its hey-day. At its peak it managed to mobilize more than 40,000 people to demonstrate against the government's intention to sign a contract with the then Czechoslovak Government to build together a dam on the Danube at Bos-Nagymaros - now part of Slovakia.

The idea of building a dam between the two countries originates in the 1950s but was developed more seriously in 1977. The power station was supposed to supply energy, help navigation and control floods. The original plan was to build two power stations - one at Bos/Gabcikovo and another at Nagymaros -, and a twenty kilometer long reservoir. The monstrous plan has all the fingerprints of the engineering ideas of the 1950s and 1960s when such constructions were built both in the developed and the third world countries, the latter often with first world "aid."

The argument was always that it would provide low cost energy. Apart from the environmental damage these dams created, even the cheap energy argument is seriously contested since the 1970s. In the Bos-Nagymaros case the very expensive construction would only produce an insignificant 2-3 per cent of the required amount of energy in both countries. The most important criticism of this giant plan is concerned with its environmental consequences. It affects the drinking and underground water supply, the local natural habitat and the river Danube.

Information concerning the construction plans were kept secret for a long time and only a limited debate existed among professionals. These experts were either engineers or biologists whose job was connected with the project. Most water engineers favored the project, but biologists were against it. The debates, however, were restricted to a small circle of professionals in conferences, attended only by those invited.

It was a journalist, Janos Varga, also a biologist by background, who stumbled on the subject by accident and decided to raise the alarm. His aim was to widen the circle of those forming an opinion and he hoped that among the wider public there would be a support against the plans. By this time it was 1984 when people were not arrested for environmental activities. First, Varga attended a meeting at the House of Technology where he attracted a core group of strong-minded people who later became the first activists of Danube Circle. They were considered dissidents at the time. The "dissident" meeting turned into a movement. Those who were present voted for a resolution to organize a group in order to raise public awareness and gain public support, put political pressure on the government and try to stop the construction.

The Danube Circle became the first national movement in Hungary to attract wide public support and is the only one which started off before the regime change and still survives. Many people joined because they had worries over the state of the environment in general and the Danube in particular. Others joined Danube Circle because they were upset about the way the government con-

106

ducted such important decisions, e.g. the complete exclusion of the public.

By 1988-1989 it mobilized a strong and successful opposition to the government's plans by organizing demonstrations with the participation of tens of thousands of people on Kossuth square in front of Parliament. The number of sympathizers and those signing petitions grew into millions. The aim of the Danube movement was to persuade the government to stop the construction of the dam. It actually reached its peak of popularity before the new regime had been established unlike any other social movement in Hungary.

The Danube Circle succeeded in stopping the construction on the Hungarian side and the original project was radically modified. But it did not stop at this goal. It has expanded its concerns and become a centre with an interest in a wider circle of environmental problems. Its complete success, however, is difficult to evaluate. Although Hungary went as far as to break the original contract signed in 1977 between the two countries and stopped the construction one-sidedly, as a result of the public pressure generated by the Danube Circle, it locked itself into a never ending argument and legal battle with Slovakia which completed its part of the project. Thus the river Danube has not escaped the environmental damage and Hungary is fighting at the European Court in The Hague.

The Danube Circle is capable of mobilizing people even now, after ten years of battle. In February and March 1999, for example, mass demonstrations stopped the government's attempt to initiate any negotiations with the Slovaks "behind closed doors." The public pressure alarmed the opposition and part of the coalition government and the negotiations had to end. The Socialist government lost the elections a few weeks later and the party forming the new government did not support any constructions or agreements with the Slovaks on this question.

The Danube Circle became a substantial political force with a considerable impact on both the Hungarian governments' decision and on public opinion. It became attractive by fighting for a concrete goal of national importance which was easily identifiable for a large section of the population whether or not they had any other type of environmental interest. Before the regime change it also took on the role of "safe" political opposition against the state socialist regime. It, however, continued to exist after the regime change and maintain its mobilizing power in the democratic period as well. Public opinion does not tolerate negotiations "behind closed doors" any longer. It demands a strong say in decision-making. This keeps the Danube Circle "in business" even a decade later.

GREEN FUTURE

Green Future is a local environmental movement, with a national reputation, concentrating primarily on problems in one of Budapest's twenty-three districts (called Nagyteteny, located in the southern outskirts of the capital, in an industrial area). This is an example of a local movement which gained a well earned reputation far beyond its boundaries.

It started off as a green club, organized by a local cultural worker of the district community centre in the summer of 1988. There were several severe environmental problems in the district, which originally, most of the population was unaware of. Those who had more access to information, such as local doctors, teachers and engineers in the local firms, gave the first enlightening talks in the green club in 1988-1989. These attracted a larger and larger audience and led to further recognition of the need for investigation by local people. The lectures "opened people's eyes," and they started to "see" the dark smog coming out of the local factory chimneys (quoted by Agnes Harsfalvi , the organizer of the lecture-series, in Pickvance 1998).

It was discovered that many firms, among them Metallochemia, Chinoin, and a large pig farm, were responsible for the heavy pollution in the district and that one of them (Metalloglobus) constituted a particularly serious danger to locals, by polluting the air, the soil and the water, used not only for drinking but also for irrigation of the small allotments. The local GPs provided evidence of above average incidence of cancer and poor childhood development in the district. There were other important issues which mobilized local people as well. One of them was the plan for a new motorway to be built through the district's densely populated housing estates. This plan had been kept secret. It only became known to the local public when the construction practically reached their doorstep.

All this information could only come to light at the time when the old political structure had started to crumble. By this time organizing social movements was no longer politically dangerous. The green club members decided to organize a movement to raise public awareness, put political pressure on the authorities and do something about the appalling situation in the district.

The triggering event for organizing a movement was a local council meeting which was to be held to discuss the environmental problems of the district with the complete exclusion of the public. The community organizers bravely decided to call a public meeting inviting the representatives of the "embryonic political parties" in opposition, which were just forming at that time, wanting to help them to put pressure on the local authorities. This was followed by several more public meetings organized with the specific aim of recruiting more people to become members of the newly formed Green Future. The movement became very popular and extremely well supported by the local population. After ten years it still exists and fulfils its original role.

Green Future succeeded in getting the major polluting firm closed down and the local council was given extra money by the central government to improve the state of the environment in the district. The motorway conflict did not lead to victory but Green Future leads the legal battle for substantial compensation to be shared out among the population for all the environmental damage occurring in the district.

The movement also became the local centre of all environmentally related issues within the district. It is a place to which people can turn for political support or for information. It is also a centre for environmental education where all people, but especially the younger generation (for example, in organized summer camps and in schools) can learn about environmental awareness. In this manner the environmental consciousness is maintained and strengthened in the district.

THE AIR GROUP

The air group originates in several university green clubs. It, however, differs from the Danube Circle in that it is not a "dissident group" as it only was organized after the regime change. In fact, the Air Group achieved fame and recognition when many already argued that the upsurge of environmental groups was over.

It was created by two university green clubs and the environmental group of the Esperanto Union. Recognizing the problem of air pollution, members of these green clubs decided to combine forces and fund a social movement. The original aim was to combat the growing concentration of air pollutants created by growing traffic and the industry. It had two aims right from the beginning: both a concrete goal and a wider agenda.

The concrete aim was to achieve cleaner air by reducing private traffic, improving the quality of public transport and providing facilities for cyclists. The wider aim was to combine environmental forces by attracting existing members of environmental groups scattered around the country who were acting fairly independently of each other. These two aims were followed from the very beginning, unlike in the cases of the other two movements where the idea of widening the movement's concern developed only at a later stage, initially mainly as a survival strategy.

Today the Air Group has 52 branches all over the country and their work is coordinated through fortnightly meetings. The opinions expressed at these meetings are then presented as the Air Group's proposal at national or local level. The Air Group became well known and popular even though it has neither engaged in "opposition" roles on the political platform, nor made any particular national demands. It however was very clever in utilizing new methods after the regime change.

The Air Group was the first which advertized itself very successfully and cleverly. Being young and ready for the new style arizing from the regime change, they decided to turn to allies in business who could help them. Budapest's largest public transport company agreed to provide the movement with free space for advertizing their cause. This newly privatized company saw the possible advantages created by the movement in promoting public transport as opposed to private cars. Thus the Air Group also benefitted by gaining widespread public knowledge of their activities through the space allocated to them without charge on all public transport vehicles which they used to promote their ideas.

These advertisements then further strengthened their opportunities to pursue their cause and the Air Group's next step was to lobby for an increased tax petrol to be earmarked for specific environmental projects. The aim of the tax was to (a) penalize road users for not choosing alternative means of transport; (b) to reduce car traffic by raising petrol prices and hence ease one of the main sources of air pollution in urban areas; and (c) to create a special fund for specifically environmental purposes.

This tax was introduced with widespread public support instead of resentment, as is usual for new taxes. The Air Group's popularity ensured that the petrol tax, though hitting the population, was accepted as a useful measure. Encouraged by this the Air Group pressed for further taxes, e.g. on trucks, to penalize unnecessary road usage. It also achieved a 25 per cent higher punitive tax on pornographic material, a culturally "polluting" aspect, published and/or sold in Hungary.

The Air Group made people suddenly feel that they were indeed suffocating in the highly polluted cities. It also benefited from the fact that the many environmental groups which sprung up around the time of the regime change already had done the pioneering work among the population by educating people and by then having raised their environmental awareness.

Since then the Air Group's major concern is to ensure that enough attention is paid to environmental investment in Hungary by any government. To achieve this they have representation and play a very active role in the Parliamentary Environmental Committee. They make sure that no green areas are eaten away by further developments and organize protest actions against out-of-town shopping centres, increased traffic or illegal constructions. Apart from this they make regular suggestions concerning the allocation of national finances through their regular and close contacts with the Ministry of Finance. The Air Group has achieved a professional level at instigating legal or financial proposals. It has developed a well organized network which operates at local and national level as well as in their 52 branches nationwide.

In sum, the Air Group's initial success was the result of their innovative way of adapting to new circumstances. They found a new approach, unknown to Eastern European social movements in the past, by utilizing business opportunities and advertizing themselves to become known. They were also new in the sense that short and long term aims were combined in their thinking right from the start. Finally, they became popular at the time when the Hungarian public was becoming aware of the environmental damage created during the previous period and was more responsive to the arguments of an environmental movement. Their continuing success is due to the fact that they have developed both the necessary expertise and a reputation which makes the authorities as well as the public respectful towards them.

CONCLUSION

Hungarian environmental movements came into existence not long before the regime change. Earlier the idea prevailed that any social movements were kept under such close political control - even in liberal Hungary - that no social movement could survive. From the mid-1980s environmental movements developed a special position. They were "exempt" from the otherwise strict control and reclassified as non-political, as not constituting potential danger to the existence of the socialist regime. This miscalculation allowed environmental groups to become a magnet for both anti-regime feelings as well as concern over the environment leading to, by 1988-1989, a mushrooming of green movements.

After the regime change some of the environmental movements lost one of their attractions - their anti-regime element. Individuals who were primarily politically minded could join the various political parties. Many green groups, however, not only survived but became respectable vis-a-vis the authorities and in the eyes of the local population. They fulfil a very important "policing" role concerning the environment today.

Hungarian environmental law changed since the regime change, bringing it in line with European standards. The national network of environmental authorities is also in place and operating according to the law. But this did not eliminate the role of non-governmental organizations. The Danube Circle, Green Future and the Air Group are good examples of some of the green voluntary organizations which at present play a very important part in raising environmental standards in Hungary.

NOTES

*On the wish of the main author, in references page information is supplied only for journal articles.

REFERENCES*

Fleischer T. 1993. "Jaws on the Danube: water mangement, regime change and the movement against the Middle Danube hydroelectric dam" *International Journal of Urban and Regional Research* 17:429-443

Juhasz J., A. Vari and J.Tolgyesi. 1993. "Environmental conflict and political change: public perception on low-level radioactive waste management in Hungary" in *Environment and Democratic Transition: Policy and Politics in Central and Eastern Europe.* Edited by A.Vari and P.Tamas. Dordrecht. Kluwer Publishers

Kulcsar L. and I. Dobossy. 1988. *Az okologiai tudat es viselkedes tarsadalmi tenyezoi.* Zarotanulmany (The social factors of ecological knowledge and behaviour. Report). Budapest. Tomegkommunikacios Kutatokozpont

Peto I., S. Szakacs. 1985. *A hazai gazdasag negy evtizedenek tortenete 1945-1985: I. Az ujjaepites es tervutasitasos iranyitas idoszaka, 1945-1968.* (The history of the four decades of the Hungarian economy 1945-1985: I. The period of reconstruction and the command economy 1945-1968). Budapest. Kozgazdasagi es Jogi Konyvkiado

Pickvance K. 1997. "Environmental movements in Hungary and Russia: a comparative perspective" *European Sociological Review* Vol. 13 Nr. 1:1-25

Pickvance K. 1998. "Democracy and opposition at grassroots level in Eastern Europe: the case of environmental movements" *Sociological Review* Vol. 46 Nr. 2:187-207

Pickvance K. 1998. *Democracy and Environmental Movments in Eastern Europe: a comparative study of Hungary and Russia.* Boulder, Colorado. Westview Press

Pickvance K. 1999. "The diversity of post-socialist Eastern European social movements" in *Urban Movements and Global Processes.* Edited by P.Hamel and M.Mayer. London. Routledge

Richardson D. 1995. "The Green Challenge: philosophical, programmatic and electoral considerations" in *The Green Challenge: The Development of Green Parties in Europe.* Edited by D. Richardson and C. Rootes. London. Routledge

Szirmai V. 1997. "Protection of the environment and position of green movements in Hungary" in *Environmental and Housing Movements: Grassroots Experience in Hungary, Estonia and Russia.* Edited by Lang-Pickance, N. Manning and C. Pickvance. Avebury. Aldershot

Varga J. ed. 1997. *A Hagai Dontes. (The Decision of the European Court in den Haag).* Budapest. Enciklopedia Kiado

Waller M. 1992. "The Dams on the Danube" *Environmental Politics* 1:121-143

DOCUMENTS

Air (Lelegzet). The monthly periodical of the Air Group 1995-1999. Budapest

Tenyek Konyve. Zold. (The Book of Facts. Green.) 1998. Budapest. Greger-Delacroix

The Limits of Growth. 1972. Report by the Club of Rome. Rome. The Club of Rome

The Blueprint of Survival. 1972. London. The Ecologist

9. The Ecological Movement as the Element of the Civil Society

Piotr Gliński
compiled and translated by Helena Flam

INTRODUCTION: THE INDEPENDENT ECOLOGICAL MOVEMENT AND ITS TARGETS PRIOR TO 1989

The independent ecological movement emerged together with the *Solidarność*-revolution. In the 1980s it was primarily a movement of protest and self-defense. It was spear-headed by informal groups as well as by the intelligentsia and counter-cultural milieus. They had two goals: the struggle against the anti-environmental policy of the authorities and the moulding of the state-independent pro-ecological public opinion.

The first nation-wide, independent organization - The Polish Ecological Club - has been active since 1981. In the later 1980s several important youth movements appeared: ranging from the movement Freedom and Peace (*Wolność i Pokój*), which was strongly engaged in politics, through the counter-cultural Green Federation (*Federacja Zielonych*) to the ecological-peace movement "I prefer to be" (*Wolę być*), which was the most moderate in its protests.[1] Numerous local pro-ecological milieus organized self-defense actions in situations threatening health and nature. They mobilized against nuclear risks, especially after the Chernobyl disaster of 1986, and against the environmental destruction caused by heavy industry so typical for the Polish centrally planned economy. Moreover, many groups focused on alternative, pro-environmental technology in the fields of energy, industry and agriculture. Independent expert milieus, composed of lawyers, space planners, economists-conservationists, also grew. The ecological movement constituted a small, but significant enclave of the civil-oppositional society emerging in Poland at the time. For this reason in the Round Table negotiations which preceded the first quasi-free political elections of June 1989 a separate ecological table was set up. It gathered several representatives of the independent ecological movement.

In contrast to many other institutions, the Polish ecological movement was relatively well-formed and differentiated even before the crucial breakthrough-year of 1989. It was prepared as it were for its further development under new political conditions. It consisted of about 135 autonomous groups and organizations which had a vast network of international contacts. It looked for new organizational formulas and even started a process of internal consolidation: the First All-Polish Meeting of the Ecological Movement was organized in Warsaw in 1989. One hundred participants attended it. They represented about 50 different pro-ecological social milieus from the entire country.

THE STRUCTURE OF THE ECOLOGICAL MOVEMENT AND THE MAJOR CONFLICT LINES

The changes which took place in 1989 made possible a dynamic growth of the movement. In 1995 there existed more than seven hundred organizations, foundations and pro-ecological groups. At the present they number one thousand.

Although intensified integration tendencies have been very clear since 1989 and will be described in the next section, the ecological movement has always been internally differentiated

(Gliński 1996:239-243). At least 12 different currents can be distinguished: (1) The Polish Ecological Club, which had 4,000-5,000 members in 1995; (2) The League for the Protection of Nature, which lists 800,000 members, but which has very few activists of whom youth constitutes 90%, and other post-communist organizations; (3) The Green Federation, which had 50 local groups in 1995; (4) defenders of animal rights and the vegetarian movement; (5) other youth groups, including students at higher institutions of learning, high school students and scouts; (6) groups practicing "deep ecology;" (7) organizations for the protection of nature; (8) local organizations; (9) educational organizations; (10) expert and specialist organizations; (11) religious and quasi-religious organizations; and (12) artistic and quasi-artistic groups. Most groups which together constitute a current have less than 20 activists each and perhaps several tens formal members. Only during confrontations does the number of those mobilized increase.

These currents can be best understood in terms of polarized, dichotomous identities which ecological groups in Poland and elsewhere assume (Diani and Lodi 1988:103; Pakulski 1991:169). *Deep radical ecologists*, concerned with achieving profound insight, contrast strongly with *ecologists of compromise*, who act upon their fears. *Ecologists of moral protest*, similarly, differ as markedly from *ecological pragmatists* as groups of *ecological "experts"* do from the groups of *"amateur" ecologists*. The *ecologists of deeds* composed of activists bent on social engagement are distinct from the *ecologists of the soul* who are recruited from the ranks of deep *radical ecologists* and who seek to perfect themselves without social engagement. Finally, the ranks of *independent ecologists* are constituted by those who co-operate with the state, self-governments, business and sponsors.

The movement is marked not only by different self-definitions of groups but also by some lines of conflict. In extreme cases, compromiseless *radical ecologists* accuse others of treason, loss of autonomy and succumbing to the manipulations of the opponent.[2] Personal conflicts, moralism, a wish to impose a set of central priorities on the entire movement as well as lack of tolerance and understanding for a variety of functions which a full-blown ecological movement needs to fulfill, together account for some remaining conflicts within the movement.

THE EXPANSION, PROFESSIONALIZATION AND INTEGRATION OF THE ECOLOGICAL MOVEMENT AFTER 1989

At the present movement, the Polish ecological movement is well grasped as a movement engaged in self-education, self-reflection and integration (Gliński 1996). Starting with the early 1990s, protests and demonstrations have been increasingly supplemented by alternative proposals of "civic" solutions and forms of action: participation in preparation and decision-making processes, such as co-operating with administration, advising legal solutions or lobbying as well as independent management of the non-governmental societal spheres in form of ecological projects.

The integration of the movement progressed in part because of the annual All-Polish Meetings of the Ecological Movement and in part because of the development of different intra-sectoral media, such as periodicals, Green Brigades (*Zielone Brygady*) or The Vegetarian World (*Wegetariański Świat*), or the internet network Bridge (*Most*). Ever more formalized movement structures and specialized information, service or financial institutes underpinned this development. The members of the movement trained themselves in nature protection law, interest mediation and negotiations as well as in management and financing of non-governmental organizations. Ecological organizations increasingly worked out rational action strategies and co-ordinated their actions and pro-ecological campaigns nation-wide.

National Campaigns

The first such action, a campaign against the construction of a nuclear plant in Żarnowiec, was a continuation of the anti-nuclear protests of the 1980s. It was crowned with success by the end of 1989. In 1990-1993 protest against a construction of a dam in Czorsztyn became loud. It temporarily attracted public attention to the problem and - what just a few still remember - forced the authorities to build sewage treatment stations around the reservoir, but in the end this protest turned out inefficacious (Gliński 1994; Gliński 1998a).

Later on, tens of different, nation-wide pro-ecological campaigns were organized. Among them we find recycling and waste management campaigns, including the well-known campaign Cleaning up the World (*Sprzątanie Świata*) as well as such as The Vistula Now (*Teraz Wisła*) whose aim it has been to return the eco-cultural identity to the local communities inhabiting the Vistula valley. Also worth mentioning is the campaign for ecological agriculture, which has been organized, together with Germans, since the 1980s. In 1999 a strong Coalition for Ecological Agriculture emerged which includes near 20 organizations. Its integrating and lobbying activities are very important. They have influenced the Polish parliament to prepare a new law that supports ecological agriculture in Poland.

Several of these campaigns ended with considerable successes. The anti-highway campaigns, which expressed support for railroads, public means of transporation and bicycles, actually brought changes favorable to the bicycle riders into the new road codex. The campaign Ecology in Constitution resulted in the introduction of several essential pro-ecological entries in the Constitution of the Republic of Poland. Anti-circus and anti-fur campaigns as well as the campaign An Animal Is Not a Thing (*Zwierzę nie jest rzeczą*) had as their final successful outcome the passing of the *Sejm* law on animal rights by the *Sejm* in 1997. Campaigns in defense of "wildlife" led to extending species protection to wolf and lynx as well as to the partial widening of the area of a nature park, Białowieski Park Narodowy. The Coalition for the Protection of the Tatra Mountains, composed of dozens of groups, achieved a spectaclular victory when, in co-operation with the Tatra National Park and enlisting the support of outstanding Polish intellectuals, including Nobel Prize winners, such as, for example, Miłosz and Szymborska, it managed to dissuade the government to promote Zakopane as a candidate for the Olympic Games 2006. In 2000 the issue of river protection in Poland, raised primarily by the *Gaja Club*, the organization that had started the Vistula Now campaign, was strongly supported by the WWF. It established a new office in Warsaw and launched a powerful international campaign against the plans of the Polish government to build a new dam on the Vistula. It also works towards saving the natural character of the Oder river.

Led by the Green Network, many ecological NGOs have also been involved in campaigns for access to civic and environmental information, for an ecological tax reform, and for "greening" Western subsidies and the national budget. The campaign against the Genetically Modified Organisms (GMOs), now run by the Ecological Institute, started in 1997 following the Green Federation's awareness-raising efforts ("Menu for the Next Millenium"). It is directed against genetically modified food and agri- and food-culture. It resulted in GMO-related amendments to the environmental legislation and greater public sensitivity as far as GMOs, intensive agriculture and unsustainable food consumption are concerned. An international seminar on the GMOs organized in Warsaw brought together West, Central and East European activists in 2000. A second report on the GMOs in Poland was also published.

During the 1990s we have also observed a number of the local Agenda 21 initiatives, many of them in co-operation with Western partners. Some recent activities also involved monitoring the EU enlargement process. A new European Information Office was established by the Institute of Sustainable Development in Warsaw in 1999. In the end of the 1990s a new, anti-globalization campaign started in Poland. Protest focused on the international economic organizations, such as the World Trade Organization, International Economic Fund and the World Bank. Polish ecologists were also very active in the Prague demonstrations in September 2000. Anti-capitalist sentiments became manifested also in other ways. Recently many Polish radical groups have joined the anti-capitalistic coalition of various populist and even rightist organizations, such as a peasant movement Self-Defense, *Samoobrona*.

Different Forms of Rational Self-Reflection and Co-ordination
Institutions and structures of co-operation - which emerge around concrete actions and campaigns - are conducive to a growing sense of constituting a community based on shared experience. The development of new communication networks as well as different meetings and disputes support the task of rational self-reflection. Among meetings which contribute to a movement-wide discourse, we find these between the movement leaders and their sponsors as well well as those among the government representatives and the movement leaders who were selected for the so-called "List of 21" - an unofficial umbrella body of 21 movement leaders elected at the All-Polish Greens' Meeting in 1996. Even the talks between the movement members and the Ministry of Nature Protection, Natural Resources and Forestry about the Co-operation Program, which took place with varying degrees of intensity between 1992 and 1997, played a similar role.

In 1999 the Polish Green Net (*Polska Zielona Sieć*), financed by European and Dutch funds, was finally started after four years of streneous preparations. It realizes the program of ten different Ecological Information and Activisation Bureaus. Its integrating capacity is considerable which is very important in light of the fact that All-Polish Greens' Meetings face an uncertain future.[3] Currently the integration process is carried out via the meetings of the Polish Green Net, although its activities are opposed by some radical clubs and by the Polish Ecological Club which jealously tries to safeguard its past networking position. Integration is also pursued by other networking organizations, such as the Green Federation, and by co-operating local and branch organizations. The integrative role played by the electronic media in this context is crucial.

In 1998 a new Environmental Lobbying Support Office was established in Poland to facilitate ecological lobbying, national campaigns and communication with state officials. Its main taks are (1) to ease contacts between ecological lobbyists, on the one hand, and members of parliament and government officials, on the other; (2) to gather and distribute information about environmental issues on the parliamentary and govermental agenda as well as about potential allies and opponents; (3) to inform about structures, rules and procedures in use in parliament and government; (4) to explore possibilities of co-operation with the national and international mass media; (5) to supply information about problems, "green" NGOs and their activities to politicians, government officials and the media.

THE ECOLOGICAL MOVEMENT, ITS TRANSFORMATION AND ITS CONTRIBUTION TO THE CIVIC SOCIETY

In sum in the 1990s one could witness a process of professionalization and attainment of civic maturity by the ecological movement. Interestingly, these processes were spontaneous, through the initiatives coming from below, often with help of international organizations and foundations, but generally without any support of the Polish government. They were not part and parcel of some transformation reform designed from above. On the contrary, the acitivities of the movement belonged to those few elements of **change from below** which were endogeneous and had an evolutionary, stable character. The contents of change are not only *stricte* ecological, but also, a fact exceptionally important in a time period of systemic change, "civic." The ecological movement contributed to the realization of one of the postulated goals of the transformation which was the emergence of civic society. Capturing the issue in a synthetic manner: in the last ten years in Poland the ecological movement underwent change from a counter-culture to a civic society, from a political opposition to societal participation, from expression to constructivism, from "joyful" creativity to professionalization, from informal structures to institutionalization.

Pro-ecological social milieus and organizations constitute enclaves of civic society which are still relatively rare in Poland. They are best seen as *interest groups* with specific *positive identity* which contrasts with a past negative identity shaped through the opposition to the system. They emerged *from below* as a result of the individual free choice to participate and are *independent* from both the government and political structures. Pro-ecological groups vary as to their degree of institutionalization as well as their capability to self-organization and self-defense. Their *social engagement* is very high.

These groups also possess a specific *public status*, their activities are generally accepted. They are also characterized by strong internal and external group *ties*. With some exceptions, they are *responsible and loyal* towards the new state and the democratic rules of the game. Most groups have renounced the use of force as well as relying on "soft" ecological terrorism. Widespread stereotypes to the contrary, these groups are "societal subjects" with well-developed "*civic virtues,*" that is, preparedness to think and act for the common good, significant *tolerance* for other groups and organizations as well as relatively well-developed capacity to *negotiate compromises*. The ecological movement does not only realize civic virtues, but also fulfills a special culture-creating function insofar as it helps to diffuse civic norms and cultural patterns to other areas of societal life.

CONCLUSION: A PROGNOSIS OF THE RADICALIZATION IN THE FUTURE

Perhaps the next stage in the development of the ecological movement in Poland will be its politicization, that is, the construction of *stricte* political structures. However, the past attempts to call into life an ecological political party did not succeed. Until 1998 there existed in Poland as many as 17 formal ecological "couch" parties, which could not show for themselves any practical pro-ecological activity. Once new laws concerning political parties were introduced, only 3 of these passive political creations survived. In the 1990s the only pro-ecological social milieu which was truly active on the political scene was the Ecological Forum[4] of the Freedom Union (*Forum Ekologiczne Unii Wolności*). It was composed of several members of parliament and closely co-opearated with pro-ecological organizations. The result of this co-operation was that parliament accepted many pro-ecological laws and amendments. Still, the movement did not generate, so far, any significant political party. Decisive here is the non-mass character of this movement. In Poland the middle class, a traditional supporter of the ecological political movements in the West, is not strong (Gliński 1998). On the other hand, 33% of the Polish youngsters declare sympathy towards ecologists and only 7% declare lack of sympathy and, thus, make ecologists rank highest among 21 subcultural groups under investigation (CBOS 1996). The question is whether this group will make itself heard in the future.

In the pre-1989 counter-cultural context, which imposed loose organizational forms and inclusive group structures on the movement, the impact of the programmatic differences was mild. The counter-culture united rather than split the movement. The representatives of the radical current, who as critics, have contributed to the broadening of the internal ecological discourse and also have played an imporant role as the guardians of basic ecological values, at the present moment turn into an essential threat to the civic character of the activities of the ecological movement in Poland. In recent years the radical current, which includes primarily *deep radical ecologists* and some participants in the Green Federation, has been acquiring strong contours. Indicating a growing cleavage in the entire ecological movement, in 1998 the First Meeting of the Radical Groups took place.

The reasons behind this new trend are as follows. First, an intensification of the ideological conflict. *Radical ecologists* do not accept the traditional model of civilizational change. They oppose the fact that the government supports the development of private, motor-driven transportation to the disadvantage of public means of transportation. They also oppose the ever greater presence of the international corporations. Secondly, there is an increasing trend towards the marginalization of the ecological issues as well as of the ecological movement by the elites, composed of politicians, journalists and intellectuals. The final reason is the absence of modern - participatory, negotiating and mediating - mechanisms for avoiding or solving eco-societal problems.

While between 1992-1995 about twenty meetings took place between the representatives of the ecological movement and the Ministry of Nature Protection, Natural Resources and Forestry (Tews 1999:83), in 1996 these meetings became less frequent and changed their character. Over time, despite many conflicts, a multifaceted working relationship emerged between the Ministry and the representatives of the ecological organizations. A central issue concerned forms of co-operation and the financing of the activities of these organizations by the Ministry. In 1996 the Ministry saw itself forced to work out a program of co-operation with the ecological NGOs. This would not have been possible without the support of the American Harvard Institute which financed the preparation of the program. A group of experts with roots in the movement won the competition to finalize this program. A supervisory board included government and movement representatives. As a result in February of 1997 a modern, complex program of co-operation entitled, "Co-operation between the Ministry of Nature Protection, Natural Resources and Forestry and the ecological NGOs," was adopted (Jendrośka et. al. 1997). In the same year the Ministry established an independent Bureau of Information and Public Communication whose one important task was to implement this program. Six basic points specified movement-state co-operation: (1) access to information; (2) involvement in the creation of policy and law; (3) participation in decision-making; (4) contribution to the control and implementation of legislation; (5) institutional support; (6) financial solutions, such as competitions for grants. Several steps were taken to prepare for the implementation of this program. A team was set up to supervise the preparatory work. Then, suddenly, the entire process was stopped. Everything indicates that it was halted by politicians unaccustomed to societal participation in democratic institutions. Ruling by the virtue of the "procedural mandate," they refused to tolerate influence gained by the virtue of the "participatory mandate." The only other positive institutional achievement - a mixed commission which the Ministry called into life in the beginning of 1998 to allocate financial means for the ecological education - was wasted, when Minister Tokarczuk filled all positions with his people. Moreover, until today the matter of public financing of the ecological movement remains on the agenda. The movement draws no benefits from such sources as the National Fund for the Protection of the Environment and Water Management (*NFOŚiGW*). The representatives of the ecological movement that sit on its supervisory board have no influence.[5] Even worse, no rules exist which would insure that citizens can make transparent or gain influence over the allocation of at least those funds which are meant for the ecological NGOs.

It is very likely that the crystallization of two separate movement currents - the radical one and the compromise-oriented - within the at the moment still rather differentiated ecological movement will be hastened by the activities of the authorities which have the potential to play a role of an external pivot. If they continue to marginalize the ecological movement and do not provide any negotiation arenas, they are bound to push the activities of the movement beyond the borders of the democratic system (Bennie and Rüdig 1994:1).

In this situation the group of "double-reject" participants of the ecological movement will expand considerably. They are "rejected" by the establishment and they "reject" the system. Seen from the point of view of transformatory changes, this constitutes a dangerous state of affairs. A violent radicalization of the part of the ecological movement threatens to destroy its achievements in the area of civic attitudes.

NOTES

1. The Green Federation exists even today, while some of the participants of the first and third movement play an important public role.

2. However, some of the very same critics are capable of pragmatism and compromise reached for the sake of the least evil for the nature, see articles by, for example, Janusz Korbel, Marta Lelek or Ewa Fin in *Zielone Brygady*.

3. As a result of a severe conflict betwen Radicals and Realos no All-Polish Greens' Meetings were held since 1997. In the first half of 2000 a serious attempt was made to bring together the two wings of the movement. Two preliminary meetings resulted in the establishment of a new Coalition for Wild Life that unites the nature protection and deep ecological organizations. But the Coalition does not affect much the basic split within the movement - a matter in which further talks are planned for the end of 2000.

4. The Ecological Forum, by the way, is the only Polish organization which for years now has co-operated with the Western Greens. In 1999 it achieved the observer status in the European Federation of Green Parties. In 2000 the Polish representative, Gabriela Szuba, was elected to the 9-member board of this federation, the EFGP.

5. Law is ignored when the duly elected representatives of the ecological NGOs are omitted in the selection of members for the advisory boards of the regional funds (*wojewodztwo*) and of the National Fund for the Protection of the Environment and Water Management (*NFOŚiGW*). The National Fund is a tax-based fund.

REFERENCES

Bennie L. G. and W. Rüdig. 1994. "The British Greens as a Social Movement" paper presented at The XIII. Congress of the International Sociological Association held in Bielefeld, Germany between July 8 and July 12, 1994

CBOS (Pubic Opinion Research Center). 1996. *Młodzież o sobie: wartości, obyczajowość, grupy odniesienia*. Komunikat z badań. Warszawa. Centrum Badania Opinii Społecznej, listopad/ November

Diani M. and G. Lodi. 1988. "Three in One: Currents in the Milan Ecology Movement" in *International Social Movement Research. Vol. 1. From Structure to Action: Comparing Movement Participants across Cultures*. Edited by B. Klandermans, H.-P. Kriesi and S.Tarrow. Greenwich, Connecticut. JAI Press, pp. 103-124

Gliński P. 1994. "Environmentalism among Polish youth. A maturing social movement?" *Communist and Post-Communist Studies* Vol. 27. Nr. 2:145-159

Gliński P. 1996. *Polscy Zieloni. Ruch społeczny w okresie przemian*. Warszawa. Wydawnictwo IFiS PAN

Gliński P. 1998. "Polish Greens and Politics: A Social Movement in a Time of Transformation" in *Environmental Protection in Transition - Economic, Legal and Socio-Political Perspectives on Poland*. Edited by J. Clark and D. H. Cole. Brookfield, USA. Aldershot, pp. 129-153

Gliński P. 1998a. "Learning by Action. The Case of the Polish Environmental Movement" *Action Learning. Praxiology: The International Annual of Practical Philosophy and Methodology* Vol. 6. Edited by Wojciech W. Gasparski and D. Botham. New Brunswick and London. Transaction Publishers, pp. 191-200

Jendrośka J. et.al. 1997. *Współpraca pomiędzy Ministerstwem Ochrony Środowiska, Zasobów Naturalnych i Leśnictwa a pozarządowymi organizacjami ekologicznymi*. Raport końcowy. Wrocław. Towarzystwo Naukowe Prawa Ochrony Środowiska

Pakulski J. 1991. *Social Movements. The Politics of Moral Protest*. Melbourne. Longman

Tews K. 1999. *EU-Erweiterung und Umweltschutz. Umweltpolitische Koordination zwischen EU und Polen*. Leipzig. Leipziger Universitätsverlag

SELECTED CONSULTED DOCUMENTS

Zielone Brygady (1994)
Serwis Ochrony Środowiska (1994)
Dzikie Życie (1997)

10. Institutionalization instead of Mobilization - The Environmental Movement in Eastern Germany

Dieter Rink
assisted by Saskia Gerber

INTRODUCTION

It was in the early 1980s that the first independent environmental activities took place in the GDR[1] - partly within the state-controlled Society for Nature and the Environment, *GNU* (*Gesellschaft für Natur und Umwelt*), and partly among environmental groups under the auspices of the Protestant Church. Yet ecology only came into the public eye in the late 1980s, when the appalling environmental situation became one of the motives behind the protests in autumn 1989. In the 1990s, environmental activities in eastern Germany - since October 1990 part of the united Germany - have died down. Environmental groups and associations appear to generate hardly any protest and their role in ecological policy is unclear.

In the early 1990s, western observers expected eastern Germany to "modernize" and catch up. They foresaw the formation of a movement sector including an environmental movement. Activists in eastern Germany believed that the issues they championed would gain in public weight because of the spread of environmental awareness and acceptance. They also thought that environmental protection would assume an important role in politics, and that their movement would become stabilized and firmly established within the field of ecological policy. They also aimed at achieving organizational independence - not only from the church and the state but also from the large environmental associations in western Germany - and at joining forces.

Ten years after the *Wende*[2] in eastern Germany, what has become of these hopes and expectations? What is the situation concerning environmental groups and organizations today? What audience is there?

The current state of research on this topic is still very sketchy. Assessments and analyses of the history of social movements in the GDR have hardly treated the history of the environmental movement in the GDR as an independent topic.[3] Here we attempt to close this gap.

THE ENVIRONMENTAL MOVEMENT IN THE GDR

The 1970s and the 1980s
In the 1970s there was no independent environmental movement in East Germany. Parts of the peace movement, however, addressed the ecological problems. The first active autonomous environmental groups were formed in the late 1970s and the early 1980s, chiefly in response to specific problems in the ecological crisis areas. Nearly all were established under the auspices of the regional Protestant churches. However, it was only after prolonged theological and social-ethical discussions that a workable grassroots structure was laid down in the early 1980s. During the process of consolidation, thematic differences arose among the environmental groups.

In January 1988, members of the Environmental Library (*Umweltbibliothek*) founded the first Green organization in the GDR. Known as the The Ark - The Green-Ecological Society (*Grün-*

ökologischer Bund Arche), it was formed with the aim of building up a network of ecological groups. The Ark co-operated with the Eastern European network Greenway, which had been set up in 1985.

The nuclear reactor disaster at Chernobyl severely shook the belief in technical progress shared by much of the population. In the wake of this catastrophe, anti-nuclear power groups were set up in, for example, Berlin, Dresden, Greifswald and Leipzig.

Official ecological debate in the GDR was mainly conducted in the *GNU*, which was founded in 1980 as the largest conservation organization in the GDR. The state-controlled *GNU* was the only attempt at grass-roots work involving groups opposed to the Party and independent intellectuals. It was part of the League of Culture (*Kulturbund*) and combined urban ecology and traditional nature conservation with the beginnings of modern environmental protection within a series of interest groups. Its initial membership of 40,000 active environmentalists had grown to 60,000 by 1989. However, the *GNU* had almost no political weight, and forms of political ecology were barely represented.

The environmental groups organized under the auspices of the Protestant Church criticized the development of industrial society, including its ecological consequences, and the concrete political and ecological situation in the GDR. This criticism was focused on the unsuccessful industrial policy, the chief target of attack being the country's energy policy – especially lignite-mining and the long-term expansion of nuclear power.

Church-affiliated dissidents linked environmental criticism to the shortcomings of the political system. Most members of environmental groups were associated with other movements. One of the environmental movement's hallmarks was its flowing transitions to, above all, the peace and human rights movement as well as the Third World movement. Working under conditions of partial illegality, the environmental groups were unable to reach a large audience. The environmental movement had a relatively small membership compared to the population, and was lacking in both professionalism and funding. Nevertheless, it represented a political and social "counter-culture" with a minimum of self-determined organizational structure.

In addition to their criticism of society, ecological groups were characterized by a high willingness to set a personal example. Their members applied new ecological approaches directly to their own lives, to put a special mark on their everyday life. They changed their own behavior amidst traditional working and living conditions.

Revolution and unification 1989-1990

In the final few months of the GDR, during and immediately after the Peaceful Revolution in autumn 1989, environmental issues became one of the major topics of discussion. The peace and environmental groups active in GDR in the 1980s were the forerunners of the citizen initiatives, and a source of both inspiration and activists. In fact there was a large identity and continuity in terms of members and ideas between the social-ethical groups and the citizen initiatives, the backbone of the political protests in autumn 1989. They viewed the state as responsible for the problems mainly caused by industry. Their foremost concern was to introduce a new, non-secretive economic and ecological policy. Various aspects of the environmental situation became topics of the mass demonstrations, especially in the often severely polluted industrial conurbations in the south of the GDR.

The environmental issues had the potential of uniting different oppositional currents. They brought people as politically mature citizens first into the churches and later out onto the streets in the disaster areas in Saxony and Saxony-Anhalt. The call for an "ecological change" was of outstanding importance in autumn 1989. The post-1989 new social reality enjoyed a substantial advance bonus, everybody believed that "from now on, everything will be different and better," in part because East Germans did not have any experience with the free market.

Immediately after October 1989 the leaders of the Ark, environmental activists from the individual church environmental groups and from the official *GNU* co-founded the Green Party of the GDR (*Grüne Partei der DDR*), based on the Western model. In March 1990, the Green Party won a number of seats in the first freely elected People's Chamber of the GDR (*Volkskammer*), and in December 1990 it entered the all-German parliament, the *Bundestag*, as part of the Alliance 90/The Greens (*Bündnis 90/Die Grünen*) faction. It actually even managed to act in parliaments as an independent political force and as part of the European Green movement.

In addition, various citizens' action groups came together to establish an independent association of ecological groups. It was from this organization that the Green League (*Grüne Liga*) emerged as an independent environmental association in eastern Germany.

THE ENVIRONMENTAL MOVEMENT IN EASTERN GERMANY IN THE 1990S

Organizational structure

The structure of the environmental movement in eastern Germany is basically composed of three main pillars:

1. **Political parties**, the main one being the Alliance 90/The Greens (*Bündnis 90/Die Grünen*). In contrast, the conservative Ecological-Democratic Party of Germany (*Ökologisch-Demokratische Partei Deutschlands, ÖDP*), New Forum (*Neues Forum*), the Natural Law Party (*Naturrechtspartei*) and the Animal Conservationists (*Tierschützer*) are negligible factors.

2. **Official associations**, the Green League being the most important environmental association. The eastern German offshoots of the League for the Environment and Conservation, *BUND* (*Bund für Umwelt und Naturschutz Deutschland*) and of the Conservation League, *NABU* (*Naturschutzbund*) are smaller and not present everywhere.

3. **Independent citizens' action groups**, some of which stem from the GDR opposition or were founded in 1990-1991.

Political parties

Alliance 90 (*Bündnis 90*) emerged as a political alliance in the run-up to the elections to the GDR People's Chamber (*Volkskammer*) in March 1990 from the political cores of the citizens' action groups. In 1991 it developed into a political party. Shortly afterwards, it merged first with the Green Party of the GDR and then with the Greens from western Germany to form the political party *Bündnis 90/Die Grünen*. Excluding *Bündnis 90*, the Green Party of the GDR had a membership of about 3,000 in 1990-1991 (Kühnel and Sallmon-Metzner 1991:197), which, following the merger and a host of resignations, grew only slightly to some 4,000 or 5,000. Although the party managed to establish itself organizationally at a low level in the 1990s, since 1994 its importance has gradually declined. Nowadays in the late 1990s it is not represented in any of the regional parliaments in eastern Germany. Moreover, since the local elections of 1999, *Bündnis 90/Die Grünen* has become insignificant in almost all local councils in Saxony, Saxony-Anhalt and Thuringia.

Although initially there was still relatively broad co-operation with environmental citizens' action groups and organizations, this has been superceded by political lobbying. Mobilization is not one of the party's activities; at most it merely supports protests such as that against the transport of nuclear waste containers.

Whereas the Green Party's rank-and-file members tended to have rather conservative values (Kühnel and Sallmon-Metzner 1991:215), merging with *Bündnis 90* strengthened the left-wing/ alternative faction. Now the eastern German *Bündnis 90/Die Grünen* association ranges from left-wing to neo-liberal in its political views, although the eastern German section of the party can largely be assigned to the *Realpolitik* faction.

By all appearances, the party's declining significance seems to continue and even accelerate under the present *SPD*/Green coalition government. So far this government has largely proved to be a disappointment for the environmental movement in eastern Germany. It has not given environmental issues the hoped-for boost, nor does it create more money or resources for large projects.

Another political party worth mentioning is the New Forum, which still continues to regard itself as a citizens' initiative, but which nevertheless meets the legal requirements set up for political parties. Since 1994 it has stood for European elections and some regional elections (Saxony and Saxony-Anhalt). It is represented on some local councils. Although it still attaches high importance to ecological policy, hardly any initiatives are forthcoming from its mini-factions or individual councillors.

Another party focusing on environmental issues is the conservative The Ecological-Democratic Party of Germany (*Ökologisch-Demokratische Partei Deutschlands, ÖDP*) which maintains an office in eastern Germany and reports having 350 eastern German members (out of a total membership of 7,500). However, functioning groups only exist in Dresden, Berlin and in the Mecklenburg region.

Associations

The largest official environmental association which is represented in all the federal states comprising eastern Germany is the Green League. It was actually established by all the church environmental groups and urban ecology groups from the *GNU* in the thick of the *Wende* in autumn 1989. It roughly represents the eastern German counterpart of the western German *BUND* (*Bund für Umwelt und Naturschutz Deutschland*) - the largest west German environmental umbrella organization. The Green League unites about 100 local groups and some 3,000 members. It had a budget of approximately DM 20 million in 1995. It maintains 20 full-time employees (as well as other staff on job creation schemes) in its German headquarters and regional offices. A fully functioning association, it publishes magazines and also sets its own projects in motion. The Green League pursues a dual strategy of confrontation and co-operation, and aims to maintain maximum independence from trade and industry. Consequently, it refuses commercial sponsorship, although it does accept state support and its job creation schemes as this does not come with any thematic strings attached (see also Bergstedt et al 1999:88-92). Shunning rigid association structures, the Green League instead strives to network environmental groups and initiatives. Nevertheless, its public image is similar to the classical associations: pursuing above all practical and political lobbying, it hardly mobilizes any form of protest.

In the early 1990s, the large west German environmental associations *BUND* and *NABU* had problems gaining a foothold in eastern Germany. Now there is a large network of groups and committees spread throughout large sections of eastern Germany. Both *BUND* and *NABU* inherited the topics and personnel after the dissolved *GNU*, taking on in particular former members who had been active in traditional conservation. In 1990 *BUND* founded the first eastern German regional associations and currently has some 7,500 members and just as many donators, a figure which is gradually increasing. *NABU*, which is more actively involved in classical conservation, had some difficulty getting off the ground, but now has 19,000 members and donators active in over 100 regional and district associations, as well as in groups focusing on specific topics and areas. However, the number of committees in both associations is small, and, despite the slightly increased membership, is on the wane. The eastern German regional associations of *BUND*, for example, are regarded as not very critical or actionistic, and a co-operative attitude towards the economy tends to predominate (Bergstedt 1998:53).

Greenpeace is only represented in eastern Germany by a few groups. It is found in Chemnitz, Dresden, Leipzig and eastern Berlin. Its 8,500 donators are very few compared to more than half a million in western Germany (Naumann 1996:63).

Independent citizens' action groups

In the 1980s, ecology was the leading concern of the East German opposition, followed by peace and human rights groups. Networking began in the mid-1980s. Following the *Wende* in 1989, in 1990 and 1991, rapid, far-reaching changes took place, which initially led to significant growth in the number of groups; in fact a veritable wave of new groups was founded. Nevertheless, the establishment of, for instance, women's groups was much more dynamic than that of the ecological groups.

These environmental groups deal with a broad range of themes and are organizationally independent, and hence act outside the official associations and political parties. Their initially close ties to the Greens, which which they once had specific concerns and members in common, have also now much loosened. The environmental groups (like many others) have profited above average from the initially generous job creation schemes set up by the Federal Labor Office (Rucht, Blattert and Rink 1997:81). After many of these job creation scheme positions expired, Section 249h of the Work Promotion Act, which came into force on 1 April 1993, enabled support to be continued for ecological projects in particular.

However, there is hardly any independent networking between these groups; this function is mainly performed by the environmental associations, especially the Green League. In addition there are also smaller networks, such as the anti-nuclear power groups (e.g. the *Anti-Atom-Plenum* in Thuringia), while others are of a regional nature. During the course of the 1990s most of these groups managed to stabilize themselves - only a few dissolved. However, the range of these groups' activities has significantly declined as a result of decreasing voluntary involvement. Their political influence is limited to the local and regional level, and must be assessed as relatively low.

Infrastructure

The partly rapid development of the independent infrastructure, aided by public funds and donations, can be regarded as the most significant achievement of the eastern German environmental movement in the 1990s. The thematic orientation of this movement has broadened. Links to the secondary labor market and even the commercial sector have emerged. These include in particular environmental centres and libraries, large and small projects, and ecological villages.

The network of environmental centres, Green Houses, ecological and conservation stations, environmental training centres and similar establishments is relatively dense and spread throughout eastern Germany. These centres are often run by environmental associations or operated by citizens' action groups, societies and other committees or individuals. Moreover, there are now 28 independent environmental libraries in eastern Germany and 45 in western Germany; since the population of western Germany is about 65 million and the population of eastern Germany about 15 million, this means that there are actually more environmental libraries per capita in eastern Germany (Müller and Quester 1999).

Above all in agricultural regions, the eastern German environmental movement has "dramatically developed a large number of project-based activities" (Meyer-Engelke et al 1998:221) in diverse fields, especially in the area of "sustainability." Some "alternative large-scale projects" designed as model projects should be emphasized. For example, the ecological project *ElbeRaum* is a joint project run by groups, associations and experts from the administration, politics and science, which was initiated in 1990 within the Green League. Its aim is to "ecologize the Elbe catchment area" – a concept which covers much more than merely remediation, conservation and environmental protection in the conventional sense. The approach used is to combine public involvement and technical expertise. The Leipzig Eastern Region Project (*Leipziger Ostraum-Projekt*) – a model project for the ecologically oriented development of a city's surrounding countryside and socio-ecological urban regeneration – is designed to achieve the long-term mobilization of local and regional self-help potentials by means of co-operation rather than confrontation between the public, the administration and the economy (Hahn and Richter 1996; Hahn and LaFond 1997; for more on the large projects, see also Ziesche 1995).

Since the early 1990s, a considerable number of ecological villages has been established in eastern Germany. Well-known examples include *LebensGut Pommritz* in Saxony, which is chiefly based on the subsistence economy ideas of Rudolf Bahro, and whose foundation owes much to support from Kurt Biedenkopf, Saxony's Minister-President. This and other "new communities" are focal points within a growing network (cf. www.ecovillages.org/germany; eurotopia 1998:68) and represent the further development of community projects and concepts from the 1960s and 1970s. The ideological reasoning behind them also includes ideas of deep ecology and can be described as "spiritual ecology." Wherever visible, aspects of natural religion are emphasized and dominate a biologistical picture of mankind and society. The impression of a type of new "simple life" reform movement featuring analogies and parallels to the earlier conservation and *Heimatschutz* movements - concerned with the preservation of the character of town and countryside and the encouragement of regional culture - cannot be overlooked (see also Geden 1996:177).

Ideology

Ever since they were set up, the east(ern) German citizens' action groups have been strongly characterized by their practical involvement in environmental protection and nature conservation. In addition, efforts existed above all in the 1980s to change individual attitudes and way of life. These approaches were frequently derived from currents in the Protestant ethics, and focused on modest living and thrift up to asceticism and renunciation. In the 1980s, often unformulated, vague ideas of reformist socialism were spread in the peace and ecological groups under the auspices of the church. After the *Wende*, their civic-society and communitarianist approaches gained a certain attraction. It is generally accepted, and our own findings confirm this, that in many groups a strong scientific viewpoint prevails - an apolitical, purely scientific understanding of environmental protection (see, for example, Kühnel and Sallmon-Metzner 1991:187). This coexists with strong traditional conservation, which is increasingly associated with *Heimatschutz*. Particularly striking is the generally widespread lack of political ecology.

One exception in this respect is philosopher Rudolf Bahro, who in 1978 was stripped of his citizenship by the GDR, and who can be regarded as the leading theoretician of environmental groups in the GDR and now also in eastern Germany. In the 1980s his book, "The Alternative" (*Die Alternative*), was also discussed by dissidents, although, admittedly, his ideas did not achieve greater influence. After his return to the GDR at the end of 1989, he spoke out for ecological concerns in the reform debate and within the process of German unification, his work being supported by the establishment of the Institute of Social Ecology at the Humbodt University in Berlin.

His book, "Logic of Salvation" (*Logik der Rettung*), published in the GDR (Bahro 1990) influenced greatly sections of the eastern German environmental movement in the 1990s. His starting point is the "search for a different state of mind and way of life [which can be] broadly [organized] on the basis of self-constraint and a corresponding sustainable closed loop materials economy." (Bahro 1990:9) Bahro sees the aim of social development to be a "cultivated subsistence economy," which is based on an environmentally sustainable economy driven by small and medium technologies. Local and regional self-sufficiency is conceived as being a constitutive element for life in manageable communities. These basic communities are to form the fundamental units of human life and be characterized by personal communication. Bahro[4] believes this goal can be brought about via "co-operation between the state and alternative culture" (see also Bahro 1991:11). Following an exchange of ideas with Kurt Biedenkopf, the Minister-President of Saxony, Bahro's institute declared itself willing to assist in the setting up of new communities, with the support of the Free State of Saxony. This resulted in the foundation of *LebensGut Pommritz* (see below).

Mobilization

Even under the repressive GDR regime successes in the environmental mobilization could be noted at the end of the 1980s, such as the pilgrimage along the River Pleisse in Leipzig and protests against the construction of a silicon plant in Dresden. Environmental issues also played a role during the mobilization in the *Wende* – especially in the first phase until the Berlin Wall came down; subsequently they were replaced by such topics as national and social policy.

Environmental mobilization reached its peak in eastern Germany after the mobilizing in demonstrations died down closing the first part of the *Wende* and during the subsequent phase in 1990-1991. Protests were directed for example against the continued operation of uranium mining by Wismut, lignite-mining in the Leipzig region and in the Lausitz, refuse imports and planned transport projects. The classical forms of mobilization of social movements were used: demonstrations and rallies, petitions, and human chains. These protests were sometimes regarded as a threat to the political system in Germany as a whole.[5]

Since 1992-1993, all in all there has been a sharp decline in actual mobilization and mobilization potential. An exception in this regard is the mobilization of the youth environmental movement in the early 1990s, for example the bicycle tour from Rostock to Bremen, in which some 5,000 young people took part, as well as the Upbeat (*AufTakt*) Festival in Magdeburg, which was attended by about 10,000 participants. Other campaigns included the German Grassroots Environmental Festival and the Youth Environmental Congress held in Göttingen over New Year 1993-1994.[6] The majority of these campaigns were admittedly organized by younger members of the environmental associations from western Germany, since eastern members were still busy setting up or reorganizing their own groups. Nevertheless, this contributed to the mobilization of young eastern Germans for environmental concerns.

However, this cannot hide the fact that since then there has hardly been any form of all-embracing environmental mobilization in eastern Germany. Instead, local and regional protests addressing individual issues still predominate. Most of these have been directed against new large-scale projects in eastern Germany such as the new large airport in Berlin, motorways, and rubbish imports from western Germany, etc. Of a broader nature are campaign days such as *Mobil ohne Auto* (Carless Mobility), Earth Day on 26 April (the anniversary of the Chernobyl disaster), and involvement in the anti-nuclear power protests. The latter include protests initiated since the mid-1990s against the transport of nuclear waste flasks to the central nuclear waste depository at Gorleben and to decommissioned nuclear power stations in eastern Germany, against which a network of eastern German anti-nuclear power groups has been formed, especially from Mecklenburg-Western Pomerania, Berlin and Saxony-Anhalt. However, the anti-nuclear power protest is dominated by autonomous groups from western and eastern Germany, which simply regard it as a battlefield against the capitalist system. The mobilization potential of the environmental movement is dwarfed by that of autonomous groups in eastern Germany.

This is unlikely fundamentally to change in the near future. Individual observers, such as Schmitt-Beck und Weins, anticipate a possible re-strengthening of the new social movements in eastern Germany once the immediate problems of the general public decline due to the economic upswing. Environmental problems represent for them a "probable starting-point for future mobilization" (Schmitt-Beck and Weins 1997:351). However, such a situation is at present unlikely. Kühnel and Sallmon-Metzner's view "... that far-reaching mobilization for ecological topics is unrealistic in eastern Germany" (Kühnel and Sallmon-Metzner 1991:216) remains valid. Their forecast that problems other than environmental issues play a larger role and that it will be difficult for the Green League to assert itself in eastern Germany has proved realistic.

TAKING STOCK AND FUTURE PROSPECTS: THE EASTERN GERMAN ENVIRONMENTAL MOVEMENT AT THE END OF THE 1990S

In comparison to other areas of life, environmental problems have declined in importance in eastern Germany during the course of the 1990s. People who are doing poorly economically are less likely to view the environment as an important area of life. Yet parallel to this, East(ern) Germans appreciate the changes which have taken place – the improvement of air and water pollution, stemming from deindustrialization, and the cleaner environment, resulting from ecological policy. It could thus be concluded that "the state" and "politics" have (at least in this field) met their responsibilities, and that individual involvement is no longer necessary.

Perhaps this is an initial explanation for the shrinking potential in the area of voluntary involvement in the eastern German environmental movement in the 1990s. The number of activists in voluntary associations and initiatives as well as the mobilization potential has only slightly increased since the 1980s.

Moreover, the movement has been weakened by its institutionalization: Many citizens' action groups have lost activists to political parties and associations, and the political core of the GDR opposition formed the political party *Bündnis 90/Die Grünen*. The eastern German environmental movement is overwhelmingly characterized by conservation and environmental work organized by official associations, a Green Party whose significance is continuously declining, a series of independent citizens' action groups, small networks of left-wing radical opponents of nuclear power, and the "green-orange spots" of new communities. Over the past few years, the ecological reformism of the

Greens has in this process lost ground to conservative trends and come under pressure in the anti-nuclear power sector from left-wing radical forces.

The environmental movement is of minor importance for ecological policy in eastern Germany, although the contradiction between relatively innovative environmental legislation and directives, and their insufficient implementation is very pronounced. McGovern therefore recommends the eastern German environmental administrations involve the environmental groups and associations "... via easier, more suitable forms of participation, in order in particular to guarantee their critical potential for conflict with other departments." (McGovern 1995:182) He also sees this as an opportunity to motivate passive and new members, and to overcome what they see as their own impotence.

The future eastern German environmental movement will remain pragmatic rather than fundamentalist. Its co-operative orientation will partly compensate for weakened mobilization. Its continued existence is ensured by its institutionalization. The main problem affecting the environmental movement will continue to be its low public and political profile (cf. also Meyer-Engelke 1998:223). The Local Agenda 21 may have a positive impact by raising the visibility of environmental groups or contributing to greater public response. However, Agenda topics are rarely suitable for mobilization, and when they are, such mobilization is constrained and limited. Local Agenda 21 has so far not led to a change in ecological policy, but simply provided a new framework for the area of debate and conflict. What the eastern German environmental movement now needs is an internal debate over its future strategy.

NOTES

1. "GDR" refers to the German Democratic Republic (East Germany), which ceased to exist with the official onset of German unification on 3 October, 1990. The term "eastern Germany" (and its adjective "eastern German") denotes the area formerly comprising the GDR in the period following 3 October 1990.

2. The *Wende* is the German term used for the events of autumn 1989, when the government of the GDR was forced to enact a number of far-reaching policy changes (including the abolition of previous travel restrictions) in response to mass demonstrations (the "Peaceful Revolution") throughout the country. The *Wende* paved the way for free national and local elections, and eventually for German unification on 3 October 1990.

3. In particular, (former) activists have tried to document their oppositional activity in the GDR, including during the *Wende* (Beleites 1991; Gensichen 1991; Jordan 1991; Jordan and Kloth 1995; Rüddenklau 1992; Hoffmann, Nooke and Gensichen 1998). By contrast, academic analyses of the history of environmental groups in the GDR in the 1980s, as well as of the Green Party and the Green League, are rare (cf. Becker 1990; Kühnel and Sallmon-Metzner 1991). As far as the 1990s are concerned, so far only a few general overviews of eastern German movements and comparative analyses of German–German movements have appeared. They only deal with selected aspects of the eastern German environmental movement (Rink 1995, 1999; Rucht, Blattert and Rink 1997; Schmitt-Beck and Weins 1997). More recent works on the environmental movement in Germany as a whole have almost completely neglected mobilization, groups and networks in eastern Germany (cf. Brand 1999; Ehmke 1998; Opp 1996, 1998; Rucht 1994, 1998).

4. The development which Bahro's ideas have undergone in the 1990s also represents recognizable trends in the dissemination of spiritual and esoteric orientations in the eastern German environmental

movement (see Bahro 1995). Some authors, and in particular left-wing critics, have for a number of years drawn attention to the closeness of his attitudes to right-wing or even fascist concepts, and pointed out that right-wing ideologies have managed to gain ground via the reception of esotericism within the environmental movement (Bergstedt 1998:149; Geden 1996:176; Ökolinx H. 28-29 1998-1999). However, virtually no direct references or links to right-wing ideologies or groups have yet been proved.
5. For example, Gabriel drew attention to the constantly high willingness to protest among the population in eastern Germany, which was partly fed by environmental motives (Gabriel 1995: 174).
6. For more on the youth environmental movement, see Bergstedt 1998:129-145.

REFERENCES

Bahro R. 1990. *Logik der Rettung. Wer kann die Apokalypse aufhalten?* Berlin. Union-Verlag
Bahro R. 1991. *Über kommunitäre Subsistenzwirtschaft und ihre Startbedingungen in den neuen Bundesländern. Denkschrift.* Berlin. Humboldt-Universität
Bahro R. 1995. *Apokalypse oder Geist einer neuen Zeit. Bleib mir der Erde treu!* Berlin. Edition Ost
Becker C. 1990. "Umweltgruppen in der DDR" in *Jugend in der DDR.* Edited by B. Hille and W. Jaide. Opladen. Leske+Budrich, pp. 216-247
Bergstedt J. 1998. *Agenda, Expo, Sponsoring - Recherchen im Naturschutzfilz.* Frankfurt a.M. IKO-Verlag
Bergstedt J., J. Hartje and T. Schmidt. 1999. *Agenda, Expo, Sponsoring. Perspektiven radikaler, emanzipatorischer Umweltschutzarbeit.* Frankfurt a.M. IKO-Verlag
Beleites M. 1991. *Untergrund. Ein Konflikt mit der Stasi in der Uranprovinz.* Berlin. Basisdruck
Brand K.-W. 1999. "Transformationen der Ökologiebewegung" in *Neue Soziale Bewegungen. Impulse, Bilanzen, Perspektiven.* Edited by A. Klein, H.-J. Legrand and T. Leif. Opladen. Westdeutscher Verlag, pp. 237-256
Diekmann A. and C. C. Jaeger, eds. 1996. *Umweltsoziologie.* Sonderheft der *Kölner Zeitschrift für Soziologie und Sozialpsychologie.* Opladen. Westdeutscher Verlag
Ehmke W. 1998. "Transformationen der Ökologiebewegung. Versuch einer Ökobilanz" *Forschungs-journal Neue Soziale Bewegungen* Vol. 11. Nr. 1:142-153
eurotopia. 1998. *Leben in Gemeinschaft. Das europäische Projekte-Verzeichnis 1997/98.* Belzig. Eurotopia-Verlag
Gabriel O.W. 1995. "Politischer Protest und politische Unterstützung in den neuen Bundesländern" in *Ostdeutschland im Wandel: Lebensverhältnisse - politische Einstellungen.* Edited by H. Bertram. Opladen. Leske+Budrich, pp. 173-205
Geden O. 1996. *Rechte Ökologie. Umweltschutz zwischen Emanzipation und Faschismus.* Berlin. Elefanten Press
Gensichen H.-P. 1991. "Kritisches Umweltengagement in den Kirchen" in *Zur Freiheit berufen. Die Kirche in der DDR als Schutzraum der Opposition 1981-1989.* Edited by J. Israel. Berlin. Aufbau-Taschenbuch Verlag, pp. 146-170
Hahn E. and C. Richter. 1996. "Leipziger Ostraum-Projekt: Modellprojekt einer ökologisch-orientierten Stadt-Umland-Entwicklung" in *Stadtökologie und Stadtentwicklung: Das Beispiel Leipzig.* Edited by J. Breuste. Berlin. Analytica, pp. 121-131
Hahn E. 1997. *Lokale Agenda 21 und Ökologischer Stadtumbau. Ein Europäisches Modellprojekt in Leipzig.* Berlin. WZB-paper FS II 97-406

Hellmann K.-U. and R. Koopmans, eds. 1998. *Paradigmen der Bewegungsforschung. Entstehung und Entwicklung von Neuen Sozialen Bewegungen und Rechtsextremismus.* Opladen. Westdeutscher Verlag

Hoffmann L., G. Nooke and H.-P. Gensichen. 1998. "Umweltschutz als ein Motiv der Bürgerrechtsbewegung in der DDR - erfüllte Erwartungen oder enttäuschte Hoffnungen?" in *Umweltschutz in Ostdeutschland und Osteuropa.* Edited by F. Brickwedde. Berlin. Analytica, pp. 160-191

Jordan C. 1993. "Im Wandel - Ökologiebewegung und Grüne im Osten" in *Die Bürgerbewegungen in der DDR und in den neuen Bundesländern.* Edited by G. Haufe and K. Bruckmeier. Opladen. Westdeutscher Verlag, pp. 240-260

Jordan C. and H.M. Kloth. 1995. *Arche Nova.* Berlin. Basisdruck

Klein A., H.-J. Legrand and T. Leif. 1999. *Neue Soziale Bewegungen. Impulse, Bilanzen, Perspektiven.* Opladen. Westdeutscher Verlag

Kühnel W. and C. Sallmon-Metzner. 1991. "Grüne Partei und Grüne Liga" in *Von der Illegalität ins Parlament. Werdegang und Konzept der neuen Bürgerbewegungen.* Edited by H. Müller-Enbergs, M. Schulz and J. Wielgohs. Berlin. Linksdruck, pp. 166-220

McGovern K. 1995. "Kommunale Umweltpolitik in den neuen Bundesländern. Innovationsbedarf und Umsetzungsprobleme" in *Deutschland Ost vor Ort.* Edited by S. Benzler, U. Bullmann and D. Eißel. Opladen. Leske+Budrich, pp. 165-189

Meyer-Engelke E., H. Schubert and D. Heuwinkel. 1998. *Beispiele nachhaltiger Regionalentwicklung-Empfehlungen für den ländlichen Raum.* Stuttgart. Raabe-Verlag

Müller J. and R. Quester. 1999. *Umweltbibliotheken. Wegweiser.* Berlin. Grüne Liga

Naumann J. 1996. "Von der Umweltbewegung der DDR zu Greenpeace-Ost" in *Das Greenpeace-Buch. Reflexionen und Aktionen.* Edited by Greenpeace. München. Beck, pp. 51-63

Opp K.-D. 1996. "Aufstieg und Niedergang der Ökologiebewegung in der Bundesrepublik Deutschland" in *Umweltsoziologie.* Edited by A. Diekmann and C. C. Jaeger. Opladen. Westdeutscher Verlag, pp. 350-379

Opp K-D. 1998. "Die Perspektive der Ressourcenmobilisierung und die Theorie kollektiven Handelns. Eine Anwendung zur Erklärung der Ökologiebewegung in der Bundesrepublik" in *Paradigmen der Bewegungsforschung. Entstehung und Entwicklung von Neuen Sozialen Bewegungen und Rechtsextremismus.* Edited by K.-U. Hellmann and R. Koopmans. Opladen. Westdeutscher Verlag, pp. 90-108

Rink D. 1995. "Neue Bewegung im Osten? Zur Entwicklung des ostdeutschen Bewegungssektors nach dem Ende der Bürgerbewegungen" *Forschungssjournal Neue Soziale Bewegungen* Heft 4:20-26

Rink D. 1999. "Mobilisierungsschwäche, Latenz, Transformation oder Auflösung? Bilanz und Perspektive der Entwicklung (neuer) sozialer Bewegungen in der DDR bzw. in Ost-Deutschland" in *Neue Soziale Bewegungen. Impulse, Bilanzen, Perspektiven.* Edited by A. Klein, H.-J. Legrand and T. Leif. Opladen. Westdeutscher Verlag, pp. 180-195

Rucht D. 1994. "Ökologiebewegungen" in *Modernisierung und neue soziale Bewegungen.* D. Rucht. Frankfurt a. M. Campus, pp. 235-290

Rucht D. 1998. "Ökologische Frage und Umweltbewegung im Spiegel der Soziologie" in *Die Diagnosefähigkeit der Soziologie.* Sonderheft der *Kölner Zeitschrift für Soziologie und Sozialpsychologie.* Edited by J. Friedrichs, R.M. Lepsius and K.U. Mayer. Opladen. Westdeutscher Verlag, pp. 404-429

Rucht D., B. Blattert and D.Rink. 1997. *Soziale Bewegungen auf dem Weg zur Institutionalisierung. Zum Strukturwandel 'alternativer' Gruppen in beiden Teilen Deutschlands*. Frankfurt a.M. Campus

Rüddenklau W. 1992. *störenfried. ddr-opposition 1986-1989. mit texten aus der umweltbibliothek*. Berlin. Edition ID-Archiv

Schmitt-Beck R. and C. Weins. 1997. "Gone with the wind (of change). Neue soziale Bewegungen und politischer Protest im Osten Deutschlands" in *Politische Orientierungen und Verhaltensweisen im vereinigten Deutschland*. Edited by O. W. Gabriel. Opladen. Leske+Budrich, pp. 321-351

Ziesche M. 1995. "Zwischen Müsli und Eisbein. Ökoprojekte in den neuen Ländern." in *Alles wird besser, nichts wird gut? Wege zur ökologischen Wende*. Edited by M. Ziesche. Berlin. Aufbau Taschenbuch Verlag, pp. 277-286

PERTINENT INTERNET ADDRESSES

http://www.adfc.de
http://www.anti-atom.sachsen.de
http://www.biohoefe.de
http://www.bund.net
http://www.difu.de/stadtoekologie
http://www.ecovillages.de
http://www.gaia.org
http://www.greenpeace.de
http://www.grueneliga.de
http://www.hddl.de/oekoloewe
http://home.t-online.de/home/oekowahn
http://www.nabu.de
http://www.oekocity.de
http://www.oneworldweb.de/castor
http://www.oneworldweb.de/moa
http://www.oneworldweb.de/organisationen
http://www.ufu.de
http://www.umweltbibliotheken.de
http://www.wwf.de

PART IV

GAY MOVEMENTS

11. Cherries Blossoming in East(ern) Germany?

Jochen Kleres

LOOKING BACK: THE MOVEMENT BEFORE 1989

As in West Germany, attempts in the GDR to establish a gay-lesbian movement began soon after the liberalization of legal norms which abolished the punishable nature of ordinary homosexuality. However, East Germany continued to insist on a special age of consent for homosexuals (§ 151 of its penal code) which was intended to prevent homosexual contact between adults and youths in general.[1] Despite some earlier attempts at liberalization, it took until 1968 for the crucial legal changes to be passed (for details, see Grau 1996, 1995:104-125). Legal changes did not alter the fact that rigid, negative moral views on homosexuality remained dominant in society and politics for quite some time. The liberalization can thus be seen as the expression of a relative intellectual progress - the recognition that gays and lesbians cannot be made responsible for their desires - rather than the result of a fundamental societal change.

Although gays and lesbians had not been completely passive prior to the legal changes, their attempts to influence policy occurred at an individual level. Those who did speak out, did so only from a neutral position - for example, only as men of medicine: The neurologist Rudolf Klimmer (1905-1977) was the central actor in this area (see Grau 1995:90-95; Kowalski 1987:23-25, Steinle 1997). Before 1968 a gay subculture existed, but no social movement developed. The subculture consisted of "cottages," parks, quasi-gay pubs and private circles. However, it was constantly threatened by police controls.[2]

After the crucial legal changes of 1968, it took another five years until the first attempts to organize a gay-lesbian movement occurred. The political context for gays and lesbians remained repressive because homosexuality was legally tolerated, but still morally condemned. In addition, the authorities had a deep suspicion of any societal initiative unintended by state institutions, further hindering the development of any form of movement (cf. Sillge 1991:84). The first steps toward a gay-lesbian movement were made in 1973 when a group of East German gays and lesbians tried to unfold a banner at the 10th World Games of Youth and Students (*Weltfestspiele der Jugend und Studenten*). State security stepped in to prevent this gesture. Attempts to establish contact with members of the British gay movement were also prevented by state security forces.

In 1974, the first group began to organize itself. The "Homosexual Community of Interest Berlin - HIB" (*Homosexuelle Interessengemeinschaft Berlin - HIB*) placed its hopes in an alliance with scientists and a communication center. Neither got off the ground due to lack of support. HIB also failed in its attempt to achieve official status as a society, giving the authorities an opportunity to turn it down. A residual group remained and functioned as an informal circle,[3] which became important again in the mid-1980s.

The 1980s witnessed the emergence of a lasting gay-lesbian movement. The atmosphere free of state intervention that was necessary to begin such actions had begun to develop. In 1982, the Homosexuality Study Group (*Arbeitskreis Homosexualität*) was founded within the Protestant

135

student community. Under the umbrella of the church, this group turned into the first lasting group for gays and lesbians in the GDR. It became the starting point of a widespread diffusion process throughout the GDR. Until the end of the GDR, similar groups were being established in most big towns in the country.

From the mid-1980s on, gay groups outside the church were merely tolerated. Such groups were usually connected to certain state-sanctioned organizations, in particular the Free German Youth (*Freie Deutsche Jugend, FDJ*) or Culture Clubs in whose premises they could have their meetings. The Sunday-Club (*Sonntags-Club*) in Berlin was the first and the most important among these. The informal circles which remained from the 1970s were crucial for the forming of the *Sonntags-Club*. As with the ecclesiastical movement, there were also attempts at diffusion.

The diffusion processes were paralleled by linking the developing groups and forming a network of co-operation. This was especially the case in the ecclesiastical movement, which organized events such as workshops at the protestant academies, or memorial services at the Buchenwald concentration camp. In addition, a higher level of co-operation emerged. Special groups were built around theoretical issues or around problems connected with HIV and AIDS. However, the secular movement pursued this strategy as well through national meetings. Generally speaking, the movement formed a functioning network that encompassed the whole country.

In terms of goals, the two parts of the movement were very similar. They differed in their fundamental orientation, which can be captured by two words: emancipation (church-affiliated) vs. integration (secular) (for more details see Kleres 2000). For both, the main task was, of course, to end discrimination. For the church-affiliated part of the movement this included the analysis of the historical roots and societal preconditions of homophobic structures and their implications as well as viewing societal structures as the ultimate cause of discrimination. The position of the secular movement was too weak for such an advanced criticism of society. It stressed the vital necessity of integrating gays and lesbians in society in order to bring socialism to real fulfillment. Only if *anyone* could unfold a freely socialist personality, could socialist society develop fully (cf. Thinius[4] summed up by Kowalski 1987:63-65). None of the groups rejected state socialism. In 1989 both parts of the movement published programmatic papers.[5] Differences between the papers are very small, concerning only details. Both papers cover an entire spectrum of issues:

1. *Legal issues*: demands for: anti-discriminatory regulations in the constitution, extension of those privileges connected with marriage also for unmarried, gay and lesbian couples,[6] possibilities of adopting children by gays and lesbians, acceptance and compensation of the gay and lesbian victims of the Nazi regime, ending discrimination in the fields of work and housing – in the distribution of jobs and living space[7] as well as granting permits to organize gay-lesbian events.
2. *Cultural issues*: demands to grant possibilities to publish gay-lesbian magazines or show more sensibility towards gay-lesbian concerns within the national association for culture (*Kulturbund*) and national cultural life, permit and support gay-lesbian communication facilities, allow for broader presence of gay-lesbian topics in the media.
3. *Ecclesiastical issues*: demands for opening the church to gays and lesbians (only in the ecclesiastical paper).
4. *Science issues*: systematic research on gay-lesbian topics.
5. *Sex education as an issue*: integration of gay-lesbian topics in the school curriculum.
6. *Health/AIDS as issues*: the character of homosexuality and pedophilia (only in the ecclesiastical paper) as an illness should be officially denied; discrimination against gays and lesbians over AIDS

should be stopped, while safer sex, along with better provision of condoms should be promoted, gay self-help AIDS-groups should be allowed.

In addition to leisure activities and education, the groups' activities also included the inner aspects of self-emancipation and of providing aid and support, thus encompassing features of socio-psychological self-help.

Herrn and Rosenbrock (1998:20) describe the general aims of most of the movement's groups as critical towards customary gay subculture. Western commercial gay subculture was seen as a form of ghettoization (cf. also Kowalski 1987:64). The groups' aims were instead integrationist, pursuing the goal of integrating oneself into society. Especially state of the ecclesiastical groups tried to root their political activities in the groups' life. A Gay Adult Education Program (*Schwule Volkshoch-schule*) reflected their self-image (interview with Stapel). It expressed a strong link between politics and gay life, which was realized in practice by regular lectures, especially by scientists.

Scientists together with artists represented the main source of outer support for both the secular and the ecclesiastical movements. These allies were an important basis for the groups' ability to act. Furthermore they secured their very existence, since they bestowed some legitimacy on homosexuality as well as on the gay groups.

In spite of the weak position of the movement within GDR-society, its achievements are considerable. Giugni (1995) distinguishes between internal impacts, including aspects of identity-building and organizational successes, and external impacts of social movements, affecting the outer environment of the movement. The very existence of the movement in an adverse political context has to be considered a success. Even more impressive are the external achievements.

Thanks to the efforts of the ecclesiastical movement three scientific Workshops on Socio-Psychological Aspects of Homosexuality could be organized by official scientific institutes from 1985 on. Other congresses were organized by the church-affiliated groups at the church-academies. These groups also participated in the regular church congresses (*Kirchentage*), which were crucial for diffusion processes (Kleres 2000). Similarly, the *Sonntags-Club* in Berlin was a particular success in initiating an interdisciplinary research unit on homosexuality at the Humboldt University in Berlin. These impacts were of considerable importance in strengthening the position and the very existence of the movement (Kleres 2000).

But the most important outcome of the era was the abolition of § 151 of the penal code by the Supreme Court (*Oberstes Gericht der DDR*) in 1987 (Grau 1988). As a result of this decision, abolishing the discriminating category of special laws for homosexuals, the age of consent was made equal to that of heterosexuals. However, it is not clear to what extent the movement contributed to this particular change - an important subject for future research.

However, all of this should not lead to the conclusion that the situation for gays and lesbians or the position of their groups changed in a radical way: In 1989, before the *Wende*, Berlin gays and lesbians were denied the right to set up their own official organization. Officials denied state discriminations, referring to legal equal rights for gays and lesbians. Gay organizations seemed unnecessary as the state did not view itself responsible for prejudices of single citizens (Grau 1995:138-139).

GAYS IN A NEW CONTEXT: FEATURES OF THE DEVELOPMENT AFTER 1989[8]

The *Wende* and reunification imposed a new political and societal system on the area of the GDR. This implied fundamental changes in the political and societal framework for the movement, which could from then on develop as freely as in Western Germany. One expected shift towards West German standards was the rise of a sizeable gay subculture in larger cities. However, on the regional and local level, subcultures seem rather underdeveloped if one takes West German cities with comparable size[9] as a standard.

On the macro-level, the national success story of the Gay Association of the GDR (*SVD*) and later: of Germany can be seen as a very promising development of the movement. The *SVD* is one of the very few organizations which expanded from the east to west and not vice versa.

Next I will describe the emergence of the *SVD*, and analyze the development of the gay movement in Leipzig. Leipzig is the largest town in eastern Germany (circa 500,000 inhabitants), serving as a centre for the region. It is said to be the most vibrant city after Berlin (which is an exception due to its dualistic east-west nature). Leipzig, along with Berlin, played a central role in the development of a gay movement in the GDR[10] - another good reason to focus on it after the *Wende*.

SVD

In 1990 the Gay Association of the GDR (*SVD*) was created in Leipzig. Its founding members were mainly recruited from the ecclesiastical movement, especially its Leipzig-based group. For instance, one of the central actors was Eduard Stapel, who was also central to the ecclesiastical movement before 1989. After Reunification, the *SVD* expanded to Western Germany, unifying with those parts of the western movement that shared its orientation towards *Realpolitik*. It is now accordingly named the Association of Gays in Germany (*Schwulenverband in Deutschland*). The *SVD* has been the only representative of gay interests at the federal level, since the western Federal Association Homosexuality (*Bundesverband Homosexualität, BVH*) disbanded in 1997. The *BVH* was an association of various (independent) gay initiatives. In contrast, the *SVD* is a mere association of interest which is not intended to serve as an umbrella organization. Since 1994 one of the spokesmen of the *SVD*, Volker Beck, has been a member of the federal parliament within the parliamentary party of Alliance 90/ The Greens (*Bündnis' 90/Die Grünen*). The only other openly homosexual member of the federal parliament is Christina Schenk. She is a member of the parliamentary party of the *PDS*, the successor to the *SED* and a former member of the GDR-movement (but not of the *SVD*). Both she and Beck have been able to use their positions as a base from which to bring homosexuality into the national discussion.[11]

According to Stapel, this new organization is just an adaptation of the old movement to the new societal and political circumstances (my interview with him). The roots of the *SVD* in the GDR-movement are still recognizable if one focuses on its programmatical positions, which is surprising considering the usual pattern of westernization of eastern Germany. This does not only refer to the basic orientation of *SVD*-politics which could be described as realist politics labelled as citizen rights politics. In a concrete comparison, many of the positions of the two programmatical papers published in the GDR (see first part) can be found on the *SVD*-agenda, of course adapted to the new societal, legal and political circumstances. To name a few points: the *SVD* demands the extension of matrimony to gays and lesbians - this is the most prominent and central demand, since many legal privileges are connected to marriage. Moreover, it demands anti-discriminatory rules in the constitution, non-discriminatory housing policies as well as fighting discrimination in the work place. An extra anti-discrimination act shall provide further improvements. Again we find the problem of acknowledgement of the persecution of gays and lesbians under the Nazi regime. Further demands concern sex education, research as well as the mass media and cultural life. Besides that, problems connected with AIDS/HIV are mentioned and the demand for the "de-pathologization" of homosexuality - the medical profession should take homosexuality off their official list of illnesses.

Leipzig
    I will leave the national *SVD* here, turning attention now more exclusively to the situation of the gay-movement in Leipzig, in order to trace out the special circumstances which have shaped the gay movement and its activities there.
    In short, the situation in Leipzig is rather contradictory. There are four major pillars of the gay-activism in Leipzig: the Homosexuality Study Group, *RosaLinde* (both of which existed before 1989), the municipal representatives for same-sex relations and the local AIDS-Help-Organization. The gay movement had considerable successes and promising developments during the first years after reunification. Today, the movement is declining, especially in terms of its mobilization capacity.

The old groups
    In 1982 Leipzig gave birth to the first lasting gay and lesbian group of the GDR. This was the Homosexuality Study Group (*AKH*) under the umbrella of the protestant student community. This group still exists and is still situated within the church, but its role has changed considerably. Before 1989 it was the first and for a long time the only institution providing an integrated social context for gays and lesbians. At least for this reason the group had no problems attracting participants. In comparison with the past, very few people attend the group's meetings now. Younger gays, who came out after the *Wende*, do not tend to join the group (cf. also Herrn et al. 1998:200). As a result, the group changed its function, now serving mainly older gays, although this is not its explicit goal. Also the political and emancipatory demand (*Selbst-Anspruch*) of the group has faded considerably. Lectures and discussions were formerly an inherent part of the group's life, but few people attend these events now. They take place separat from the normal group meetings. As far as the contents are concerned, political events have not disappeared completely but are rare. Only hesitantly does the group try to revitalize itself. Some younger gays were convinced to participate in the steering committee (*Leitungskreis*) of the group. The group plans to change its name from the somewhat dry *AKH* to *ESGay*.[12] Finally, a "go-out" group was recently organized. But the group's attempts to gain public attention for these new features are rather few. Maybe in the end the group will find a new role, providing an alternative to commercialized and sexualized subculture not only for those who cannot (because of age) but also for those who chose not to participate in it (see also Herrn et al. 1998:146-148).
    RosaLinde is the second group that has remained from GDR-times. It is a secular initiative that was connected with an *FDJ*-club. The range of group activities has declined in the same way as the AKH, although there have been various attempts to revitalize the group. After the *Wende*, *RosaLinde* managed to get premises as well as financial aid from the local authorities and other official institutions which guarantees it some stability. Furthermore it has been acknowledged as an organization for the benefit of the community and obtained legal status as a charity. This has created fiscal advantages for people who donate money to *RosaLinde*. This acknowledgement by official institutions is not a matter of course for German gay initiatives, varying as it does from one federal state to another. In spite of these conducive circumstances, the group's activities have declined. For long periods, the main activity has been a weekly disco which still attracts many people and is one of the most central institutions of the gay subculture in Leipzig. *RosaLinde* has regularly tried to offer other services and attractions, such as film evenings, self-defense groups or relaxation groups. But

all this was short-lived and petered out after some time. Generally speaking, attendance at issue-focused events is very low (Herrn et al. 1998:149). *RosaLinde* has the best organizational and infra-structural preconditions for serving as a gay switch board. Unfortunately, its attempts to play this role resonate poorly with the "scene." Recently a new wave of efforts to vitalize *RosaLinde* by broadening its cultural activities has been launched as a new full-time volunteer was added. Future success will depend heavily on the financial support from the state which could turn this volunteer position into a paid job.

New groups and institutions

During the first years after the *Wende,* many initiatives emerged and raised expectations about future developments. In particular, during these first years, a considerable range of institutions emerged that formed a good infrastructure for gay needs. Leipzig was the first city in Germany to install two representatives of the gay and lesbian community in the city administration, the so called Representatives for Same Sex Ways of Life (*Beauftragte für gleichgeschlechtliche Lebensweisen*). This achievement must be seen in the context of the time immediately after the Wende which was the time of the Round Table discussions. Various minorities were represented at their own Round Table for Minority Politics (*Runder Tisch für Minderheitenpolitik*).

They demanded representation for gays and lesbians (amongst others), but failed at first. After the city council was constituted, the Green Party provided the *SVD* as well as the Independent Women's Federation (*Unabhängiger Frauenverband, UFV*) with a seat. The constant commitment, especially of the *SVD*-member of the city parliament, and the combined pressure by the gay and lesbian groups in Leipzig, finally led to the installation of two representatives in the municipal administration in 1991.

These representatives mediate between the administration and gays and lesbians, although their formal powers are often restricted due to the federal structure which moves some problems to supra-local state institutions. In spite of these restrictions, their activities have contributed to considerable successes, which should be very beneficial to the situation of gays and lesbians even outside Leipzig. Among these are (see also *Beauftragte* 1998):

• sufficient attention to gay-lesbian topics in the syllabus for sex education, providing the legal basis for the work of a group of young gays and lesbians visiting schools and educating youths about same-sex relations. The group is organized by the representatives of the gay and lesbian community in the municipal administration.

• creation of an infrastructure to face anti-gay-lesbian violence. This includes a working group against hate-crimes consisting not only of gays and lesbians, but also of a commissioner of the local police. This commissioner furthermore serves as an ombudsman for gay and lesbian victims. Besides that, the SVD has established a help line for the victims of hate-crimes.

• the gay and lesbian representatives have fought for recognition and financial support for gay-lesbian initiatives. Here, successes are considerable too. Gay-lesbian clubs are now acknowledged as working for the benefit of the community which brings them fiscal advantages.

• other activities concern problems of finding public housing, the problems of bi-national couples[13] or political refugees persecuted because of their homosexuality.

• finally the representatives act to co-ordinate and sometimes even stimulate the gay-lesbian initiatives in Leipzig. For this reason, they regularly organize meetings which function as a sort of Lesbian and Gay Advisory Committee (*Lesben- und Schwulenbeirat*).

140

Although these accomplishments are quite impressive, they should not be seen as a measure of the movement's mobilization capacity. According to interviews with the representatives, backing for their activities is rather low. Participation in the Advisory Committee is limited and its meetings take place only irregularly. A similar institution on the Saxony state level, bringing together all Saxon groups, has dissolved due to diminished interest in co-operation among the participating groups.

Another organization with central importance is the local AIDS-Help-Organization (*AIDS-Hilfe Leipzig, AHL*). This emerged from informal organizational structures, dating back to the GDR. Already in 1986-1987 within the church-affiliated group in Leipzig (*AKH*), initiatives for greater sensibility towards AIDS/HIV were started. Later, the increasing links and co-operation between the gay-lesbian groups of the GDR allowed a special group for AIDS/HIV-related issues to emerge. The *AHL* was established in April, 1990. At first it was intended to be a group of gays for gays, considering the notion of self-help, but it quickly changed its character and broadened its range of activities, away from this exclusively gay approach. This was due to increasing participation of (heterosexual) women in the *AHL*-work as well as pressure from public institutions, connecting their support and financial aid to some degree with the broadening of focus. Today, the work for gays is one aspect of a broad range of activities (youth, women, foreigners).

For the gay-"scene," the *AHL* gained importance not only because of AIDS-prevention, but also due to structural aspects. A gay meeting-café, held twice a week, and other *AHL* or *AHL*-related groups play an important role. These are a leather/SM-group and a group for deaf gays, (both of which were formerly *AHL*-groups but are now independent clubs), and coming-out-groups. In addition to these stable groups, others emerged, but dissolved again after some time (transsexuals, theatre or video). The Saxon *SVD*-chapter is also housed in the same building. Therefore the notion of a rainbow-house surfaced in the past, but did not have the vitalizing effect which was obviously intended.

Queer, a monthly, gay magazine launched in 1993, dealt solely with eastern Germany and represented local gay activities. It started as an AHL project but quickly gained independence. It expanded over regional boarders and was then published in Saxony, Thuringia and Saxony-Anhalt. After constant financial problems, it unified in 1998 with a West German gay newspaper and is now the biggest gay-lesbian periodical in Germany.

After *Queer* parted ways with the *AHL* in August 1994 following significant quarrels, the *AHL* published its own paper, named *Querele*, emphasizing more AIDS/HIV-related issues. Although it started as a monthly as well, it is now published only once or twice a year due to financial problems and lack of personnel.

From a theoretical point of view one could describe the development of the *AHL* as a process of differentiation. Compared to other movement institutions, the role of the *AHL* in this process is the most important. This might be linked to the high grade of professionalization of the *AHL*-staff (three full-time social workers and one administrator) giving *AHL* the greatest capacity to organize and back further initiatives. In turn, this makes it apparent that much of this differentiation development is based on the commitment of professionals rather than of mobilized volunteers.

Mobilization

Considering these major pillars of the gay-"scene," there seems to be sufficient institutional infrastructure to organize other activities. But surprisingly, attempts to do so are often unsuccessful in the long run due to too little resonance. Even if they persist for some time, this is often only because of the commitment of single persons. As soon as these move away from their jobs, the resulting gaps are difficult to fill.

The Leipzig Christopher Street Day (CSD)[14] celebrations illustrate this well. Leipzig had its first CSD in 1992. The number of participants declined constantly from 300 to 400 in the first years to some 100 to 200 in recent years. Finally the groups in Leipzig lost interest in organizing further events and from 1996 Leipzig has had no CSD of its own. Also the notion of a central event for the whole of Saxony, each year in another town, failed to come to fruition. In spite of that, an alternative type of mass event, the Fall Gay Cravings/*HerbstGayLüste*, has taken place since 1997. It is rather apolitical, offering cultural and social features, such as a disco night or sports championships. But at present, it seems that the *HerbstGayLüste* faces similar problems - lack of co-operation and little interest - especially on the part of commercial facilities. This is striking, since other eastern German states *(Länder)* managed to maintain the tradition of CSDs, organizing central events for each state *(Land)* and since Leipzig had a strong political movement before the *Wende* and witnessed promising developments just after the *Wende*.

Since 1993 a group of gays organized monthly events in a non-commercial cinema, but it stopped its activities in 1996 because of poor attendance. An advisory telephone line for gays suffered from a lack of resonance as well and finally stopped running. A quick browse through old issues of *Queer* shows many other groups of special interest - whether independent or connected to other organizations, e.g. the *AHL* or *RosaLinde*, which have been planned or even ran for some time but failed in the long run. For instance, there were several unsuccessful attempts by the regional *SVD* chapter to organize a group for research on the gay historical past of Leipzig. A group for transsexuals within the *AHL* had no success. *RosaLinde* tried to offer regular film evenings, but could not attract enough people. A course for self-defense was organized by *RosaLinde*, but finally faded away after some years. A local chapter of Homosexuals and the Church *(Homosexuelle und Kirche)* was set up in 1996, but has scarcely been noticed except for its contribution to the protestant church congress *(Deutscher Evangelischer Kirchentag)* which took place in 1997 in Leipzig.

A monthly radio show was launched when a local citizen radio program received permission to broadcast in 1995. After some rather active years with constant efforts to popularize the program, it has recently declined in visibility as well as in program variety, due to personnel changes. The local *SVD* chapter did not manage to become an important factor for the gay-"scene" in Leipzig. Neither its history group nor its elderly gay group found sufficient support. Its regular meetings for members in a gay pub were hardly attended. The *SVD* regularly rejects involvement in the broader gay and lesbian community in Leipzig because it sees its local culture as apolitical and itself as political. In July 1999 the regional *SVD*-chapter dissolved because of the national organization opened its membership to lesbians. The critics found this decision undemocratic. The second reason was a lack of personnel.

But it would be wrong not to mention that there are also groups which seem to have established themselves successfully. A good example is the sports club Pink Lions *(Rosa Löwen)*. It organized several extraordinary activities, including a gay night in the municipal sauna, which was well attended. For a long time, its activities have been seen as an example of success by the rest of the community. The second successful group is the gay choir The Cherry Blossoms *(Die Kirschblüten)* which continually gathers new members.

Commercial facilities

Bringing commercial facilities into the picture, several "experts" say that, though there have been ups and downs after the *Wende*, a commercial subculture seems to have established itself among gays.

Today Leipzig has two well-established discos as well as two others which do not enjoy wide popularity. Two gay saunas have opened and are well visited. There is only one strictly gay pub in town. Others are mixed. A local bookstore offers a variety of gay literature in addition to other kinds of literature. An exclusively gay bookstore gave up after attacks from Neo-Nazis.

Although there are also several shops in the city owned by gays, co-operation between commercial (whether explicitly gay or only gay-owned) and the non-commercial initiatives remains problematic. Commercial facilities neither strongly participate in nor much sponsor the CSD-events or the *HerbstGayLüste*.

DETERMINANTS OF THE DEVELOPMENT AFTER THE *WENDE*: EMPIRICAL DATA AND SOME SPECULATIONS

Using Leipzig as a key case, it has been argued that a set of differentiated institutions is in place that could easily be used to organize gay life and political activities. Access to these institutions is guaranteed through the two municipal representatives who have secured many legal and informal rights for gays and lesbians.

But the gay movement has lost groups and members, while its range of activities has narrowed. While its institutional frame is sufficient, it is not put to best use. The broad decline of the gay movement may be evidenced by the unwillingness to co-operate, the disappearance of the CSD events with their political implications, the disappearance of political contents from the group work and the lack of a backing for gay subculture. If successes are gained, they are mostly due to the activities of single persons who can rarely draw on support of a broader community. Even *Queer* regularly voices a complaint that the Leipzig gay subculture is dead. There is clearly a general depoliticization and commercialization of the gay subculture. The following are several plausible explanations - some of them contradictory and so in need of much further testing.

Liberalization and De-Mobilization

It is often argued that liberalization of attitudes towards gays is conducive to depoliticization (Duyvendak 1995:167-169; Roth 1998:355). Speaking of all of Germany, Hinzpeter (1997) argues that discrimination against gays has diminished considerably during recent years. He proclaims the end of the gay movement mobilized by discrimination (see also Roth 1998:355 and Duyvendak 1995: 177). Indeed, **discrimination by the state** seems to be on decline.[15] The anti-sodomy paragraph 175 of the Penal Code (which specified a special age of consent for gays in West Germany) was abolished in 1994. In many problematic cases in Leipzig, the municipal gay and lesbian representatives (see above) were in a position to use their influence in the municipal government to achieve solutions in a pragmatic way. In the national mass media as well as in some local ones gays enjoy growing visibility.

As scant as empirical research on **popular attitudes** towards homosexuality in eastern Germany is, it nevertheless casts a shadow on the optimistic view that discrimination is on decline. Shortly after the *Wende*, Starke pointed to declining tolerance of homosexuality among youth. He believed that "new intolerance [was] about to emerge." (Starke 1994:197) This trend continued in the years that followed as right-wing extremism became an ever more widespread phenomenon in eastern Germany. Later studies showed a higher degree of anti-gay violence in the new, eastern German as compared to the old, western German federal states (Bochow 1994:98). Also Kling and Müller (1997:35), who rely on surveys conducted among homosexuals, support the thesis that propensity to anti-gay violence increased in the eastern part of Germany since the *Wende*. They show, moreover, that discriminatory experiences are in fact still widespread among gays and affect almost all aspects of life (Kling and Müller 1997:31-43).

Post-*Wende* developments in Leipzig reflect these eastern German trends. First came anti-gay violence associated with the rise of a right-wing skinhead "scene." The years 1991-1993 witnessed substantial aggression against gays which, although it has subsided, still claims its victims. Several incidents revealed negative attitudes on the part of the police.

However, although anti-gay violence and police discrimination are evident in eastern Germany and in Leipzig, they do not lead to mobilization. Police discrimination against gays led to the establishment of an anti-violence initiative in Leipzig, but in the long run no mobilization followed. A police raid on a gay club in Halle, a town close to Leipzig, immediately before the regional CSD in Saxon-Anhalt, had only some short-term mobilizing effects. Finally, the constant threat for the municipal gay and lesbian representatives to be reduced to only one person or discarded completely could also politicize gays in Leipzig, but it does not do so.[16]

Legal and political support for gays and lesbians it seems, does not necessarily stabilize the gay movement and at the same time it lets political action seem unnecessary. According to the same-sex representatives, some mobilization was achieved as long as concrete goals, such as the installation of same-sex representatives, were pursued. From the very moment that these goals were achieved, mobilization declined rapidly so that it became difficult to inject life into the newly established institutions.

AIDS/HIV

Contrary to many fears immediately after the *Wende*, the number of people with AIDS/HIV did not increase to match Western levels. Between 1990 and 1997 the number of positive HIV-Tests decreased in the West from 6,308 to 4,287, but increased only from 55 to 307 in the East (cited in Herrn et al. 1998:9, see also Bochow 1994:80-81).

AIDS had a considerable mobilizing effect in West Germany before the re-unification (Hinzpeter 1997:82-83; for some other countries see Duyvendak 1996). It was also relevant in shaping identities. As Herrn et al. (1998:135) point out there are still many eastern German gays who believe their region to be an epidemiological island. This belief has distinctive consequences for their preventive behavior - preference for eastern German sex partners. For these reasons, AIDS/HIV could not serve as a mobilizing factor in the east.

Against this background it is also more understandable why the *AHL* as an institution changed its approach from "by-gays-for-gays" to "gay-along-others." Although the *AHL* is important for the "scene" in Leipzig and is willing to engage for gays in Leipzig also in a broader sense, it is conceivable that it could have attracted more gay people, if its capacities were not so much tied to straight issues.

Lost Sense of Security and Migration after the Wende

Following the *Wende*, most eastern Germans have had to cope with regaining their lost sense of security and with finding a new place in transformed society. These tasks gain priority over other aspects of life, including engagement in a gay community. Dramatically increased unemployment levels in eastern Germany seem to have created a climate of equally increased competition. Many gays are less likely to live openly gay since they perceive their homosexuality as a potential stigma, easy to instrumentalize. The economic decline in eastern Germany is furthermore paralleled by signi-

144

ficant income reductions which probably hinder participation in a commercialized subculture (Herrn et al. 1998:125-126; Krakow 1998:31).

Several "experts" I interviewed conveyed the impression that shortly after the *Wende* many gays left Leipzig and eastern Germany in order to go to Berlin or other western German cities with their broad subculture (see also Herrn et al. 1998:129-130). Those who migrated had a strong orientation to the subculture and open gay life style found in the West. Those who stayed are less likely to participate in gay activities or to mobilize.

Intra-movement dynamics: Subculture, commercialization and identity

Before the *Wende*, mobilization mainly relied on the use of social networks. These have declined in size. Tearooms as an infrastructural basis have also decreased in number since municipal administration closed old public lavatories, replacing them with modern versions which are no longer usable as tearooms. However, other institutions emerged, that could easily serve as an equivalent to the old networks as a means of mobilization: *Queer*, radio, better access to straight mass media, and free opportunities to place posters in town. Surprisingly, these opportunities are rarely used by the gay groups in Leipzig. This is true in particular for the *AKH*. This group makes few public relations efforts. Its program is published every half year on a small and inconspicuous flyer.

But it is also the groups' functions that have changed during the last ten years. In the GDR, groups like the *AKH* provided the only opportunity to live an integrated gay life. More fundamentally they were also of considerable importance for finding a partner (see also Herrn et al. 1998:21). They provided selective incentives, which were very effective in mobilizing people, though not yet in a political sense. The changing subculture with a growing share of commercial facilities, together with the possibility of visiting larger western German cities, neutralized this selective incentive. Hence, gay groups must look for new positions and functions in the new society to attract new members, a task which is not accomplished by the *AKH*. Subcultural movements are characterized by strong reliance on internal identity construction (Kriesi et al. 1995:84-85; Roth 1998:354-355). They provide positive identities which constitute the main incentive for an individual to mobilize. This perspective gives rise to a conceptual problem, however: What distinguishes social movements from mere sub-cultures if both construct identities? According to Duyvendak (1995:165) social movements politicize identities in contrast to subcultures which provide solely cultural identities. Gay movements become threatened as soon as commercial subculture opens up the possibility of living positive identities outside the emancipation-movements (Roth 1998:358). From this perspective it is plausible that the rise of a commercial gay subculture in eastern Germany after the *Wende* contributed to the decline of a political gay movement.

However, this is not the whole story. Duyvendak describes how gay movements can handle the tension between politics and the market. He concludes that "in order to 'survive,' this movement should not distance itself too far from its subcultural basis" (1998:165). The *SVD*, which easily can be understood as the political extension of the eastern German movement, refuses to link the political and the subcultural parts of the movement. This then would explain its decline. Institutions like *RosaLinde* became considerably depoliticized and commercialized, although they too have the potential to link subcultural and political issues.

We also have the issue of eastern German gay identity. It is possible that a special kind of identity shaped by the GDR movement has remained and/or been co-shaped by the post-unification developments. This special identity works against the development of a distinct gay movement after the *Wende*. Empirical data supports this notion. Herrn et al. (1998:130-131) describes the eastern

German preference for gay-straight mixed facilities. This tendency may be a remnant from the GDR-times when exclusively gay pubs or discos were not allowed. It can also be seen as a continuation of the East German gay movement which was integrationist, marked by a significant criticism of the subcultural structures in the West. This West subculture was seen as bourgeois, blocking the way to an integrated development of a (socialist) personality (Kowalski 1987:64, see also Herrn et al. 1998:20). Thus it seems likely that a peculiar gay difference-denying identity was formed (see also Starke 1994b:163).

The post-*Wende* institutions seem to hinder mobilization in one more way: The reunified state is far from being as restrictive as its predecessor. State discrimination has declined considerably. To speculate: gay people who in the past focused on a powerful state, today miss a clear opponent against whom they can define their identity. The persistence of this orientation might then also explain why gay activists have not as yet picked up, for example, the homophobic society as a mobilizing issue for the movement. Further research is needed to throw more light on these questions.

NOTES

* I would like to thank the editor whose support and encouragement contributed considerably to this article. I would also like to thank my interviewees for their willingness to provide information. For linguistic help I would like to thank Eron Witzel and the editor.

1. Unlike in the old § 175, which was replaced by this new law, women were also included.
2. Research on this particular aspect is not advanced at all. It is only rumored that the police and/or the state security attempted to apply the so-called pink lists at that point of time, i.e. systematically collected data on homosexuals. As gay-lesbian groups emerged later on, the state security apparatus tried to gather information about people involved in these groups and thereby also about their sexuality. As far as attitudes among members of the security apparatus are concerned, they probably matched general societal and official attitudes. This apparatus did not have its own policy on homosexuality. Rather it implemented what the party-state ordered (Stapel 1999). For more details for the pre-1989 period, see also Kleres 2000.
3. In particular a group of lesbians associated with Ursula Sillge managed to meet regularly at the House of Health (*Haus der Gesundheit*) in Berlin, but quickly dissolved again as group activities were increasingly regimented by psychologists and doctors. In an attempt to organize a GDR-wide meeting of lesbians, the *HIB* let the addresses of some activists circulate through the whole country.
4. Thinius argued this way during the first "Workshop on Socio-Psychological Aspects of Homosexuality" (see below) in 1986. He was member of a research group at Humboldt University (see below) and stood close to the *Sonntags-Club*.
5. By the church-affiliated groups (and also by some seculars) in July 1989: For Acknowledgement and Equality of Lesbians and Gays (*Für Anerkennung und Gleichberechtigung von Lesben und Schwulen*) (in Soukup 1990); by the secular groups in September 1989: Demand Catalogue of the Secular Lesbian and Gay Groups aiming at the further Integration and Equality of Homosexual Citizens (*Forderungskatalog zur weiteren Integration und Gleichstellung homosexueller Bürger*) (in Sillge 1991).
6. The secular text mentioned explicitly the registration of gay/lesbian partnerships at registration offices.
7. Living space was provided by the state in the GDR. Common flats were usually given only to

married couples, while gay and lesbian couples found it nearly impossible to share a common flat.

8. The account presented below is based on expert interviews I conducted with some key figures of the movement and on an analysis of the eastern German monthly *Queer*, from 1993, when it started, to 1997, when it changed into a national publication. More research has to be done in order to do justice to these complex developments.

9. Leipzig and Dresden are the largest towns in eastern Germany after Berlin. They can be compared to Nuremberg or Hanover in western Germany.

10. In the following I will only rarely refer to lesbians. Although there have been exclusively lesbian initiatives (e.g. in Berlin), lesbians and gays were engaged in a common movement before 1989, also in Leipzig. However, in the late 1980s lesbians left the church-affiliated group to establish their own structures. Their movement deserves its own analysis.

11. In 1999 the *SVD* broadened its focus to include lesbians. Thus it is now named *LSVD*.

12. *ESG* is the German abbreviation for Protestant Students' Community (*Evangelische Studenten Gemeinde*).

13. Compared with heterosexual couples there are relative disadvantages for gays and lesbians, e.g. if they want to share a common council flat. Besides that, for bi-national couples it is not possible to marry and thereby get a residence permit for the foreign partner. Although for formal-legal reasons this latter problem cannot be the object of local political decision making, the representatives can for single cases often successfully act as an advocate of gay-lesbian interests.

14. In the entire world, CSD's (or Gay Prides, as they are also called) are organized to remember the events of 1969, when in Christopher Street in New York the riots of gays against their suppression marked the beginning of the post-war gay(-lesbian) movement in the USA and elsewhere.

15. As the growing success of the *SVD* indicates.

16. This also indicates problematic attitudes in parts of the municipal administration (see also Kling and Müller 1997:39) .

REFERENCES

Bochow M. 1994. *Schwuler Sex und die Bedrohung durch AIDS - Reaktionen homosexueller Männer in Ost- und Westdeutschland*. Berlin. Deutsche AIDS-Hilfe

Duyvendak J.W. 1995. "Gay subculture between Movement and Market" in *New social movements in Western Europe. A comparative Analysis*. Edited by H. Kriesi, R. Koopmans, J. W. Duyvendak and M. G. Giugni. London. UCL Press, pp. 165-80

Duyvendak J.W. 1996. "The Depoliticization of the Dutch Gay Identity, or Why Dutch Gays Aren't Queer" in *Queer Theory/Sociology*. Edited by S. Seidman. Cambridge. Blackwell Publishers, pp. 421-38

Giugni M.G. 1995. "Outcomes of New social movements" in *New social movements in Western Europe. A comparative Analysis*. Edited by H. Kriesi, R. Koopmans, J. W. Duyvendak and M. G. Giugni. London. UCL Press, pp. 207-37

Grau G. 1988. "Entscheidung des Obersten Gerichts der DDR zur Homosexualität. Kommentiert von Günther Grau" *Zeitschrift für Sexualforschung* Vol. 1 Nr. 2:162-165

Grau G. 1995. "Sozialistische Moral und Homosexualität. Die Politik der SED und das Homosexuellenstrafrecht 1945 bis 1989 – ein Rückblick" in *Die Linke und das Laster. Schwule Emanzipation und Linke Vorurteile*. Edited by D. Grumbach. Hamburg. MännerschwarmSkript Verlag, pp. 85-141

Grau G. 1996. "Im Auftrag der Partei. Versuch einer Reform der strafrechtlichen Bestimmungen zur Homosexualität in der DDR 1952" *Zeitschrift für Sexualforschung* Vol. 9. Nr. 2:109-130

Hinzpeter W. 1997. *Schöne schwule Welt. Der Schlußverkauf einer Bewegung.* Berlin. Querverlag

Herrn R. and R. Rosenbrock. 1998. *Schwule Lebenswelten im Osten: andere Orte, andere Biographien.* Abschlußbericht. Berlin. Wissenschaftszentrum Berlin für Sozialforschung

Kleres J. 2000. "Gleiche Rechte im Sozialismus" *Forschungsjournal Neue Soziale Bewegungen.* Themenheft 3/2000. *Queering Democracy.* Opladen. Westdeutscher Verlag

Kling U. and K. Müller. 1997. *Studie zur Lebenssituation von Lesben und Schwulen in Sachsen-Anhalt.* Berlin.

Kowalski G. von. 1987. *Homosexualität in der DDR. Ein historischer Abriß.* Marburg. Verlag Arbeiterbewegung und Gesellschaftswissenschaft

Kriesi H., R. Koopmans, J. W. Duyvendak and M. G. Giugni. 1995. *New social movements in Western Europe. A comparative Analysis.* London. UCL Press

Rosenbrock R. 1998. "Aids-Politik, Gesundheitspolitik und Schwulenpolitik" in *Verqueere Wissenschaft?: Zum Verhältnis von Sexualwissenschaft und Sexualreformbewegung in Geschichte und Gegenwart.* Edited by U. Ferdinand, A. Pretzel and A. Seeck. Münster. Lit, pp. 365-378

Roth R. 1998. "(K)Eine Atempause. Neue Soziale Bewegungen als Kontext der Schwulen- und Lesbenbewegung" in *Verqueere Wissenschaft?: Zum Verhältnis von Sexualwissenschaft und Sexualreformbewegung in Geschichte und Gegenwart.* Edited by U. Ferdinand, A. Pretzel and A. Seeck. Münster. Lit, pp. 351-364.

Sillge U. 1991. *Un-sichtbare Frauen. Lesben und ihre Emanzipation in der DDR.* Berlin. Christoph Links Verlag

Soukup J. J., ed. 1990: *Die DDR. Die Schwulen. Der Aufbruch. Versuche einer Bestandsaufnahme.* Göttingen. Schriftenreihe des Waldschlösschens

Stapel E. 1999. *Warme Brüder gegen klate Krieger. Schwulenbewegung in der DDR im Visier der Staatssicherheit.* Magdeburg. Landesbeauftragte für die Unterlagen des Staatssicherheitsdienstes der ehemaligen DDR in Sachsen-Anhalt

Starke K. 1994a. "Schwulenbewegung in der DDR. Interview mit Eduard Stapel" in *Schwuler Osten. Homosexuelle Männer in der DDR.* Edited by K. Starke. Berlin. Christoph Links Verlag, pp. 91-110

Starke K. 1994b. *Schwuler Osten. Homosexuelle Männer in der DDR.* Berlin. Christoph Links Verlag

Steinle K.-H. 1997. "Homophiles Deutschland – Ost und West" in. *Goodbye to Berlin: Hundert Jahre Schwulenbewegung; Eine Ausstellung des Schwulenmuseums und der Akademie der Künste.* Edited by Schwules Museum Berlin and Akademie der Künste Berlin. Ausstellungskatalog. Berlin. Verlag Rosa Winkel, pp. 195-203

DOCUMENTS:

Beauftragte für gleichgeschlechtliche Lebensweisen. 1998. Arbeitsbericht 1998. Leipzig.

INTERVIEWS:

| Matthias Kitlitz | former *AKH*-activist | Leipzig | June 11 1998 |
| Eduard Stapel | *SVD*-chairman | Bismarck | November 22 1998 |

Ursula Sillge	fromer activist of the *Sonntags-Club*	Berlin	December 05 1998
Hync Richter	*AKH*-activist	Leipzig	March 18 1999
Kathrin Sohre	municipal representative for same-sex ways of life	Leipzig	April 27 1999
Peter Thürer	Social worker for the *AHL*	Leipzig	May 17 1999

12. Self-Articulation of the Gay and Lesbian Movement in Hungary after 1989*

Mihály Riszovannij

INTRODUCTION: AFTER THE CHANGE OF REGIME

The self-organization of gays and lesbians in Hungary dates back to the period before 1989.[1] In the beginning of the 1980s some private circles of "conscious" gays contacted Western activists and in 1987 Homosexual Initiative (*Homosexuelle Initiative - HOSI*) Wien organized a regional international meeting for gay activists in Budapest. These first steps, although they were watched by the security forces, cannot be considered an oppositional activity: they were not taken against the ruling system and did not formulate claims against it. On the other hand, this activity was not intended as an "alternative way of socialist life style" like it was the case in East Germany (Thinius 1994).

Homérosz, the first homosexual organization in Hungary was founded in 1986. Its full name was: *Homérosz Lambda National Organization of Homosexuals in Hungary*. It was registered in 1988 before the fall of communism. Its goal was to promote AIDS-prevention among gay men and to organize leisure activities, excursions and counselling. In 1991 its members published a magazine called *Homérosz* that had only two issues.[2] *Homérosz's* confined homosexuality to the private sphere, but fought to achieve minimal tolerance of society, without strengthening visibility and activism. The organization was considered "homophile," although this term was borrowed from a quite different historical and cultural context, the USA of the 1950s.

At the beginning of the 1990s, differences in style and aims emerged. Some members decided to separate, and in 1991 they founded the *Lambda Budapest Friendship Society. Lambda* activists aimed at fewer but more concrete things: publishing a magazine for gays and participating in the organization of gay events. But they acted in a more radical and direct way engaging in conflicts with state organizations. *Homérosz,* which was supported by the National Health Care Organization (*NEVI*), tried to avoid any kind of open criticism.

For a long time, there were only these two officially recognized, that is, registered, gay organizations in Hungary. Besides the steps towards building a community, they (co-)organized some public actions, such as World AIDS Days, and initiated changes in the legal system to eliminate discriminatory passages. At the same time, at the beginning of the 1990s, several smaller groups were organized to meet the special demands of religious people, married homosexuals, hikers. These groups have not been registered and avoided publicity. They deal with certain aspects of community-building.

In 1991, a gathering of homosexual students was organized at the Eötvös Loránd University in Budapest. As a group active at a "work place," they caused aversion among the authorities of the university. Their flyers were torn down and they were given a warning not to "advertise sex." The reason for that grotesque decision was their *name*: the word "homosexual" contained the word "sex," so the Vice-Dean saw a promotion of sexuality in it. This group existed

150

approximately till 1995. They offered meetings, organized lectures, invited famous guests. Later, some members of the university group became founders or activists of other gay and lesbian organizations.

An Attempt at Centralization: The Case of Szivárvány

The separation of the Hungarian gay and lesbian movement, the lack of sufficient public measures and legal programs made many people rethink the possibilities of action. In 1994, the "Rainbow" (*Szivárvány*) Association was founded (*Szivárvány Társulás a Melegek Jogaiért =Rainbow Association for Gay Rights*). *Szivárvány* made an attempt to change former structures and styles. On the one hand, its founders wanted to be a co-ordinating forum bringing smaller groups together (just as their Czech or Polish counterparts). On the other hand, they planned to launch new projects to enhance community-building, legal remedy and a more critical reflection on sexuality in the whole society. They wanted to recruit an energetic and active staff which would not be afraid to appear in public. They appealed to the Court for official registration. The application was turned down for two reasons. The word *meleg* appeared in the name of the organization and no minimum age-limit was set for the members.

The first "reason" reveals a typical problem of language-policy and the question of self-naming. In Hungarian, like in other languages, there are several words that denote people who are attracted to the same sex, but each of them has different stylistic features and connotations. Because of its medical-official overtone, the word "homosexual" became less and less frequently used by homosexuals. The pejorative word *buzi* (similar to English *fag*) did not gain acceptability like English *queer* or German *Schwul* did. In the US and Germany homosexual people started to use these pejorative expressions for themselves (inversion) and in the process the negative connotation disappeared. In Hungarian, however, the use of the word *buzi* remained offensive as it is rarely used within the community itself. The third choice was the word *meleg* ("warm," from the German *warmer Bruder*). It has neither medical nor pejorative connotations, and, furthermore, is used for self-naming by both men and women. So the leaders of *Szivárvány* were right to choose the word *meleg*. The Court however thought the word was too confidential and was not compatible with the standard Hungarian norm. *Szivárvány* turned to the Linguistic Institute of the Hungarian Academy of Sciences which came to the conclusion that the word *meleg* cannot be disapproved on linguistic or stylistic grounds. This expert opinion resulted in that only one reason for the denial was left.

The other, more severe, objection was the age limit. Although in Hungary the age of consent for homosexual relationships is 18, the organizers of *Szivárvány* did not take it into consideration because the association was founded not to facilitate (sexual) contacts but for legal protection. The Court's most astonishing objection was that within the organization a morally "bad pattern" could disturb the psychosexual development of the members who are under 18. This caused a great stir and initiated public reflection on the general right of association (Kis 1997). Many prominent Hungarians signed a support statement. Eventually the denial became effective. After this point, though the decentralization of the movement remained, the possibilities for further steps had to be reconsidered. The results, and so the current spectrum of the gay and lesbian organizations will be shown below.

Opening the Domestic Partnership for Same-Sex Couples

The unfathomable features of the attitudes towards emancipatory politics can be observed in the variety of sometimes positive, sometimes negative official decisions. The modification of the paragraph regulating domestic partnership, one of the most succesful achievements of the gay and lesbian movement, was induced by a civil initiative. It was not preceded by any social protests or demonstrations, nor any public "discourse." In 1993 *Homérosz* appealed to the Constitutional Court for a decision on whether the passage of the law saying that a domestic partnership is a relation "between a man and a woman" is anti-constitutional or not. After three years the Court declared that this passage is anti-constitutional and ordered the parliament to modify it within a year. The modification took place in May 1996, without any debate. Except for a demagogue speech of a populist politician, the parties agreed to the modification because it did not directly affect laws considering marriage, family and children. The event had greater echo outside of Hungary because it was not only unique in Eastern Europe but was rare in Western Europe too. This modification, however, does not mean that there were substantial changes in the views on sexuality. A few years later, in 1999, this unexpected succes was followed by a "Concept on Family Policy" which declared homosexuality to be a "deviance endangering families." Furthermore, the age of consent remains higher for homosexuals (18 years of age) compared to heterosexuals (14 years) - a state of law which contradicts EU-norms and -proposals.

Steps towards Publicity

One of the characteristics of gay and lesbian organizations in general is that, besides private events, they all organize public programs, (protest) actions, or events that can be visited by anyone. In Hungary, this process of literal coming out was gradual, too. At the beginning of the 1990s cultural events were the major area of gay and lesbian publicity in the form of book presentations as well as film- and theater-premièrs. These events were officially not "gay" but were "marked" by the presence of gays and lesbians. The first opportunity to demonstrate presence in the street was the International World AIDS Day, held on the 1st of December, 1991.[3] Although it is not an especially gay event, a great number of homosexuals take part in it.

The first exclusively gay and lesbian public event was the "Pink Picnic," an open-air meeting in the Buda Hills in 1992. It was no longer a reserved excursion but an organized event offering several programs and using gay and lesbian symbols in public. But it was far from public: apart from some tourists who got lost, only those people went there who looked for it. Of course, the symbolic meaning of the Picnic (which takes place annually) was enormous, some people even called this event "the Gay Pride Day." But the real Pride Day, including the obligatory Parade, arrived later. The next step after the Picnic was to organize cultural festivals, with films, panel discussions, lectures, etc. The first Gay and Lesbian Film Festival was organized in 1993, in connection with the World AIDS Day and the second one in June 1997, at the same time when Western gay and lesbian communities organize their Pride Days, but without a Parade. The first Pride Parade was held in September 1997, prepared without much publicity. Between 200 and 250 persons took part in the first gay and lesbian march which was a great succes at that time. With this step an international gay and lesbian festival was established in Hungary and the most important act of mass public appearance was accomplished too. During this process the main supporters were such international institutions like the Central European University, the Goethe Institut or the Institut Français. They provided room and hosted these cultural events. In 1998 the Festival (enriched by exhibitions, reading out literary works, round-table talks) and the Pride

Parade were unified in the Gay and Lesbian Pride Week and, hopefully, set a precedent for the future.

THE GAY AND LESBIAN MOVEMENT IN THE END OF THE NINETIES

Although *Homérosz*, the first organization of Hungarian homosexuals, had taken the first steps and started several - succesful - initiatives, by now it has lost its dynamism. As the founding of *Szivárvány* showed, *Homérosz* was not able to serve as a potential co-ordinator either. In the middle of the 1990s, it existed only formally, without any public activities. The former activists either lost their interest or started new projects outside *Homérosz*. The "new generation," socialized politically after 1990, has not even joined it, but rather other organizations, like *Háttér* (see below). In their last meeting, in 1999, the remaining members of *Homérosz* decided to dissolve their organization. Today the Hungarian gay and lesbian movement is made up of the following registered organizations:

Lambda Budapest

As mentioned above, founders of *Lambda Budapest* separated from *Homérosz* in 1991. One of its most important activities has been publishing "The Others" (*Mások*), Hungary's only gay magazine, since April 1991, in about 3,000 copies. The number of the actual readers are difficult to estimate because copies usually circulate in small groups of friends. *Mások* tries to cover nearly every aspect of gay life in Hungary. It publishes news from Hungary and abroad, comments on governmental decisions that concern gay people, follows the media discourse about homosexuality, informs its readers about cultural programs, publishes reviews of books, films and performances, and, last but not least, features a large section of personal advertisements. Thus, the magazine is the most important forum for gay people in Hungary as it is the only way of finding information on and expressing opinions about gay life. The latter is realized by a section called "readers' letters."

The editors of *Mások* are very sensitive to any homophobic statements coming from the media or the field of politics. They protest against discriminatory decisions, such as the Constitutional Court's decision that maintained the difference between the age of consent for heterosexuals and homosexuals. The editors also write petitions together with other organizations, as was the case with the debate in parliament on the registered partnership. They raised their voices against the inexcusable tone of some politicians. The magazine puts people who need legal or any kind of help in touch with experts. The editors are consistent in their principles, put great emphasis on coming out and have a liberal orientation. This is not always approved of, not even within the gay community and is the reason for sometimes quite fierce "political" criticism of the readers.

Meleg Háttér

The final denial of the registration of *Szivárvány* by the Supreme Court divided the activists. There were some who considered the reasons for the denial to be unacceptable and, demanding legal remedy, turned to the Human Rights Commitee of the European Parliament, whereas those who pressed for immediate action suggested a compromise in order to become registered and to start organizational work. Thus in 1995 they formed a new group called *Háttér - (Support) Society for Homosexuals* and declared that every member has to be over 18. They

153

aimed at launching projects concerning gay and lesbian people. As first they established a telephone helpline that provides mental care and gives information on gay and lesbian life. They recruited staff which consisted of volunteers and educated them with the professional help of psychologists and psychiatrists. The candidates also took part in workshops dealing with consultation and HIV/AIDS-prevention. The helpline started its operation by Christmas 1995 and has been working since then every day for 5 hours with 2 operators daily. Since the beginning of its operation, *Háttér* has launched many additional projects such as HIV/AIDS-prevention, specifically for gays and lesbians (compiling and spreading condom-packs and advisory material). It co-organizes a discussion group for young lesbians and gays, called *Flamingo*. *Háttér's* members participate in conferences on family law and on other relevant topics. They also organize training for social workers.

Háttér is not introverted and it does not restrict homosexuality to the private sphere. It is the major organizer of nearly every gay and lesbian event (cultural festivals, Gay Pride Day, World AIDS Day), has relationships with international gay and lesbian organizations and its representatives participate in international courses and conferences. *Háttér* is a member of the International Lesbian and Gay Association (ILGA) and of the International Gay and Lesbian Youth Organization (IGLYO). In 1996 it was the co-organizer of the first IGLYO East European Regional Conference in Budapest. In 1997 in Cologne at the ILGA World Conference one of its members was elected to the ILGA Board. Members of *Háttér* became familiar with movement strategies and community forms in the West and were able to convey Western experiences to gay and lesbian people in Hungary, making it possible for them to make comparisons, to reflect, or, in certain cases, to adopt useful ideas. In June 2000 *Háttér* edited a book on the topic of sexual orientation in the EU and in Hungary which is in part a transaltion of an ILGA-publication. It has been distributed to the members of parliament, lawyers and other organizations.

Lesbians in Hungary: Coming to Terms

When dealing with homosexual organizations, it makes sense to analyze how women take part in a homosexual movement, how much they are (under-)represented and how, if at all, they can co-operate with gay men.[4]

In Hungary, lesbians are much less visible than gay men. In the commercial subculture, they are sometimes only "tolerated guests." No exclusively lesbian places of entertainment exist. However, some initiatives towards "women only" programs have been taken, but opening bars exclusively for women failed for financial reasons: the number of guests was so small that it lead to bankruptcy.

As for public opinion, homosexuality, first of all, means male homosexuality. Stereotypes describing homosexuality (like the transvestite, the seducer or the paedophile) and homophobic statements are almost always related to gay men. This certainly does not mean that lesbians are not exposed to homophobia, or that they are not endangered in certain occupations because of their sexuality. Male dominance usually means excluding lesbians from the category of "homosexuality." A remarkable example: during a talk-show on TV a well-known (male) actor responded to the question "Would you feel that your child is in danger if he/she were educated by a homosexual teacher?" by saying that he had nothing to do with this problem because he had two daughters...

One of the consequences of concealment is that even though stereotypes about lesbians are not as strict as those about gay men, there are no images of lesbians that are closer to reality.

In reports on lesbians there is an over-sexualizing tendency; the first thing they are asked about is their attitude towards men. One of the most common questions is whether they have ever thought of having sexual intercourse with men or not, and if not, why. As original pictures of lesbian lives are not available, they are illustrated by the male heterosexual image of "lesbianism" - female striptease dancers embracing each other.

In order to change this, lesbians started to organize themselves. The question was whether or not they wanted to co-operate with gay men. Experience during the past years shows that the co-operative tendency dominates. One of its grounds is the lesbians' strained relationship with feminist organizations. Although feminism has a tradition in Hungary, after the change of regime it was difficult to re-establish it. Feminist groups have few members and are exposed to strong prejudice. They are often charged with "male-hatery" and denounced as lesbians. Feminist organizations do not act on lesbians' behalf in spite of the fact that they have active lesbian members. Although lesbians sometimes use the infrastructure of the feminist groups, their presence is not acknowledged by feminists in public events or round-table discussions. Their special needs or problems are not part of feminist programs.

Lesbians have taken part in the activities of Hungarian homosexual organizations since the beginning. In the early period the situation was similar to that in East Germany. Men predominated but there were a few - active - women as well. Because of the lack of a separatist feminist tradition, such as in West Germany in the 1970s and early 1980s, their shared position in many conflicts (like discrimination by the law or, to a certain extent, common prejudices), the advantages of appearing together in applications for financial support and, for the most part, the lack of enough women who are ready to act, the co-operation with gay men is very strong. Unfortunately, even nowadays the proportion of women in mixed groups is much less than the "theoretically demanded" 50%. The situation is similar to that in the homosexual media. The magazine *Mások* has never become a gay *and* lesbian medium. Although the editors are open towards female authors and they always publish their articles dealing with lesbian issues, most of the topics and all of the illustrations aim at gay men. Consequently the readers are mostly men, and any kind of innovation, such as pictures of women in the magazine, to win the interest of lesbians is impossible. The editors believe that the male readers would quit long before the magazine could gain a sufficient number of lesbian readers.

In *Háttér* the proportion of women has always been significant, currently approximately one third of the members. They are also represented in the board. *Labrisz*, the first lesbian publication, was also started by women from *Háttér*. In order to articulate their special needs, some of them founded the women-only *Labrisz Lesbian Assotiation* in 1999. Among its aims there is (1) the publication of a magazine and a book series (the first volume appeared in 2000) that are to strengthen lesbian visibility; (2) finding public settings for discussion; (3) networking with international lesbian organizations; (4) building a vital lesbian community; and (5) taking part in the organization of common gay and lesbian events. The major part of these aims focuses on founding new communities, but they are not averse to publicity or to determined action. Recently the *Assotiation* received funding for an education project which has enabled the activists to start a letter campaign addressed to all secondary schools. In the letter they ask school teachers to invite them to hold classes at their schools so that they can inform both teachers and students about homosexuality. They want to challenge homophobia, stereotypes and ignorance at school in this particular manner.

Other Initiatives

The *Habeas Corpus Working Group*, founded by *Szivárvány*'s former members, is not an explicitly gay and lesbian organization, but for their interests it is a relevant one. As its name suggests, it mainly deals with problems connected to the human body and provides legal remedy to those who suffer disadvantages or insults because of their sexual orientation, body traits, nourishment, smoking habits, etc. Although at the first glimpse *Habeas Corpus* limits sexuality to one's body it actually draws attention to some hidden relations and social mechanisms that control and regulate the body and, through this, sexuality. This organization consists of only a few but enthusiastic activists. They have organized a series of public lectures ("Habeas Corpus Evenings") on social aspects of sexuality since 1997, provided legal assistance and even suggested modifications of the law. They do not consider themself a homosexual organization and tend to overstep the categories of sexual identity, suggesting that it is of minor importance. That is why their role is significant not in building up the community but in anti-discriminatory politics.

CHARACTERISTICS OF THE GAY AND LESBIAN MOVEMENT

Mobilizing Power

Depending on whether we speak about people who appear at public events or think of those who are reached by the activities of gay and lesbian organizations and hereby may join the community, our mobilization estimates will differ. In 1999 at the Gay Pride Parade, there were an estimated 300 people, but at the cultural festival more than 3,000 tickets were sold. In 2000 the number of participants in the Parade, which began with a demonstration before the parliament where a petition against the anomalies in the legal system was handed over, went up to 2,000 people. If we look at accessibility in a broader sense, we can refer to about 500-600 callers at *Háttér's* helpline monthly or to the 3,000 readers of *Mások*. There are great differences between the number of gay men and lesbian women as well as between the number of participants at open versus closed events. The representatives of lesbian women stress that their group, which consists of about 50 members, not only attend the monthly discussions, called "*Labrisz* Evenings," regularly, but nearly all of them attend the Gay Pride Parade, whereas hundreds of gay men join the half-open events, such as the New Year- and Easter-Parties or ship-tours, but few of them take part in the Parade itself.

Number of Members, Structures, Symbols

The number of activists in the gay and lesbian movement is rather small. The largest organization is *Háttér*, with approximately 60 members. Most of them work at the helpline or in other projects. *Lambda's* leaders report 20 members who are mainly the authors of the magazine. *Labrisz* was founded by 12 women. At present they are at the stage of recruiting members. We should add, however that many people work for two or more organizations so there are overlaps, but also that these organizations are not political parties and do not have (and do not encourage) passive membership, so that these numbers indicate activists. The majority of the organizations have tried several organizational structures and, finally, they chose the "president + board" form because it makes the organizing process and responsibility-sharing easier.

During the past years gay and lesbian people in Hungary learnt and borrowed a lot of elements from symbols used in Western gay and lesbian communities. A generally known and used symbol is the rainbow flag. *Lambda Budapest* puts the Greek letter "lambda" on their flag. On the emblem of *Háttér* a pink triangle can be made out. The origin of this symbol has never brought about any controversies within gay or lesbian communities, everybody who likes it, uses it. Lesbians, as the name of their organization and magazine shows, use *Labrisz*, the hatchet with two edges, the ancient greek symbol of female power. These symbols appear at gay and lesbian events as parts of decorations or banners.

Protest Forms, Recourse to Violence
    Aside from one incident during a hiking trip, none of the gay and lesbian organizations have ever resorted to violence. Forms of protest include petitions to state-institutions, protest-letters to the media, non-violent demonstrations and speeches. None of the activists has ever been insulted publicly. This is due to the fact that most of them avoid publicity and there are no open gay and lesbian institutions that can be reached easily except for bars, but these are not a part of the social "scene," such as a community centre or a book-shop. There was, however, a remarkable event in 1992 when the police appeared in the flat of the editors of *Mások*. Referring to an investigation into a murder act, they demanded the subscribers' and the advertisers' lists. As the editors refused, they were "invited" to the police station. Since they managed to contact a reporter of the Hungarian Radio, the event became news. As a result, the two editors were released. Of course, the lack of violence against organizations and their activists does not mean that gay or lesbian people are not injured mentally or physically, sometimes even by the police. The phenomenon of gay-bashing (connected to cruising and prostitution) is present in Hungary as well, but these events are seldom made public, and are less documented/investigated. Co-operation between the police and gay organizations, such as is found in Germany, for example, is not yet found.

Relationships with Politicians, Parties and Business
    As for the politicians, the majority of them relegates sexuality and sexual identity to the private sphere, trying to avoid taking a stand on these issues. In party programs we cannot find any reference to homosexuals with the exception of the extreme right wing "Party of Hungarian Truth and Life" (*MIÉP*), which declared that anyone who is homosexual, "freemason" or atheist may not be the member of the party. Being commited to human rights, the "Association of Free Democrats" (*SZDSZ*) has protested against any discrimination of minorities, but until recently it was not too self-confident regarding gays and lesbians. In their speeches and publications, some of their leaders support anti-discriminatory politics but they try to speak/act as private individuals, not as leaders of a party. Nearly nothing is mentioned in support of gay and lesbian identity or efforts at community building. Sometimes local organizations of the party help gay or lesbian groups and may offer space for events. The *Hungarian Socialist Party*, since it is the biggest party in Hungary, has a decisive word in every case, is not sure yet whether it should support gay and lesbian rights like its counterparts in Western Europe. Conservative parties, with reference to traditional family values, reject making an issue of homosexuality and of the equality of homosexual relationships.
    Solidarity with homosexuals or speaking publicly at gay and lesbian events is considered risky for a politician because he/she would be in "danger" of denounciation for being homo-sexual. Party politicians say that open support repels votes. It might be a good sign of change that the leading personalities of the *SZDSZ* made public appearances and spoke at the Gay and Les-

bian Cultural Festival's opening ceremonies in 1999 and 2000. On the occasion of the Pride Parade 2000 the president of the *SZDSZ* for the first time officially met with a delegation of gay and lesbian activists to discuss their current problems.

Business keeps away from advertising regularly in gay magazines, as it is afraid of loosing non-gay customers. Unlike the companies in Western Europe and the USA, the representatives of multi-national companies have not understood yet the potential consumer force of many gay men. So in Hungary gay and lesbian organizations and publications can hope for little financial support from commercial organizations. Occasional donations from business people who sympathise with the movement constitute rare exceptions.

Public Resonance

Because of the lack of a gay and lesbian umbrella-organization and spokes(wo)men on gay and lesbian issues, journalists or researchers who are interested in authentic information can turn to the few activists (the "professional homosexuals," as one of them put it) who are willing to appear in public. A number of newspapers quote from *Mások*, positively or negatively, depending on their point of view. There have been many articles and reports about *Háttér* and the members are often asked about partnerships, adoption or (according to the public stereotype) paedophilia. For a few years, the Gay and Lesbian Cultural Festival and the Pride Parade have become a central topic in the media - a serious public resonance, even if the reports and especially their illustrations (focusing on the few transvestites) are biased. In the extreme right wing media, the issue of homosexuality and the results of anti-discriminatory policy are considered as an "attack on the Hungarian nation" leading to "moral decay." The supporters of the gay and lesbian movement, such as the liberal politicians and thinkers, are said to be the executors of a "nation-corrupting policy." The homophobic discourse is connected to a nationalist, anti-Western discourse.[5]

Financial Resources

In Hungary most of the NGOs have financial difficulties but, when the money is distributed, gay and lesbian organizations have worse acces to funds because of social prejudices. None of them has permanent or long-term state support, even if they can prove that their activities are of public use (as is the case with *Háttér's* helpline). *Lambda Budapest* covers its costs from selling *Mások*. Although AIDS-prevention is a constant and recurrent topic in the magazine, the National AIDS Committee, which is responsible for distributing the money for AIDS-prevention, gives only occasional financial support to them. *Háttér* is a non-profit organization so it fully depends on subsidies. During the years it turned to a number of foundations and committees and received money from the EU Phare-Program, the Foundation of the Dutch Embassy, the parliament, the General Assembly of Budapest, the Soros Foundation, etc. Their support, however is occasional and is not enough for an optimal operation. The organizers of *Labrisz* also turned to Western foundations. A special source is the 1% of the income-tax paid every year to NGOs. The more gays, lesbians and their supporters know of this source, the more money they can secure.

Relations to other Organizations, Allied Movements

The co-operation with religious institutions is hindered by the hidden and sometimes open homophobia of the Catholic and the Protestant Churches. Even the gay and lesbian religious groups cannot - openly - mediate between the churches and the movement. Minority organizations are similarly resistant even if the resolution of problems of multiple discrimination, such as gay or lesbian gypsies, could be solved in a co-operative form. The participation in sex education and AIDS prevention is accidental, depending on the number of invitations of activists, mainly those of *Háttér's*. Even the professional social or health-care organizations with which *Háttér* has contacts are very often homophobic and reject both co-operation and the exchange of experiences.

In addition to *Habeas Corpus*, a "body-political" organization, another allied association is the "Association for the Rights of Liberty" (*Társaság a Szabadságjogokért*), which deals with the legal aspects of sexuality, abortion, drugs and diseases. It helps people who have conflicts with the law for these reasons.

The possibilities of co-operation between the gay/lesbian and the feminist movement should be re-considered on both sides. Feminists often emphasize that the problem of sexual minorities cannot be solved without re-thinking gender and criticizing patriarchy. But feminists are often one-sided, too, when they are campaigning for women's rights and do not press the issue of (homo)sexuality nor represent lesbians. On the other hand, those gay men, who espouse sexist views should be more involved in rethinking general problems of gender and give more space to lesbians in their organizations. These two processes and the elimination of mutual prejudices may bring about a co-operation that is now successfully working in the Western world.

SUMMARY

The Hungarian gay and lesbian movement plays a significant role in stimulating societal tolerance and the process of rethinking the attitudes towards sexuality and gender. At present it does not make any clear distinction between politicial activism and community building. Its activities include both institution-building and encouraging participation. In this sense, it is not a traditional *mass* movement, but should be considered as a movement promoting social change. As for the future, its members should work more intensively towards creating conditions conducive to a free choice of sexual identity, for legal equality, and for proper community networks with-in a civil society. This seems to be a bit distant in Hungary, but we can say that the organizations are over the initial steps. More people, however, are needed who are willing to appear publicly and are ready to act. This, in turn, requires civil space, a gay and lesbian community, which can help its members to accept their own sexuality as well as to articulate and assert their interests. It follows that these things are interdependent. It is important that those who are in charge of representing other people's interests should act on the basis of the same principle against the (sometimes quite authoritative and unpredictable) official decisions. The development of the gay and lesbian movement as well as the legal and social situation of gays and lesbians are important questions and, in the context of catching up with Europe and joining the EU, a test for Hungarian democracy.

NOTES:

* I would like to thank Bea Sándor, Géza Juhász, László Láner and László Mocsonaki for their help in data collection and their critical comments.

1. For the social history of homosexuality, see Toth 1994.
2. One of the leaders of *Homérosz*, a psychiatrist, who was the first homosexual to appear publicly on television, often talked about the origin of homosexuality from a psychoanalytic-biologist perspective. This is why some experts labelled him an "essentialist."
3. It has taken place every year since 1991.
4. For an analysis of lesbians within the civil society, see Kremmler 1998.
5. About the public discourses in details, see Riszovannij 2001.

REFERENCES

Kis J. 1997. "A Szivárvány-teszt" (The Rainbow-Test). In the auhtor's *Az állam semlegessége* (The Neutrality of the State). Budapest. Atlantisz, pp. 335-362

Kremmler K. 1998. *Lesben und Zivilgesellschaft im postsozialistischen Ungarn*. Magisterarbeit, Institut für Europäische Ethnologie. Humboldt Universität. Berlin

Riszovannij M. 2001. "Media Discourses on Homosexuality in Hungary". In *Gender in Transition in Eastern and Central Europe Proceedings*. Edited by Gabriele Jähnert et al. Berlin. Trafo Verlag, pp. 254-260

Takács J. 1997. "(Homo)Sexual Politics. Theory and Practice" in the special issue of *REPLIKA - Hungarian Social Science Quarterly* entitled *Ambiguous Identities in the New Europe*. Budapest, pp. 93-103

Thinius B. 1994. *Aufbruch aus dem grauen Versteck - Ankunft im bunten Ghetto. Randglossen zu Erfahrungen schwuler Männer in der DDR und in Deutschland Ost*. Berlin. BVH

Tóth L. ed. 1994. *A homoszexualitásról* (On Homosexuality). Budapest. T-Twins

13. A Child of a Young Democracy: The Polish Gay Movement, 1989 - 1999*

Krzysztof Kliszczyński
expanded by Helena Flam

The most recent 4th of July was celebrated as the 10th anniversary of regaining librty in Poland. The ten years which have passed since the semicontested elections of June 1989 were the times of great changes for the Polish gay society.[1]

Ten years ago the word "gay" did not exist in Poland at all - people of homosexual orientation were called scornfully "faggot;" there was no *legal* gay organization, no gay newspapers, and no clubs. Homosexuality was a taboo - it appeared only in gross jokes or as a cheap piece of sensationalism from police files. Gay community, with its approximately several hundred thousand members (Adamska 1998:135,53), one of the most numerous Polish minorities, lived deeply hidden. Only its *samizdat* testified to its existence in the last decade before the downfall of communism. It was necessary to subvert communism in order for Polish gays to overcome their fear and demand their rights. There is no exaggeration in saying that the Polish gay movement is a child of our young democracy.

IT IS NOT JUST A MATTER OF LAW: THE STATE-AUTHORIZED RAID AND MOBILIZATION PRIOR TO 1989

Before 1989 it was very difficult to find any information about the homosexual movement in Poland. It does not mean that it did not exist - it was just hidden. People from the homosexual movement of the past say that their organization was a greater secret than the trade union "Solidarity" (*Solidarność*)[2] once it was banned.

This state of matters is rather surprising since from the legal point of view Poland was one of the first few European countries to decriminalize homosexual relations among adults. The first criminal code of independent Poland which was modelled after the Napoleonic code and was passed in 1932 broke completely with the then obligatory practice of repression. The wording of the code, however, did not change people's attitudes towards sexual minorities. Also during the interwar period (1918-1939) homosexuality remained a taboo, reserved only for "artistic" circles.

At the time of the Second World War Poland did not escape Nazi repression directed against gays, but luckily it was not as intense as in Germany. During communist rule (1945-1989) decriminalization of sexual relations was merely the effect of a foresight of the legislators from 1932. According to the official state ideology, homosexuality was a symptom of "Western depravity" and did not fit socialist morality. Using the tactics of silence, as was also the case with drug addiction, the government tried to create an impression that homosexuality simply did not exist.

Although already towards the end of the 1960s and in the liberal 1970s sporadic serious articles about homosexuality appeared in prestigeous journals (Adamska 1998:118-119), when the trade union "Solidarity" was legalized first changes in the press attitudes towards this "problem" could be noted. In 1981, for example, an important weekly, "Politics" (*Polityka*), published an article about the negative attitude of Poles towards homosexuality and described the inconspicuous gay subculture in Warsaw (see Pietkiewicz 1981 and Selerowicz 1994). The imposition of the martial law on December 13, 1981 put a break on these first attempts to lift the "conspiracy of silence," a silence which lasted until AIDS appeared in the arena of international politics. In 1985 *Polityka* once again let Polish gays speak (see Darski 1985). The title of the article was "We are different" and constituted the first attempt to have a public discussion about the gay situation in Poland. It strongly contrasted with sensationalist or medical-scientific reports on homosexuality prevalent at the time. Journalists or experts dominated the media until the end of the 1980s when this trend was broken (Adamska 1998:119,121). Typical of the new approach was a television program aired by TVP/II in 1987 in which the activists of the Warsaw Homosexual Movement participated.

In this discussion context the first attempts to establish formal gay organizations were made. The Austrian organization Homosexual Initiative Wien (*Homosexuelle Initiative - HOSI*), owing to its geographic proximity, was able to help the incipient gay movement on this side of the Iron Curtain. It took care of its co-ordination. The attempt to bring into existence a gay organization met with a very unfavorable reaction on the part of the communist authorities, however. In November 1985 the police carried out an all-Polish operation, "Hyacinth," on the order of the Minister of Home Affairs (see also Sklerowicz 1994:22 and Adamska 1998:99). Operation "Hyacinth" consisted of the compulsory registration of personal data of hundreds of gays. In larger towns they were whisked from their clubs, interrogated and fingerprinted. Interrogators asked about friends and lovers. They set up archives. The official reason was the apparent criminal tendency of the gay society and the threat of AIDS. Gays are convinced, however, that the real intention behind the operation was to intimidate potential movement leaders and thus to prevent any gay organizing.

Gays responded with mobilization to this act of state repression. In 1985-1986 the first coming out in the press, the first gay paper *Filo Express*, and the first informal gay group formation all took place (Adamska 1998:99). In 1987 the first gay centers finally were created - in Warsaw, Gdańsk, Łódź and Wrocław. Two of them, "The Warsaw Homosexual Movement" and a group from Wrocław, were admitted to ILGA, the International Lesbian and Gay Association.

At the turn of 1987 and 1988 activists decided that it was time for the legalization of the movement. People from The Warsaw Homosexual Movement applied for legal registration in Warsaw. Despite considerable concessions (for example, the word "homosexual" was removed and the name of the organization was changed to the "Society for Preventing and Fighting with AIDS"), the authorities refused to register this "dangerous" association.

THE FIRST NATIONAL ORGANIZATION AND ITS LOCAL HEIRS

In the 1989 Polish parliamentary "June" elections, which subverted the communist system, as well as the "Autumn of nations" in Central Europe finally brought the long expected turning point. In October the same year in Warsaw a founders' meeting of The Lambda Association of Groups, all-Polish gay and lesbian organization, took place. On February 23, 1990 the Provincial Court in Warsaw registered this first Polish gay organization.

According to its statutes, Lambda activities focused on three areas:
- Propagating social tolerance towards homosexuality,
- Forming positive consciousness of homosexual men and women *(work in this field consisted in helping gays to self-acceptance and coming out),*

- Propagating preventive actions against the expansion of AIDS and co-operation in struggle with this "dice" with other institutions.

The first three years after the peaceful revolution were the euphoric years in the development of the Polish gay movement. By 1992 Lambda Groups spread to 15 big cities. For a certain period of time 7 gay magazines were published (among others "Warsaw Gay News" in English). Many gay bars, restaurants and discos appeared. Some of them went bankrupt soon after they were opened. When the Lambda Association still worked as an all-Polish organization, it joined a series of concerts organized under the banner: *"Love - don't kill."* Many musicians openly declaring themselves as gays took part in those concerts.

During the whole time of its activity The Lambda Association of Groups, founded on the basis of earlier informal activities and continuing the traditions of the movement from before 1989, was not very formalized. There were no exact member lists and one of the reasons for the existence of so many Lambda Groups whose number has been changing from year to year was the fact that three people were enough to establish one. Weakly co-ordinated, with very few permanent activists, and limited access to new communication technologies, this first national gay organization found it difficult to consolidate itself (Adamska 1998:133-134). From the point of view of one of its prominent critics, the editor of *Inaczej*, the Lambda Association did not manage to set up an effective organization nor supply a group of respected and flexible leaders; on the contrary, step by step most discussions turned into arguments and bitter mutual accusations (Wróblewski 1999). As the leaders failed to gain respect of their gay and lesbian following, the organization declined, even though several resuscitation attempts were made. It also had to face a measure of hostility coming from the commercial gay press. In view of its inertia and very poor attendance at the national meetings, its activists decided to dissolve it in 1996.

Although a national Association was replaced by many local organizations, there is much continuity in terms of activists and facilities they occupy. At the present, the following gay or gay-and-other organizations exist (see also Adamska 1998:131-133):

- "Lambda-Warszawa" Association (*Lambda-Warsaw*) in Warsaw,
- "Lambda-Poznań" Association in Poznań,
- "Lambola" Association in Olsztyn,
- "Rainbow" Association (*Tęcza*) in Wrocław,
- "Gdańsk Initiative" Association (*Inicjatywa Gdańska*) in Gdańsk,
- "Allos" Association in Katowice (still in process of organization),
- A Group of Lesbians and Gays from Świętokrzyski Region in Kielce (still in process of organization),
- "OLA-Archives" in Warsaw (a lesbian group),
- "Be with Us" Association (*Bądź z Nami*) in Warsaw (engaged in AIDS prevention),
- "Tolersex" Association in Warsaw,
- "Youth Aid Association" (*Towarzystwo Pomocy Młodzieży*) in Warsaw - an organization financed by local government also providing help to young gays and lesbians.

All these organizations (both entirely gay and only partly focused on homosexual problems) pursue the aims previously pursued by the Association of Lambda Groups - propagating tolerance towards gays and supplying aid to the members of this minority. The fact that there is no one national gay organization fortunately does not influence the quality of gay activities (but see note 4). It is much easier to work where members live. Sometimes it is also less difficult to receive funds from a local sponsor for a local organization than from a national institution.

PUBLIC MASS MEDIA AND THE GAY PRESS

The lack of positive information was one important reason for the creation of the grotesque stereotype of a homosexual - a stereotype of a pervert who depraves juveniles or of a campy queer. Well aware of this, today gay and gay-and-other organizations disseminate information relying on leaflets as well as on TV and radio programs in which gays take part. Contacts with the press and groups interested in homosexuality are cultivated. Politicians as well as journalists note, however, that public television has renounced the task of spreading information about homosexuality (Wróblewski 1999). In this respect, the press and local radio stations do much better.

In spite of all these changes, just like in the regular press, so on the radio and television, old themes and stereotypes are constantly re-warmed: present-day situation of gays, their life styles and problems, tolerance (Adamska 1998:120-122). Old themes are joined by some new variations: the problem of homosexual teachers, homosexual marriage and child adoption by homosexuals.

Active members of gay organizations understand the importance of having their own papers which counter the main-stream to some extent. Today four monthly magazines - "Differently" (*Inaczej*) from Poznań, "Fellow" (*Facet*) from Gdańsk, "New Men" (*Nowy Men*) and "Geyser" (*Gejzer*) from Warsaw - live a relatively secure existence. They are all available in official distribution and internal bulletins of individual organizations. The first two have high literary and intellectual standards. Many other papers and magazines did not make it (see Adamska 1998:135-139 for contents analysis).

AID CENTERS

The other field of gay organizational activity is the work on behalf of gays and lesbians which expresses itself in the establishing of various aid centers. Very good example of such a center may be the Warsaw "Rainbow" Center managed by the "Lambda-Warsaw"Association. As one of few groups in Poland, this organization keeps open a helpline for gays, lesbians and their families. The staff operating the phoneline consists of specially trained volunteers; information about the line is published everyday in every Warsaw daily and other mass media. The "Rainbow" Center also organizes professional support groups, a therapeutic group run by a psychologist, meeting groups for socializing and a Christian-ecumenical group which focuses on homosexual problems in light of religion. This group organizes also its own retreat with priests well disposed towards homosexuality. The "Rainbow" Center has also a gay library and press archives.

Like the other groups, the Warsaw Center offers also some amusements - in form of tourist trips, bivouacking or social meetings, but these are not a very important activity sphere at the Center. Instead social life is organized by a rather well-developed net of gay clubs - discos, pubs, restaurants. Most of them are in Warsaw and Poznań, the least - in eastern Poland. This region can be called the real "gay desert" - there are no gays organizations at all.

An important statutory aim of the national Lambda Association of Groups - prevention and treatment of HIV/AIDS - was partly taken over by non-gay institutions, such as, for example, The Governmental National Co-ordination Bureau in Matters of AIDS (*Krajowe Biuro Koordynacyjne ds. AIDS*). It does not mean that gay organizations do not work in this field at all, but rather that their actions are limited to the distribution of leaflets about safer sex and organizing meetings dedicated to this problem.

Most Polish gay organizations are also members of All-Polish Agreement of Gay and Lesbian Organizations (*Ogólnopolskie Porozumienie Organizacji Lesbijsko-Gejowskich*) by an informal agreement reached in March 1998. It co-ordinates national operations. The existence of national campaigns plays an important role for foreign organizations, such as the United Nations Organization Department, and for government institutions, such as, for example, the National Co-ordination Bureau. These institutions help Polish gay movement financially and by organizing helpline or "street programs" which promote safer sex in informal gay-meeting places, in clubs, discos and pubs, all financed by the UNDP.

LOBBYING FOR AN EXPLICIT NON-DISCRIMINATION CLAUSE

While writing about the Polish gay movement it is impossible to omit the wide sphere of law and politics. The first sign of dissonance between the world of politics and the gay society came with a statement of Vice-Minister of Health, Kazimierz Kapera, from the National Catholic Alliance party (*Zjednoczenie Chrześcijańsko - Narodowe, ZChN*). During his appearance on public TV in 1991, he used the word "perverts," when talking about gays. Three days later liberal Prime Minister, Jan Krzysztof Bielecki, dismissed this vice-minister. The fact that the same politician was included in the current coalition government as Minister-Plenipotentiary for Family Issues must be seen as a sign of political insensitivity to the gay community. Obviously, it is just a single example, but it is very meaningful. Right-wing and national social milieus, very often supported by the Catholic Church, define homosexuality as "morally non-ordered" and so still display a xenophobic attitude.

In response to the resolution of the European Parliament, which urged European governments to grant legal status to gay relationships, some Polish newspapers started a campaign equating this resolution with a promotion of perversion. A large part of Polish society (and of some politicians) is unfavorable if not hostile towards gays. This attitude is not, of course, typical for all Polish citizens. To the youth from big academic centers homosexuality is a matter of fact. In other places, especially in the country and small villages, stereotypic fears of and hostility towards the "different" still prevail.

Trying to counter these negative views and feelings about homosexuality, Polish gays became engaged in the biggest - and so far the only - action of political lobbying concerned with the non-discrimination clause in the new Constitution. In 1992 the Polish parliament began the work on a bill of the Constitution. The first project of the Bill (prepared as the Charter of Rights and Freedoms by President Lech Wałęsa) had a clause prohibiting discrimination based on sex, racial, national, ethnic or religious ground, but it did not include "sexual orientation." The gay community mobilized. Many letters and petitions were addressed to the parliament. Pressure was put on the Constitutional Commission. A special "Report about Discrimination" (1994) was prepared. It took until April 1994 for the Constitutional Commission to add the phrase "sexual orientation" to the non-discrimination clause. However, an unexpected change of government neutralized this unquestionable success of the gay community. In May 1993, after parliament dismissed the government of

Prime Minister Hanna Suchocka, President Lech Wałęsa dissolved parliament. The new parliament elected in fall the same year started anew the task of working out a new Constitution. After the elections, pressure on the Constitutional Commission was renewed, but this time it did not bring positive effects. The Constitution passed in 1997 has a general non-discrimination clause saying that *"nobody can be discriminated in his or her political, social or economic life on whatever ground and for whatever reason"*[3] - it does not explicitly forbid discrimination on the grounds of sexual orientation.

Why did the mobilization of Polish gays have such an incidental character? In my opinion, gays still have not acquired the democratic habit so widespread in Polish society. The constant fear of coming out and being rejected still constitutes an obstacle to open mobilization.[4] Having said this, lobbying is ineffective and lacks legitimacy when there are only five to ten active people. Yet most Polish gay organizations have only a few active members. An average politician, interested only in votes, has no reason to pay any attention to them. Neither do they command political power nor do they possess any protest potential.

The fear of rejection is also the main reason why there are no public demonstrations or public performances. There are, of course, some Gay Pride events organized in Western style, but they have been transformed into closed private performances in gay clubs or discos.[5] Even in 1998 the nth attempt to organize a national Gay Pride Day in Warsaw ended in a fiasco - as every year instead of a great, proud and public celebration, one joined a quasi-private party in a lesbian-gay club (Adamska 1998:152). Potential participants do not dare to join in the open, they observe the events from a safe distance. A celebration in an "own" club does not demand coming out. The time for several thousand people strong demonstrations of sexual minorities in Poland has not yet come.

CONCLUSION: PUBLIC AND INSTITUTIONAL ATTITUDES TOWARDS GAYS

In closing this article, I would like to mention one more issue - the question of perception of the gay movement by the authorities and society. It seems that the authorities (both central and local) have accepted the existence of homosexual groups as part of a rich public life. The co-operation with local governments is quite good. They often support local gay organizations, especially in organizing aid centers. Central government stands mostly for "political correctness." However, the attitude of Polish society differs very much from the official position on this question. As much as 86% of all adults claim that they do not know any gays, but no less than 63% would be very willing to forbid homosexuals to apply for public office. Seventy nine percent would prohibit their teaching. Most oppose the question of gay marriages or child adoptions. There are, however, also some positive changes - in 1992 only 17 percent of Poles accepted homosexual relations, in 1994 as many as 40 percent did. It means more than one hundred increase in acceptance,[6] but the overall picture remains rather negative.

Reluctance towards gays becomes expressed by the fact that almost every opening of a gay club becomes an occasion for the local community to mobilize in protest against it under the pretext of noise or immorality. They are also police controls in gay bars, such as the "Jambalaya"- club in Poznań, and insulting texts on walls of gay centers.

Also the standpoint of the Catholic Church has not much changed. Since a few years it again aggressively opposes the resolution of the European Parliament which allows homosexual marriages and adoption of children by homosexual couples on the grounds that they negate the essence of marriage and family (Adamska 1998:104-105). When in 1997 the Informal Group of Christian Gays and Lesbians (acting within the "Lambda-Warsaw" Association) asked the Polish Primate to open the priesthood to homosexuals, cardinal Józef Glemp answered that he did not see any problems of that group... Some homosexual believers defend themselves by holding on to their faith while rejecting the Catholic Church and/or standard interpretations of specific fragments of the Bible by this Church (Adamska 1998:107-110). They form their own groups,[7] such as The Group of Christian Lesbians and Gays that established itself in Warsaw in 1994. Homosexual Catholics also note the smallest positive changes in the attitude of the Catholic Church to homosexuality: the new Cathechism of the Catholic Church carries message of tolerance in one of its three points on homosexuality. They also see hope in the fact that although the Pope condemned the resolution of the European Parliament concerning homosexuals, he nevertheless stressed that the Catholic Church opposes discrimination of homosexuals on the grounds that every human being deserves respect.

It seems that the opening of Poland towards the West, free movement of ideas and rise of the education levels will help the gay movement. But the hardest step gays must take themselves - they must stop being afraid and confront the external world with words: *"I'm gay and I'm good!"*

NOTES

* I would like to thank Małgorzata Niemiec and the editor for translating this article.

1. The author is writing about the parliamentary elections, which took place on June 4, 1989. By the terms of political agreement between the communist government and the opposition, the elections were semicontested: only 35 percent of the seats in the lower chamber of parliament were contested, in the high chamber all were contested. After the unexpected victory of the opposition, "Solidarity" started to rule and Tadeusz Mazowiecki, a long-term, prominent opposition member, became the first non-communist Prime Minister.
2. See the article "Występek, choroba, odmienność" *(Offense, disease, dissimilarity)* in a weekly magazine Meetings *(Spotkania)*, 1992, 2-8 of August, nr.27.
3. Article 32.2 of the Polish Constitution from April 2, 1997.
4. In a letter intended for this volume Sergiusz Wróblewski, the editor of *Inaczej*, a historian by education and a journalist by choice, writes: The pressure exercised by the Polish gays on the Polish parliament at that time consisted of letters sent to parliament by small gay organizations, each consisting of less than 20 persons. And to make things worse only 100 gays responded to a call to send postcards to the chairman of the Constitutional Commission. Politicians of the post-communist party, *SLD*, who worked for including "sexual orientation" in the clause, felt let down by the weak gay support. They were also disappointed to hear that it was impossible to organize a 100-person strong gay demonstration. Leading liberal Polish politicians friendly towards gays, such as, for example, the late Professor Zofia Kuratowska, repeatedly but to no avail have called for organizing at least a federated gay organization capable of conveying the image of unity and strength. As Kliszczyński so Wróblewski believes that most Polish politicians are aware of that the Polish gay movement is weak and not worthy of taking electoral risks. Wróblewski also notes that at the national level the post-communist party has been very supportive of the movement for gay rights since 1989. In contrast, several post-Solidarity parties have taken to rationing freedoms, while the Freedom Party *(Unia Wolności)*, which enjoys a liberal image in the West, has not worked out a

clear-cut line with respect to homosexuality because of internal disagreements on this issue and because of its aspirations to turn into a Christian Democratic type of a political party. (Wróblewski has interviewed about 60 prominent public figures about their views on lesbian and gay rights. He prepared two different reports on these rights for the Polish *Sejm* and Senate - the two legislative bodies. He contacted the editor of this volume too late to play a role of a full-fledged contributor).

5. The First Gay Pride took place on in Warsaw on June 11, 1995. Let me note here briefly that Polish gay symbols do not differ from the Western symbols: a pink triangle (seldom used), a Greek letter lambda, a rainbow-hued flag - which is the origin of many names such as the "Rainbow" Center or Association "Rainbow" (*Tęcza*) - or rainbow-hued laurel award given for special merits for gay movement.

6. Data from a research project on the social acceptance of homosexuality conducted by CBOS, Public Opinion Research Center in August 1994. This research was later discontinued.

7. One of these groups supplied a list of discrimination acts commited by the Church to the "Report about Discrimination" (Adamska 1998:108).

REFERENCES

Adamska K. 1998. *Ludzie Obok. Lesbijki i Geje w Polsce*. Toruń. Graffiti BC
Darski K.T. 1985. "Jesteśmy inni" (We are different) *Polityka* Vol. 23 Nr. 47 (November), p.8
Pietkiewicz B. 1981. "Gorzki fiolet" (Bitter Purple) *Polityka* Vol. 21 Nr. 8 (February), p.8
Selerowicz A. 1994. *Leksykon kochających inaczej*. Poznań. Softpress

DOCUMENTS

Kliszczyński K. "Być innym" (To be different). Warszawa, manuscript
CBOS (Public Opinion Research Center). 1994. "Społeczna akceptacja homoseksualizmu. Komunikat z badań." Warszawa. *Centrum Badania Opinii Społecznej*, sierpień/August
Raport o dyskryminacji ze względu na orientację seksualną. (Report about Discrimination based on Sexual Orientation). 1994. Praca zbiorowa przygotowana przez Stowarzyszenie Grup Lambda. (Edited volume prepared by the Lambda Association of Groups). Warszawa.
"Występek, choroba, odmienność" (Offence, disease, dissimilarity), *Meetings* (*Spotkania*), 1992, 2-8 sierpnia/Aug., nr. 27
Wróblewski S. "Komentarz" a comment on Kliszczyński's article, dated August 9, 1999.

INTERVIEWS

Brodacki Piotr	activist in Warsaw and national Lambda	Warsaw	June 12 1999
Kostrzewa Yga	Vice-president of the Warsaw Lambda Association	Warsaw	May 10 1999
Pawlęga Michał	President of the Warsaw Lambda Association	Warsaw	May 10 1999
anonymous		Poznań	June 14 1999
anonymous		Wrocław	June 27 1999

14. An Uncomfortable Conclusion

Helena Flam

If we consider the characteristics of the Central European movements presented in this volume, we come up with their very focus on the "professional" forms of protest coupled with little mobilization and a quest for institutionalization. As uncomfortable as it is, the question of why there is so little mobilization cannot be ignored, the more so that in Central Europe there is no scarcity of general issues, such as the commercialization of the spirit, environmental destruction, gender inequality or homophobia, which all have a demonstrated mobilizing potential. Women have been losing their share of the labor market and wages in Poland, eastern Germany and the Czech Republic ever since 1989. Politicians cut radically the numbers of nursery schools and kindergartens, while they made abortions much more difficult. Under-represented even before 1989, after peaceful revolutions women have largely disappeared from the ministerial, political and trade union elites. Ten years after peaceful revolutions there is actually less gender equality than before (see also Einhorn 1993; Funk and Müller 1993; Rueschemeyer 1994; *Czech Sociological Review* 1999). Many specific issues, moreover, such as individual assaults against and public inattention to gay-lesbian rights are left unattended.

A "resource mobilization" approach, in particular its advanced version which takes changing political opportunity structures into account (Kitschelt 1986; Flam 1994), implies that in a new democratic context with abundant resources, new social movements should expand. The same approach also introduces the concept of *issue entrepreneurs,* individuals who play the role of major mobilizing actors, capable of constructing discontent. Their activities, much more than actual deprivation or grievances, account for the rise of social movements according to the "resource mobilization" approach. As this approach predicts, social movements have expanded in Central Europe since 1989, but, contrary to its theoretical thrust, only narrowly, mainly in terms of the sheer number of issue entrepreneurs and nonprofit organizations. This entrepreneurial and organizational growth is not accompanied by mass mobilization. How can one explain this phenomenon?

As I argued in the introduction key cleavage lines and the overabundance of burning issues help to understand weak mobilization to some extent. Even more convincing I find the idea that weak mobilization of the movements discussed in this volume cannot be explained within a single framework. Rather we have to acknowledge the fact that in Central Europe we find both social movements aiming to stablize their political influence and those still struggling for recognition. Even though they are active within the same nation-state, their differ in many ways from each other.

The chapters contained in this book suggest that the solidly pre-1989 social movements, such as the environmental movement, aim to retain their political influence and thus their access to the state. In the course of the last decade, many of their organizations came to resemble interest groups. They have turned themselves into experts and lobbyists. They rely on domestic but also on Western and international resources. It could be argued that these very resources make unnecessary the efforts to mobilize the public and to solicit individual financial contributions. In contrast, social movements, such as the gay and lesbian movements, which still struggle for recognition, are more dependent on mobilization and protest, if they are to lay foundations for a new collective identity. But to these movements and their members, although they operate in new or re-born democracies, homophobic and repressive social and political contexts are part of their everyday reality. Depending on their own internal dynamics and the contrasts in their socio-political contexts, they differ in their mobilization levels. The eastern German movement that has been institutionalized as well as commercialized is led by the older generation of gays not bent on mobilizing. The Hungarian movement displays the opposite tendency. In this case more militant younger gays and lesbians set up their own organizations and work hard to push the movement and its members towards ever more openness. The Polish movement, finally, oscillates between mobilization and de-mobilization, assertiveness and withdrawal.

Although this movement-duality helps us to understand why one and the same nation-state and one and the same democracy breeds so different social movements, it still leaves us part-blind. We need a framework that would help us understand why some but not other groups of people in Central Europe mobilize.

IN DEFENSE OF THE OLD IDENTITIES

Let us take the extreme case, that of religious movements. Whatever current spiritual needs there may be in eastern Germany or Poland, it is quite obvious that no established churches nor new sects can satisfy them. Instead *status quo* prevails in both countries. In eastern Germany there has been no rise in the number of Protestants or Catholics. Only between 30-40% of the population are members of these denominations. In Poland, the Catholic Church remains dominant with more than 90% of the population in its fold. However, most of these Catholics, an entire 72%, remain passive. A few years after 1989 new sects realized that they would probably lead only a marginal existence in this part of Europe.

Hartmann's compelling explanation for the lack of religious mobilization is that the context of job insecurity and high unemployment figures is hardly conducive to new movements. To generalize his argument: in Central Europe most people are struggling so hard to make a living and, I would add, defend their traditional identities, that they are blind to such ideas as women lib or the politics of difference.

Several types of evidence speak in favor of this thesis. First, as Gliński, Jehlička, Pickvance and Rink show, the only movements which can mobilize at all are the environmental movements which had some importance even before 1989. Joining in does not suggest a break with the past or a search for a new identity. In contrast, women's movements which have not had any recruitment successes before 1989 are more or less stagnant. Women in Central Europe have a more co-operative and egalitarian view of gender relations than their Western counterparts, and it is this *status quo* they actually want to safeguard. This implies that, to the accompaniment of shrill cries or resigned whispers of Western and domestic feminists, they insist upon upholding their old identities as women in the new context which, as Saxonberg points out, will make it increasingly difficult. Pető's chapter makes the point about the insistence on continuity with the past most explicitly. But the same goes for two gay movements depicted in this book. Most Polish and German gay leaders want to consolidate movement gains. Few of

170

their followers dare to press for more tolerance in culturally repressive contexts. Kleres' argument that extremely high unemployment rates and hard competition for jobs make insistence on gay rights into a risk factor brings us back full circle - to Hartmann's argument.

Whether we think of Central Europeans as people concerned about upholding their old identities under adverse conditions or as strategic players acting on volatile job markets, we have to conclude that their constructions of reality are largely immune to new social movements.

Let us approach the same issue from a different perspective: this volume is silent about worker or farmer protests. Yet these are actually more in evidence than mobilized new social movements, at least in Poland. Their protest has been in the news ever since 1989. A detailed study carried out by Ekiert and Kubik shows that in Poland protest events between 1989 and 1993 concerned "mostly economic demands made by well-defined social groups... It was therefore much more similar to the class-based French pattern than the German, Dutch or Swiss 'new' protest industries..." (Ekiert and Kubik 1999:331,328). In fact against their expectations it turned out that "most of the protest actions were sponsored or led by the 'old,' well-institutionalized organizations...such as labor unions, peasant organizations, and social and political movements" (Ekiert and Kubik 1999:332). Gorlach's recent study (2000), which shows that the Polish farmers' movement changed its organizational base and its discourse between 1989 and 1999, also pinpoints that this long-established social group with a clear-cut identity had no problems mobilizing when it saw its interests threatened by the new context. In eastern Germany, similarly, we witness not only a unionized, militant workforce ready to strike, to the surprise of union leaders (Holz, Pioch and Vobruba 1994; Bialas 1994). We also see the organizing and periodic protests of the unemployed - a novelty in Germany. Like those of workers and farmers, these protests are of a defensive type.

At first glance the Hungarian case should compel one to soften this line of argumentation. Although in Hungary as in Poland or East Germany trade unions and other traditional unions played an extremely important role as protest initiators and organizers (22.5% of all protest events), they actually ranked second to "new" social movements and NGOs (38.3% of all protest events) between 1989 and second half of 1994 (Szabó 1996:503,510). As I already mentioned in the introduction to this book, however, the environmental movement alone stood for 5-8% of all protests, but it was financed by the Dutch. Without this type of foreign assistance, it seems, the protest share of the "new" social movement would have been much smaller and the differences between the protest shares of trade and other traditional unions, on the one hand, and "new" social movements, on the other, less impressive.

The last piece of evidence: The post-communist parties have the most stable and in many cases the largest member-base compared to their competitors (Segert and Machos 1995: 301-302; Stöss and Segert 1997:412-421). The unexpected electoral successes of these former communist parties in Central Europe are (often interpreted as) an expression of widespread restitutive sentiments. In eastern Germany, Hungary and Poland people vote on the communist successor parties to protest against harsh reforms whose effects they suffer (Cook and Orenstein 1999:47; Rueschemeyer and Wolchik 1999:117-119). The re-born Czech Social Democratic party, which received a third of the total vote in 1998 and thus became the most voted for party, constitutes an exception to this rule since it is not post-communist (Rueschemeyer and Wolchik 1999:124). This party and the communist successor parties share one trait in common, however.

Although they do not want to turn back the wheel of history, they promise less severe economic and social policies. They pledge to reduce the high costs of modernizing and when in power some actually do so (Cook and Orenstein 1999:90,99; Rueschemeyer and Wolchik 1999:134-135). In Hungary and in Poland the "successor parties have adopted a clear electoral strategy to appeal to relatively weak social groups..." (Cook and Orenstein 1999:74)[1] Similarly, the Czech Social Democrats "have appealed to those more likely to be hurt by the shift to the market. Thus, their main supporters have been found among industrial workers and those with lower skill and educational levels. The social democrats' electoral supporters are also older..." (Rueschemeyer and Wolchik 1999:124). Comparative research projects also suggest that those who believe that they had lost status in the new context are the most likely to support these parties (Matějů 1998:199).

In sum, many different pieces of evidence combine to make the view that the quasi-restitutive social movements (see Tilly 1975) and quasi-restitutive political party mobilization are at least as important as, if not more important than, the "new" social movements in Central Europe today. As "socialist" states in this region withdraw their protection from the hitherto privileged groups and as market forces ruthlessly penetrate their traditional "life-worlds" and upset their livelihoods, farmers and workers, the very groups which had well-established identities for a long time prior to 1989, do not hesitate to make themselves heard. Central Europe today gives a new twist to Habermas' traditional "identity-approach" to social movements![2]

NOTES

1. This is not to deny that, as Cook and Orenstein (1999:74) assert, "their core constituency and membership has been located among the managerial and professional groups associated with the communist regime."
2. Habermas' *Telos* article reflects an attempt to deal with the traditional as opposed to the "new" social (movement) identities (see Cohen 1985:709).

REFERENCES

Bialas C. 1994. "Gewerkschaftlicher Organisationsaufbau und Transformation der Lohnpolitik im Prozeß der deutschen Einheit: Die IG Metall in den neuen Bundesländern 1990-1993" Max-Planck-Gesellschaft. Arbeitsgruppe Transformationsprozesse in den neuen Bundesländern an der Humboldt-Universität zu Berlin. Forschungsbericht, Nr. 1

Cohen J. L. 1985. "Strategy or Identity: New Theoretical Paradigms and Contemporary Social Movements" *Social Research* Vol. 52 Nr. 4:663-716

Cook L. J. and M. Orenstein. 1999. "The Return of the Left and Its Impact on the Welfare State in Russia, Poland, and Hungary" in *Left Parties and Social Policy in Postcommunist Europe*. Edited by Cook L. J., M. A. Orenstein and M. Rueschemeyer. Boulder, Colorado.Westview Press, pp. 47-108

Czech Sociological Review. 1999. Vol. VII, Nr. 2 (special issue devoted to gender questions in the Czech Republic, guest editor: Marie Čermáková)

Einhorn B. 1993. *Cinderella Goes to Market. Citizenship, Gender and Women's Movements in East Central Europe*. London. Verso

Ekiert G. and J. Kubik. 1999. "Protest Event Analysis in the Study of Democratic Consolidation: Poland, 1989-1993" in *Acts of Dissent. New Developments in the Study of Protest.* Edited by D. Rucht, R. Koopmans and F. Neidhardt. Lanham, Maryland. Rowman and Littlefield Publishers, pp. 317-348

Flam H. 1994. *States and Anti-Nuclear Movements.* Edinburgh. Edinburgh University Press

Funk N. And M. Müller, eds. 1993. *Gender Politics and Post Communism. Reflections from Eastern Europe and the Former Soviet Union.* New York. Routledge

Gorlach K. 2000. "Nowe oblicze chłopstwa: protesty rolników polskich w latach 90" in *Jak Żyją Polacy.* Edited by H. Domański, A. Ostrowska and A. Rychard. Warszawa. Wydawnictwo IFiS PAN, pp.281-312

Holz K., R. Pioch and G. Vobruba. 1994. "Verteilungskonflikte in politischen Integrationsprozessen: Das Beispiel des Tarifkonflikts in der sächsischen Metallindustrie" in *Europäische Integration und verbandliche Interessenvermittlung.* Edited by V. Eichener and H. Voelzkow. Marburg-Verlag, pp. 575-595

Kitschelt H. 1986. "Political Opportunity Structures and Political Protest: Anti-Nuclear Movements in Four Democracies" *British Journal of Political Science* 16:57-85

Matějů P. 1998. "In Search of Explanations for Recent Left-Turns in Post-Communist Countries" in *Eliten, politische Kultur und Privatisierung in Ostdeutschland, Tschechien und Mittelosteuropa.* Edited by I. Srubar. Konstanz. Universitätsverlag Konstanz, pp. 183-229

Rueschemeyer M., ed. 1994. *Women in the Politics of Post Communist Eastern Europe.* New York. M.E. Scharpe

Rueschemeyer M. and Sh. L. Wolchik. 1999. "The Return of Left-Oriented Parties in Eastern Germany and the Czech Republic and their Social Policies" in *Left Parties and Social Policy in Postcommunist Europe.* Edited by Cook L. J., M. A. Orenstein and M. Rueschemeyer. Boulder, Co. Westview Press, pp. 109-144

Segert D. and C. Machos. 1995. *Parteien in Osteuropa.* Opladen. Westdeutscher Verlag

Stöss R. and D. Segert. 1997. "Entstehung, Struktur und Entwicklung von Parteiensystemen in Osteuropa nach 1989 - Eine Bilanz" in *Parteiensysteme in postkommunistischen Gesellschaften Osteuropa.* Edited by D. Segert, R. Stöss and O. Niedermayer. Opladen. Westdeutscher Verlag, pp. 379-428

Szabó M. 1996. "Politischer Protest im postkommunistischen Ungarn 1989-1994" *Berliner Journal für Soziologie,* Vol. 6 Nr. 4:501-515

Tilly Ch. 1975. "Revolutions and Collective Violence" in *Handbook of Political Science.* Vol. 3. Edited by F. I. Greenstein and N. Polsby. Reading, Massachusetts. Addison-Wesley, pp. 483-549